Fernald Library
Colby-Sawyer College
New London, New Hampshire

Presented by

WALLACE K. EWING

D1479161

The Sociology
of
Language

The Sociology of Language

of

Language

•

AN INTERDISCIPLINARY
SOCIAL SCIENCE APPROACH
TO
LANGUAGE IN SOCIETY

• • •

JOSHUA A. FISHMAN
Yeshiva University

NEWBURY HOUSE PUBLISHERS   *ROWLEY, MASSACHUSETTS*

COLBY-SAWYER COLLEGE
NEW LONDON, N.H. 03257

NEWBURY HOUSE PUBLISHERS, INC.

LANGUAGE SCIENCE
LANGUAGE TEACHING
LANGUAGE LEARNING

68 Middle Road, Rowley, Massachusetts 01969

01064

Copyright © 1972 by Newbury House Publishers. All rights reserved.
No part of this publication may be reproduced in any form without
permission from the publisher.

Library of Congress Card Number: 75-142802

ISBN: 912066-16-4

Printed in the United States of America.   First Printing: August, 1972

FOREWORD

Joshua A. Fishman has made many contributions to the
sociology of language. Not the least of them is to provide the
subject with its first modern text. That there is need for a
text is due in no small part to Professor Fishman's own
efforts. A decade or so ago, the subject was but an interest in
the eyes of a few men, so far as active investigation was
concerned. Today it is a rapidly growing and rapidly
developing field. In several major areas of the field —
language loyalty, language development, bilingualism — Professor Fishman has been a leader in research; at the same time
he has worked to build the field as a whole.

The field of the sociology of language is defined here as a
focus upon "the entire gamut of topics related to the social
organization of language behavior." Later it is urged that
"The entire world of socially patterned variability in language
behavior still remains to be explored." Here, I think, is
indeed the crux of the matter. We are concerned here with a
perspective upon the whole of matters concerned with

language, a perspective that will prove revolutionary in its ultimate implications, if a field indeed is built, and the great world of new problems is adequately explored. It is proposed to investigate everything concerned with language from the standpoint of social function. Rather than take the category of language as given, or as handed on from the normal practice of grammar-writing, it is proposed to take what counts as 'a language', as a relevant form of language, as problematic. As is pointed out in the text, the notion of bilingualism must really be extended to comprise all the varieties that are part of the linguistic repertoire of speakers. It may prove desirable to adopt a new term for the more general concept, so as to avoid confusion with the usual meaning of 'bilingualism', but the essential point is that the existence of a multiplicity of linguistic varieties, and of patterns of choice among them, is a fundamental, universal phenomenon. Switching among ways of speaking is the equivalent in sociolinguistic research of contrast among speech sounds in phonology; it is the 'commutation test' of sociolinguistic research. With that test, forms of speech, ways of speaking, will become apparent that escape the notice of ordinary analysis. Such ways of speaking, shown by the fact of switching, of choice, to be functionally relevant and to have conventional meaning, will enable us to relate our knowledge of language much more closely to the practical problems of society, and to understand much more adequately the many roles of language in human life.

Professor Fishman discusses the famous 'Sapir-Whorf hypothesis' of the influence of linguistic form on behavior and world view, ending with a conception of the relation between language and behavior as one of interdependence, rather than any form of one-way domination. He also points out that the 'relativity' of language is a question not only of the structure of language, but also of the structure of the use of language. It is an interesting question as to whether the structure of the use of language may not itself reflect world view, underlying values, deeply shared cultural presuppositions; even whether, aspects of the structure of language, and aspects of the structure of the use of language, may not both be involved in reflecting, shaping, or otherwise relating language and cultural outlook, and along common lines. Whether or not such a link can be shown, it is essential to recognize, as Professor Fishman makes clear from the outset, that 'meaning' in language cannot be confined to the kind of 'referential meaning' that alone is usually taken into account in linguistic analysis—the kind of meaning that is involved in naming, factual reporting, and the like. Expressive and symbolic meanings are an integral part of the study of meaning in regard to language. The sociology of language necessarily deals with this fact, and much of its contribution to understanding the human significance of language will flow from this.

Of the many things to be done, the many opportunities for creative research, perhaps none is more significant than the development of an adequate typology (and hence a theory) of situations of language change. Professor Fishman stresses this point, rightly pointing out that simple-minded explanations, such as appeal to an unexamined concept of 'prestige', simply do not hold water. Debunking such excuses for analysis is essential, but, as Professor Fishman also stresses, it is only the first step. A vital part of the development of an adequate typology will be an adequate typology of speech communities, with all that that implies in terms of the need for fresh descriptions and analytic dimensions. The old equation of speech community with language community, such that a common language implied, and indeed defined, the notion of speech community, hopefully is gone for good. We have hardly the rudiments, however, of a theory to replace it. Such a theory requires many analyses of speech communities in terms of concepts such as are presented here, verbal repertoire, domain, and the like.

One major theme of the book is the need for cooperation among disciplines, the use of complementary skills, even joint training, so as to attack many of the problems of a sociology of language adequately. This view cannot be too warmly applauded. It is of the essence of the study of the social organization of language behavior to bring together related disciplines. This new field indeed may play a leading part in the convergence of social science disciplines now under way. In the past the demarcation between sociology and anthropology seemed mostly a matter of practice, not of principle—a division of labor as between regions, and a different hierarchy of preference as to methods. Now that sociologists are again significantly interpretational and comparative in perspective, and many anthropologists are working in their own backyards; with methods akin to ethnography and linguistics gaining prominence in sociology, and mathematics and statistics playing an increasing role in anthropology, there is little justification for maintenance of a boundary. The parcelling out of the study of man among competing clans may serve petty interests, but not the supervening interest of mankind itself in self-understanding and liberation. It is not merely a courtesy for Professor Fishman to acknowledge the role of other technical disciplines than sociology, just as it is not a mere courtesy (or curious accident) that someone whose background is in anthropology, folklore and linguistics should be writing a foreword for a scholar with roots in sociology. It is a sign of the integrative nature of the field of research which Professor Fishman presents in this book.

Dell Hymes
University of Pennsylvania
January, 1972

PREFACE

The rapid growth of interest in well-nigh *every* aspect of language in society has prompted me to prepare the following revision, expansion and reformulation of my former *Sociolinguistics: A Brief Introduction* (written in 1968 and published in 1970). My own classroom and research experience, that of several other colleagues, and a careful examination of the considerable research literature of the past four years, all point to the same fact: this field is now attracting students and scholars with considerably more sophistication in social research and social theory than was the case just a few years ago. As a result, a somewhat more quantitative treatment, as well as one that is theory oriented is now frequently possible, not only in connection with topics and materials that were previously presented, but, in addition, in connection with several new topics not hitherto considered.

At the very time this version sees the light of day my monograph on *Language and Nationalism* is being set in type. The relationship between all three publications therefore deserves a word of comment. The choice between *Socio-*

linguistics: A Brief Introduction and the present somewhat longer volume may well be made on the basis of the extent to which students and instructors are themselves at home in the world of social research methods and social behavior theories. In either case, one or another of the recently completed volumes of "readings" might also be utilized (or even stressed) so that students are not merely presented with conceptual integration but with the detail of research findings and theoretical elaborations. Thereafter, in a second quarter or semester, *Language and Nationalism* might well serve as an integrative core text, and, in its turn, be supplemented by a variety of detailed readings on language maintenance and language shift, language treatment and language planning. In this fashion a full year's introductory work on the sociology of language becomes possible, rather than merely a single semester based upon introductory texts at one or another of two rather different levels.

Still other sociolinguistic teaching and learning materials are increasingly becoming available, many being of a much more specialized and topically focused nature than any of those mentioned above. Many of these are suitable for those interested in a second full year of sociolinguistic preparation. As a result, the sociology of language is now sufficiently well provided with teaching-learning materials to permit it to become an area of at least "minor" if not "major" concentration in a goodly number of institutions of higher education. As such, its growth over the meager span of a decade has been most heartening. As one who has contributed to this development I remain eager to learn from the reactions and contributions of my students and colleagues, these being the major stimulants that I encounter in my constant quest for an ever more powerful and integrating sociology of language.

Joshua A. Fishman (Yeshiva University)
Jerusalem, June 1972

Visiting Professor, Hebrew University, and
Co-Director, International Research Project
on Language Planning Processes

CONTENTS

SECTION   V

SOCIETAL DIFFERENTIATION
AND REPERTOIRE RANGE   55

SECTION   VI

SOCIETAL BILINGUALISM: STABLE AND
TRANSITIONAL   91

SECTION   VII

LANGUAGE MAINTENANCE
AND LANGUAGE SHIFT   107

SECTION VIII

SOCIOCULTURAL ORGANIZATION: LANGUAGE CONSTRAINTS AND LANGUAGE REFLECTIONS

SECTION IX

APPLIED SOCIOLOGY OF LANGUAGE

SECTION X

LINGUISTICS: THE SCIENCE OF CODE DESCRIPTION ... AND MORE (Addendum for Non-linguists)

געלען, פֿונעם גאַנצן האַרצן

INTRODUCTION

Man is constantly using language—spoken language, written language, printed language—and man is constantly linked to others via shared norms of behavior. The sociology of language examines the interaction between these two aspects of human behavior: the use of language and the social organization of behavior. Briefly put, the sociology of language focuses upon the entire gamut of topics related to the social organization of language behavior, including not only language usage per se but also language attitudes and overt behaviors toward language and toward language users.

1.1 SOCIOLINGUISTIC HEADLINES

The latter concern of the sociology of language—overt behavior toward language and toward language users—is a concern shared by political and educational leaders in many parts of the world and is an aspect of sociolinguistics that frequently makes headlines in the newspapers. Many French-Canadian university students oppose the continuation of public education in English in the Province of Quebec. Many Flemings in Belgium protest vociferously against anything less than full equality—at the very least—for Dutch in the Brussels area. Some Welsh nationalists daub out English signs along the highways in Wales and many Irish revivalists seek stronger governmental support for the restoration of Irish than that made available during half a century of Irish independence. Jews throughout the world protest the Soviet government's persecution of Yiddish writers and the forced closing of Yiddish schools, theaters, and publications.

Swahili, Filipino, Indonesian, Malay, and the various provincial languages of India are all being consciously expanded in vocabulary and standardized in spelling and grammar so that they can increasingly function as the exclusive language of government and of higher culture and technology. The successful revival and modernization of Hebrew has encouraged other smaller communities—the Catalans, the Provencals, the Frisians, the Bretons—to strive to save *their* ethnic mother tongues (or their traditional cultural tongues) from oblivion. New and revised writing systems are being accepted—and at times, rejected—in many parts of the world by communities that hitherto had little interest in literacy in general or in literacy in their mother tongues in particular.

Such examples of consciously organized behavior toward language and toward users of particular languages can be listed almost endlessly. The list becomes truly endless if we include examples from earlier periods of history, such as the displacement of Latin as the language of religion, culture, and government in Western Christendom and the successive cultivation of once lowly vernaculars—first in Western Europe, and then subsequently in Central, Southern, and Eastern Europe, and finally in Africa and Asia as well. Instead of being viewed (as was formerly the case) as merely fit for folksy talk and for common folk, the vernaculars have come to be viewed, used, and developed as *independent* languages, as languages suitable for *all* higher purposes, and as languages of state-*building* and state-*deserving* nationalities. All of these examples too feed into the modern sociology of language, providing it with historical breadth and depth in addition to its ongoing interest in current language issues throughout the world.

1.2 SUBDIVISIONS OF THE SOCIOLOGY OF LANGUAGE

However, the subject matter of the sociology of language reaches far beyond interest in case studies and very far beyond cataloguing and classifying the instances of language conflict and language planning reported in chronicles, old and new. The ultimate quest of the sociology of language is pursued diligently and in many universities throughout the United States and other parts of the world, and is very far from dealing directly with headlines or news reports. One part of this quest is concerned with describing the generally accepted social organization of language usage within a speech community (or, to be more exact, within speech and writing communities). This part of the sociology of language—*descriptive sociology of languages*—seeks to answer the question "who speaks (or writes) what language (or what language variety) to whom and when and to what end?" *Descriptive sociology of language* tries to disclose the norms of language usage—that is to say, the generally accepted social patterns of language use and of behavior and attitude toward language—for particular social networks and communities, both large and small. Another part of the sociology of language—*dynamic sociology of language*—seeks to answer the question "what accounts for different rates of change in the social organization of language use and behavior toward language?" *Dynamic sociology of language* tries to explain why and how the social organization of language use and behavior toward language can be selectively different in the *same* social networks or communities on two different occasions. Dynamic sociology of language also seeks to explain why and how once similar social networks or communities can arrive at quite different social organizations of language use and behavior toward language.

These two subdivisions taken together, i.e., descriptive sociology of language *plus* dynamic sociology of language constitute the sociology of language, a *whole* which is *greater than the mere sum of its parts.*

1.3 LANGUAGE IS CONTENT;
THE MEDIUM IS (AT LEAST PARTLY) THE MESSAGE

Newspaper headlines with all of their stridency may serve to remind us of a truism that is too frequently overlooked by too many Americans, namely, that language is not merely a *means* of interpersonal communication and influence. It is not merely a *carrier* of content, whether latent or manifest. Language itself *is* content, a referent for loyalties and animosities, an indicator of social statuses and personal relationships, a marker of situations and topics as well as of the societal goals and the large-scale value-laden arenas of interaction that typify every speech community.

Any speech community of even moderate complexity reveals several varieties of language, all of which are functionally differentiated from each other. In some cases the varieties may represent different occupational or interest specializations ("shop talk," "hippie talk," etc.), and therefore contain vocabulary, pronunciation, and phraseology which are not generally used or even known throughout the broader speech community. As a result, the speakers of specialized varieties may not always employ them. Not only must they switch to other varieties of language when they interact in less specialized (or differently specialized) networks within the broader speech community of which they are a part, but most of them do not even use their specialized varieties all the time with one another. On some occasions, interlocutors who *can* speak a particular specialized variety to one another nevertheless do not so, but instead switch to a different variety of language which is either in wider use or which is indicative of quite a different set of interests and relationships than is associated with their specialized variety. This type of switching represents the raw data of descriptive sociology of language, the discipline that seeks to determine (among other things) who speaks what variety of what language to whom, when, and concerning what.

The varieties of language that exist within a speech community need not all represent occupational or interest specializations. Some varieties may represent social class (economic, educational, ethnic) distinctions within coterritorial populations. "Brooklynese" and "cockney"

English within New York and London, respectively, do not connote foreignness or even a particular section of the city as much as lower-class status in terms of income, education, or ethnicity. Nevertheless, many individuals who have left lower-class status behind can and do swich back and forth between Brooklynese and more regionally standard New York English when speaking to each other, depending on their feelings toward each other, the topic under discussion, where they happen to be when they are conversing, and several other factors, all of which can exhibit variation and, as a result, can be signaled by switching from one variety of English to another.

A speech community that has available to it several varieties of language may be said to possess a *verbal repertoire*. Such repertoires may not only consist of different specialized varieties and different social class varieties, but may also reveal different regional varieties (Boston English, Southern English, Midwestern English, and other widely, and roughly, designated dialects of American English are regional varieties), if the speech community is sufficiently large so that enclaves come to arise within it on a geographic basis alone. Furthermore, multilingual speech communities may employ, for the purpose of *intragroup* communication, all the above types or varieties of language within each of the codes that the community recognizes as "distinct" languages (e.g., within Yiddish *and* Hebrew, among most pre-World War II Eastern European Jews; within English *and* Hindi, among upper-class individuals in India today, etc.).

Regardless of the nature of the language varieties involved in the verbal repertoire of a speech community (occupational, social class, regional, etc.) and regardless of the interaction between them (for initially regional dialects may come to represent social varieties as well, and vice versa) descriptive sociology of language seeks to disclose their linguistic and functional characteristics and to determine how much of the entire speech community's verbal repertoire is available to various smaller interaction networks within that community, since the entire verbal repertoire of a speech community may be more extensive than the verbal repertoire controlled by subgroups within that community. Dynamic sociology of language on the other hand seeks to determine how changes in the fortunes and interactions of networks of speakers alter the ranges (complexity) of their verbal repertoires.

All in all, the sociology of language seeks to discover not only the societal rules or norms that explain and constrain language behavior and *the behavior toward language* in speech communities, but it also seeks to determine the symbolic value of language varieties for their speakers. That language varieties come to have symbolic or symptomatic value, in and of themselves, is an inevitable consequence of their functional differentiation. If certain varieties are indicative of certain interests, of certain backgrounds, or of certain origins, then they come to represent the ties and aspirations, the limitations and the opportunities with which these interests, backgrounds, and origins, in turn, are associated. Language varieties rise and fall in symbolic value as the status of their most characteristic or marked functions rises and falls. Varieties come to represent intimacy and equality if they are most typically learned and employed in interactions that stress such bonds between interlocutors. Other varieties come to represent educated status or national identification as a result of the attainments associated with their use and their users and as a result of their realization in situations and relationships that pertain to formal learning or to particular ideologies. However, these functions are capable of change (and of being consciously changed), just as the linguistic features of the varieties themselves may change (and may be consciously changed), and just as the demographic distribution of users of a variety within a particular speech community may change.

The step-by-step elevation of most modern European vernaculars to their current positions as languages of culture and technology is only one example of how dramatically the operative and symbolic functions of languages can change. Similar changes are ongoing today:

> Since the preservation of adequate control over the labour force loomed so large in the minds of the early planters, various devices have evolved, of which the maintenance of castelike distance was perhaps the one most significantly

affecting race relations. One thinks immediately of the frequently cited admonition in the *Rabaul Times* of August 8, 1926, by a veteran Territorian, "Never talk to the boys in any circumstances. Apart from your house-boy and boss-boy, never allow any native to approach you in the field or on the bungalow veranda." This free advice to the uninitiated planters was, no doubt, intended to preserve "White prestige," but it was also conceived as a protective device to "keep labour in its place." So also the Melanesian Pidgin, which had come into being as a medium of interchange in trade, subsequently acquired, on the plantations, the character of a language of command by which the ruling caste "talked down" to its subordinates and "put them in their place." A wide range of plantation etiquette symbolizing proper deference by workers toward their masters and expressed in expected form of address and servile conduct gave further protection to the system and any signs of insubordination or "cheekiness" on the part of the workers might be vigorously punished and rationalised by the planter as a threat to the system. (Lind 1969, p. 36)

Yet today, barely half a century since Melanesian Pidgin began to expand, it has been renamed Neo-Melanesian and is being groomed by many New Guineans to become their country's national language, and as such to be used in government, education, mass media, religion, and high culture more generally (Wurm 1961/62).

The sociology of language is the study of the characteristics of language varieties, the characteristics of their functions, and the characteristics of their speakers as these three constantly interact, change, and change one another, both within and between speech communities.

SECTION II

SOME REASONS WHY THE SOCIOLOGY
OF LANGUAGE HAS ONLY RECENTLY
BEGUN TO DEVELOP

Given the obvious importance of the sociology of language, given its apparent interest for all who are interested in either or both of its parent disciplines (as well as for all who wish better to understand events and processes all over the world), and finally, given the substantial applied promise of the sociology of language for educational and governmental use, it is quite natural to ask: why is the sociology of languages only now coming into its own? Actually, the sociology of language, as a field of interest within linguistics and the social sciences, is not as new as its recent prominence may suggest. The nineteenth and early twentieth centuries witnessed many studies, and many publications that belonged to this field are cited in Hertzler 1965. Nevertheless, it is quite true that the disciplinary priorities and biases of both fields were such that those earlier attempts were prematurely set aside, and only recently has momentum been attained in this field to enable it to attract and train specialists devoted to it per se (Ferguson 1965, Fishman 1967b).

9

2.1 INVARIANT BEHAVIOR

Linguistics has classically been interested in completely regular or fully predictable behavior. The *p* in "pin" is always aspirated by native speakers of English. The *p* in "spin" is always unaspirated. This is the kind of entirely determined relationship that linguistics has classically sought and found—to such an extent that a highly respected linguist wrote a few decades ago: "If it exists *to some degree,* it's not linguistics" (Joos 1950). The implication of this view is quite clear: linguistics is not interested in "sometimes things." The phenomena it describes are either completely determinable occurrences or nonoccurrences. Wherever some other lesser state of determinacy was noted, e.g., in usage, this was defined as "exolinguistic," as "free variations" that were outside of the realm or the heartland of linguistics proper.

The social sciences, on the other hand, were (and remain) singularly uninterested in apparently invariant behavior. Any such behavior could only prompt the observation "So what?" from the social sciences, since their preserve was and is societally patterned *variation* in behavior and the locations of those factors that parsimoniously explain and predict such variation. If one were to observe to a social scientist that the *same* individuals who *always* wore clothing when they were strolling on Fifth Avenue *never* wore any when they were bathing or showering, his reaction to this brand of societal invariance would be "So what?"

Given the above basic difference in orientations between its two parent disciplines, it is not even necessary to add that linguistics was classically too code-oriented to be concerned with societal patterns in language usage, or that sociology was classically too stratificationally oriented to be concerned with contextual speaking (or writing) differences *within* strata. Fortunately, both fields have recently moved beyond their classical interests (see Figure 1), and as a result fostered the kinds of joint interests on which the sociology of language now depends.

2.2 MODERATELY VARIABLE BEHAVIOR

Linguistics has, in recent years, plunged further and further into "sometimes things" in the realm of language behavior.

Some of the same speakers who say "ain't" on certain occasions do *not* use it on others, and some of the same cotton pickers who have such a colorful and unique vocabulary, phonology, and grammar on occasions also share other varieties with their many non-cotton-picking friends and associates. This is the kind of societally patterned variation in behavior that social scientists not only recognize and understand, but it is the kind they are particularly well prepared to help linguists study and explain. When such behavior is reported, the social scientist is oriented toward locating the smallest number of societal factors that can account for or predict the usage variation that has been reported.

FIGURE 1. The Changing Interests and Emphases of Linguistics and the Social Sciences with Respect to Variation in Behavior (after Labov).

Type of Behavior	Linguistics	Social Sciences
Invariant	Classical Interest	No Interest
Moderately Variable	Recent Growing Interest	Classical Interest
Highly Variable	Possible Future Interest	Recent Growing Interest

2.3 HIGHLY VARIABLE BEHAVIOR

Finally, and even more recently, even more complex societally patterned variation in behavior has come to be of interest to the social scientist. This behavior is so complexly patterned or determined that a goodly number of explanatory variables must be utilized and combined, with various quantitative weights and controls, in order that their total impact as well as their separate contributions can be gauged. This kind of highly variable and complexly patterned societal behavior obviously exists (and plentifully so) with respect to language too. However, linguists generally lack the skills of study design, data collection, and data analysis that are required in order to undertake to clarify such multiply determined language behavior. At this level, more than at any other, the corpus of language per se is insufficient to explain a major proportion of the variation in language behavior that obtains. Nor are a few demographic (age, sex, education), or a few contextual (formality-informality in role relationships), or a few situational factors sufficient for this purpose. Rather, predictors of all these kinds are needed, and to the extent that this is so, their joint or combined use will result in far greater explanatory or predictive power than would any two or three of them alone. The social sciences themselves have only rather recently become accustomed to working with large numbers of complexly interrelated and differentially weighted variables. This is obviously a level of analysis which will become available to the sociology of language only if there is genuine co-operation between linguists and social scientists.

The sociology of language is thus a by-product of a very necessary and very recent awareness on the part of linguistics and the social sciences that they do indeed need each other in order to explore their joint interests in a productive and provocative manner. This cooperative attitude has yielded important results in the few years that it has been actively pursued (Grimshaw 1969, Hymes 1967a) and we may expect even more from it in the future when a greater number of individuals who are themselves specialists in *both fields simultaneously* (or in the joint field per se) will have been trained.

2.4 VARIABILITY AND PREDICTABILITY

While it is, of course, true that the more variable behavior is, the more numerous the factors are that need to be located in order to account for it in any substantial way, the less predictable the behavior is until the proper factors have been located and combined or weighted in the most appropriate ways. Ultimately, however, if the quest of rigorous data collection and data analysis is successful, as high a level of predictability or explanability may be attained with respect to complexly determined and highly variable behaviors as with the far less and the somewhat less complexly determined and variable ones. Thus, the methodological differences that have existed between linguistics and sociology have been primarily differences in the extent to which a very few well-chosen parameters could account substantially for the behaviors that the respective disciplines choose to highlight. Ultimately, all disciplines of human behavior—including linguistics and sociology—strive to locate and to interrelate the most parsimonious set of explanatory-predictive variables in order to maximally account for the variability to which their attention is directed.

With respect to societally patterned language behavior, there is doubtlessly variability that can be well-nigh perfectly accounted for by a very few well-selected intracode positional factors. Social scientists should recognize such behavior, for it not only leads them to a recognition of linguistics per se but to the clearer realization that the entire world of socially patterned variability in language behavior still remains to be explored—and to be explored by linguists and social scientists together—after the variability explainable on the basis of intracode factors alone has been accounted for. However, at that level of inquiry it is *not* possible to simply put linguistics aside and, turning to more exciting and difficult tasks, simply to "do social science." Studies of more complexly determined and more highly variable socially patterned language behaviors still require rigorous descriptions and analyses of language usage per se, and for such analyses the social sciences will always be dependent on linguistics.

SOME BASIC
SOCIOLINGUISTIC CONCEPTS

The sociology of language deals with quite a range of topics: small group interaction and large group membership, language use and language attitudes, and language-and-behavior norms as well as changes in these norms. We expect to deal with all of these topics, at least briefly, in this presentation, and necessarily, to introduce the technical terms and concepts which specialized fields of discourse inevitably require. However, before moving into any of these more specialized substantive topics there are a number of basic sociolinguistic concepts that are of such general intertopic utility that we had best pause to consider them here, rather than to permit them to remain as primitives any longer.

3.1 LANGUAGE-DIALECT-VARIETY

The term *variety* is frequently utilized in the sociology of language as a nonjudgmental designation. The very fact that an objective, unemotional, technical term is *needed* in order to refer to "a kind of language" is in itself an indication that the expression "a language" is often a judgmental one, a term that is *indicative* of emotion and opinion, as well as a term that *elicits* emotion and opinion. This is an important fact about languages and one to which we will return repeatedly. As a result, we will use the term "variety" in order not to become trapped in the very phenomena that we seek to investigate, namely, when and by whom is a certain variety considered to be a language and when and by whom is it considered something else.

Those varieties that initially and basically represent divergent geographic origins are known as *dialects* (Ferguson and Gumperz 1960; Halliday 1964b). It is in this purely objective sense of the word that it is used in such terms as *dialectology* and *dialect geography* within linguistics, and it is in this sense that the sociology of language employs it as well. However, dialects may easily come to represent (to stand for, to connote, to symbolize) other factors than geographic ones. If immigrants from region A come to be a large portion of the poor, the disliked, and the illiterate in region B, then their speech variety (dialect A) will come to stand for much more than geographic origin alone in the minds of the inhabitants of region B. Dialect A will come to stand for lower social status (educationally, occupationally) than will dialect B. In this way what was once viewed only as a *regional variety* (in the sense that at a particular time its undifferentiated speakers were merely viewed as being concentrated in a particular area) may come to be viewed (and to function) much more importantly as a *social variety* or *sociolect* (Blanc 1964) once social differentiation comes to the fore. Furthermore, if the speakers of variety A are given hardly any access into the interaction networks of region B, if they marry primarily only each other, engage primarily in their original regional customs, and continue to value only each other's company, they may, in time, come to consider themselves a different society, with goals, beliefs, and traditions of their own. As a result, variety A may no longer be viewed as a social variety, but rather as an *ethnic* or *religious* variety, and indeed, it may come to be cultivated as such to the point of being viewed as a separate *language* (Kloss 1967; Fishman 1968c). However, within the community of A speakers there may come to be some who have learned B as well. They may utilize A with each other for purposes of intimacy and in-group solidarity, but they may also use B with each other for occupational and deferential purposes. Thus for them, A and B will be contrasted and complementary *functional varieties*, with B also being (or including) a *specialized* (occupational or other experiential) *variety*, and therefore in some ways different from variety B as used by others (Weinreich M. 1953).

The above theoretical sketch has more than general didactic value. It represents the route that many varieties —regional and social—have traveled in the past and the route on which still others are embarked at this very time (Haugen 1966c; Deutsch 1966). Nevertheless, it is the *general* point that is of particular value to us at this juncture. Varieties may be viewed as regional at one time and social at another. Varieties may be reacted to as regional within the speech community of their users and as social (or ethnic) by outsiders. Varieties may have additional functional uses for some of their users that they do not have for others who possess fewer contrasted varieties in their verbal repertoires. Thus, the term variety—unlike the term dialect—indicates no particular linguistic status (other than difference) vis-à-vis other varieties. A dialect must be a regional *subunit* in relation to a language, particularly in its vernacular or spoken realization. "Language" is a superordinate designation; "dialect" is a subordinate designation. Both terms require that the entire taxonomy to which they pertain be known before they themselves can be accepted. The sociology of language is interested in them only in so far as members of speech communities contend over which is which, and why. As the result of such contention varieties hitherto considered to be dialects may throw off their subordination and be "promoted" by their speakers to official and independent status, whereas formerly independent languages may be subordinated. The term variety, on the other hand, merely designates a member of a verbal repertoire. Its use implies only that there are other varieties as well. These can be specified by outsiders on the basis of the phonological, lexical, and grammatical differences that they (the varieties) manifest. Their functional allocations, however—as languages or as dialects—are derivable only from societal observation of their uses and users rather than from any characteristics of the codes themselves.

Varieties change over time, but varieties are also *changed*, either by drift or by design. Varieties that have been used in palaces and universities may later come to be used only by the rural and unlettered. In this process their lexicons may well become impoverished, hundreds or thousands of the terms once needed dropping into disuse. At the same time lexicons and grammars as well as phonologies may become much influenced by other temporarily more prestigious and possibly genetically unrelated varieties. Conversely, varieties that had never been used outside of the most humble speech networks may be elevated in function, increased in lexicon, and purified or enriched in whatever direction their circumstantially improved speakers may desire (Kloss 1952 and 1967; Fishman 1968c). All varieties of all languages are equally expandable and changeable; all are equally contractible and interpenetrable under the influence of foreign models. Their virtues are in the eyes (or ears) of their beholders. Their functions depend on the norms of the speech communities that employ them. These norms, in turn, change as speech communities change in self-concept, in their relations with surrounding communities, and in their objective circumstances. Finally, such changes usually lead to changes in the varieties themselves. Speech communities and their varieties are not only interrelated systems; they are completely interdependent systems as well. It is this interdependence that the sociology of language examines.

3.2 MAJOR TYPES OF ATTITUDES AND BEHAVIORS TOWARD LANGUAGE

One of the best known societal behaviors toward language is *standardization*, i.e., "the codification and acceptance, within a community of users, of a formal set of norms defining 'correct' usage" (Stewart 1968). Codification is typically the concern of such language "gatekeepers" as scribes, storytellers, grammarians, teachers, and writers, i.e., of certain groups that arise in most diversified societies and whose use of language is professional and conscious. Given codification as a goal, this desired "good" is formulated and presented to all or part of the speech community via such means as grammars, dictionaries, spellers, style manuals, and exemplary texts, whether written or oral. Finally, the acceptance of the formally codified (i.e., the standardized) variety of a language is advanced via such agencies and authorities as the government, the educational system, the mass media, the religious institutions, and the cultural "establishment." The standard variety then becomes associated with such institutions, the types of interactions that most commonly occur within them, and the values or goals they represent (Haugen 1966a).

Note that not all languages have standard varieties. Note also, that where a standard variety does exist, it does not necessarily displace the nonstandard varieties from the linguistic repertoire of the speech community for functions that are distinct from but complementary to those of the standard variety. Note, additionally, that there may be several competing standard varieties in the same speech community. Note, finally, that hitherto nonstandard varieties may themselves undergo standardization, whereas hitherto standardized varieties may undergo destandardization as their speakers no longer view them as worthy of codification and cultivation. Standardization is not a property of any language per se, but a characteristic societal treatment of language, given sufficient societal diversity and need for symbolic elaboration.

Another common societal view of language is that which is concerned with its *autonomy*, i.e., with the uniqueness and independence of the linguistic system, or at least of some variety within that system. *Autonomy* is often of little concern to speech communities whose languages differ markedly from each other. These may be said to be autonomous by dint of sheer *abstand* or linguistic distance between them (Kloss 1952; Kloss 1967). On the other hand, where languages seem to be quite similar to each other —phonologically, lexically, and grammatically—it may be of great concern to establish their autonomy from each other, or at least that of the weaker from the stronger. Were such autonomy not to be established, it might occur to some that one was "no more than" a dialect (a regional variety) of the other, a subservience which may become part of a rationale for political subservience as well.

A major vehicle of fostering autonomy views concerning a language is its standardization. The availability of dictionaries and grammars is taken as a sure sign that a particular variety is "really a language." However, the availability of dictionaries and grammars not only *represents* autonomy, but also cultivates and increases it by introducing new vocabulary and stressing those phonological and grammatical alternatives that are most different from those of any given autonomy-threatening contrast language. "Heroes are made not born." The same is true of the autonomy of genetically (historically) related languages. Their autonomy has to be worked on. It is not autonomy by *abstand*, but rather by *ausbau* (by effort, and, often, by fiat or decree), and pertains particularly to their standard (and most particularly to their written standard) varieties.

It is a characteristic of the newly rich to supply their own ancestors. In a similar vein those speech communities, the autonomy of whose standard variety is based most completely on *ausbau*-activity, are also most likely to be concerned with its *historicity*, that is with its "respectable" ancestry in times long past. As a result, many speech communities create and cultivate myths and genealogies concerning the origin and development of their standard varieties in order to deemphasize the numerous components of more recent vintage that they contain (Ferguson 1959b). As a result of the widespread preference for historicity, currently utilized (and recently liberated or standardized) varieties are found to be derived from ancient prototypes that had largely been forgotten, or are found to be the language of the gods, or to have been created by the same miraculous and mysterious forces and processes that created the speech community itself, etc. Thus a variety achieves historicity by coming to be associated with some great ideological or national movement or tradition (Fishman 1965c). Usually, historicity provides the ex post facto rationale for functional changes that have transpired with respect to the verbal repertoire of a speech community.

Finally, a speech community's behavior toward any one or another of the varieties in its linguistic repertoire is likely to be determined, at least in part, by the degree to which these varieties have visible *vitality*, i.e., interaction networks that actually employ them natively for one or more vital functions. The more numerous and the more important the native speakers of a particular variety are the greater its vitality and the greater its potential for standardization, autonomy, and historicity. Conversely, the fewer the number and the lower the status of the native speakers of a variety, the more it may be reacted to as if it were somehow a defective or contaminated instrument, unworthy of serious efforts or functions, and lacking in proper parentage or uniqueness. As usual, such biased views are likely to be self-fulfilling in that when the numbers and the resources of the users of a given variety dwindle they are less likely to be able to protect its standardization, autonomy, or historicity from the inroads of other speech communities and their verbal repertoires and language-enforcing resources.

Given these four widespread patterns of societal belief and behavior toward language, it is possible to define seven different kinds of varieties, depending upon their absence or presence at any given time (Figure 2). Note, however, that any speech community may include in its repertoire a number of such varieties which are differentiable on the basis of the four widespread belief-and-behavior systems just discussed. Furthermore, occupational, social class, and other experiential subvarieties are likely to exist within most of the varieties listed in Figure 2. Indeed, the members of any given community may not agree as to whether standardization, autonomy, historicity, and/or vitality are absent or present in connection with one or more of the varieties in their repertoire. After all, these dimensions are highly evaluational, rather than objective characteristics of language varieties per se, and as such, variation in evaluations may be expected both synchronically (at any particular time) as well as diachronically (across time).

In some speech communities deference due an interlocutor with whom one stands in a particular role relationship may be indicated by switching from one social class variety or from one dialect to another. In other speech communities this very same function may be realized by switching from a dialect to the standard variety (which latter variety, alone, may possess formal verb forms and pronouns of respect). In yet another speech community a switch from

FIGURE 2. Evaluations of Different Types of Language Varieties (Stewart 1968)

ATTRIBUTES*				VARIETY-TYPE	SYMBOL
1	2	3	4		
+	+	+	+	Standard	S
−	+	+	+	Vernacular	V
−	−	+	+	Dialect	D
−	−	−	+	Creole	K
−	−	−	−	Pidgin	P
+ .	+	+	−	Classical	C
+	+	−	−	Artificial	A

*1 = standardization, 2 = autonomy, 3 = historicity, 4 = vitality

one language to another (or from a dialect of one language to the standard variety of another) may be the accepted and recognized realization pattern for deferential interaction. While the precise nature of the switch will depend on the repertoire available to the speech community, switching as such and the differentia and concepts by means of which it may be noted and explained are of constant interest to sociolinguistic method and theory.

3.3 SPEECH COMMUNITY

Speech community (a term probably translated from the German *Sprachgemeinschaft*), like variety, is a neutral term. Unlike other societal designations it does not imply any particular size or any particular basis of communality. A speech community is one, all of whose members share at least a single speech variety and the norms for its appropriate use. A speech community may be as small as a single closed interaction network, all of whose members regard each other in but a single capacity. Neither of these limitations, however, is typical for speech communities throughout the world and neither is typical for those that have been studied by sociologists of language.

Isolated bands and nomadic clans not only represent small speech communities but speech communities that also exhaust their members' entire network range, while providing little specialization of roles or statuses. Such speech communities usually possess very limited verbal repertoires in terms of different varieties, primarily because one individual's life experiences and responsibilities are pretty much like another's. Nevertheless, such similarity is likely to be more apparent than real. Even small and total societies are likely to differentiate between men and women, between minors and adults, between children and parents, between leaders and followers. Indeed, such societies are likely to have more contact with the "outside world" than is commonly imagined, whether for purposes of trade or exogamy (Owens 1965). Thus, even small total societies reveal functionally differentiated linguistic repertoires (and not infrequently, intragroup bilingualism as well) based upon behaviorally differentiated interaction networks.

Such small and total (or nearly total) societies differ, of course, from equally small or even smaller family networks, friendship networks, interest networks, or occupational networks within such larger speech communities as tribes, cities, or countries. In the latter cases the interaction networks are not as redundant as in the former (i.e., one more frequently interacts with *different* people in one's various roles as son, friend, work colleague, party member, etc.). However, varieties are needed not only by diverse small networks, but also by large networks of individuals who rarely, if ever, interact, but who have certain interests, views, and allegiances in common. Thus, not only are network redundancy and network size attributes that characterize and differentiate speech communities, but so is the extent to which their existence is experiential rather than merely referential.

One of the characteristics of large and diversified speech communities is that some of the varieties within their verbal repertoires are primarily experientially acquired and reinforced by dint of actual verbal interaction within particular networks, while others are primarily referentially acquired and reinforced by dint of symbolic integration within reference networks which may rarely or never exist in any physical sense. The "nation" or the "region" are likely to constitute a speech community of this latter type and the standard ("national") language or the regional language is likely to represent its corresponding linguistic variety.

Many American cities present ample evidence of both of these bases—verbal interaction and symbolic integration—for the functioning of speech communities. Every day hundreds of thousands of residents of Connecticut, upstate New York, and various parts of Pennsylvania come to New York City to work and shop. In terms of waking hours of actual fact-to-face verbal interaction these speakers of dialects that differ from New York City English may talk more, and more frequently, to New Yorkers than they do to inhabitants of their places of residence and to speakers of their local dialects. How then can we explain the fact that not only do most of them differentially utilize the markers of their local dialects (and not only during the evenings, weekends, and holidays when they are at home rather than at work), but the simultaneous fact that many of them can and do also employ a more regionally neutral variety, which is their approximation to "Standard American," as distinct from New York City English on the one hand and Lower Connecticut Village English on the other? Obviously, the "Standard American" of these commuters to New York City cannot be based on much verbal interaction with a separate network known as "the American people." Nor can it be based upon any other interaction network, however referred to, whose speakers use "Standard American" and it alone. There is no other alternative but to conclude that the speech community of "Standard American" represents a reference group for the denizens of Connecticut villages, while "Standard American" itself is a variety that has the functions of "symbolic integration with the nation" in their linguistic repertoire.

Thus, some speech communities and their linguistic repertoires are preserved primarily by communication gaps that separate them from other communities and their repertoires. Other speech communities and their repertoires are preserved primarily by the force of symbolic (attitudinal) integration even in the absence of face-to-face interaction.

Many speech communities contain networks of both types. Many networks contain both kinds of members. Societal norms that define communicative appropriateness can apply with equal force and regularity regardless of whether direct interaction or symbolic integration underlies their implementation.

As mentioned earlier, the standard variety of a language is likely to be that variety that stands for the nation as a whole and for its most exalted institutions of government, education, and high culture in general. It is this variety which comes to be associated with the mission, glory, history, and uniqueness of an entire "people" and, indeed, it is this variety which helps unite individuals who do not otherwise constitute an interaction network into a symbolic speech community or "people." Thus it is that standard varieties and larger-than-face-to-face speech communities are historically and functionally interdependent. While interaction networks of speakers of standard varieties doubtlessly do exist (literati, scholars, social and educational elites, etc.), these are likely to arrive at somewhat specialized usages, on one hand, as well as to require a nonstandard variety, on the other hand, if they are to engage in more intimate and informal kinds of interactions as well. Thus, the standard language per se, without further differentiation or accompaniment, is most fitted for communication across large but referential (or noninteracting) networks, such as those involving the mass media, governmental pronouncements, legal codes, and textbooks. The standard variety is the "safest" for those communications in which a speaker cannot know his diversified and numerous listeners (Joos 1959). However, the more the communication is expected to live on, independently of both speaker and listener (or sender and receiver), over an appreciable period of time, the more it will be viewed as archaic (or classical) rather than merely "standard."

A basic definitional property of speech communities is that they are *not* defined as communities of those who "speak the same language" (notwithstanding Bloomfield 1933), but rather as communities set off by density of communication or/and by symbolic integration with respect to communicative competence *regardless of the number of languages or varieties employed* (Gumperz 1964a). The complexity of speech communities thus defined varies with the extent of variation in the experiential and attitudinal networks which they subsume. Speech communities can be so selected as to include greater or lesser diversity on each of these grounds. In general the verbal repertoire of a speech community is a reflection of its role repertoire (in terms of both implemented and ideologized roles). This reflection pertains not only to repertoire *range*, but also to repertoire *access* and *fluidity*.

Speech communities with a larger role repertoire reveal a larger verbal repertoire as well (Gumperz 1962). Communities most of whose members are restricted in daily experiences and in life aspirations will also tend to show little linguistic range in terms of differentiable varieties. This tends to be the case not only in the small, total communities that were mentioned earlier, but also, some suspect, in large, democratic, industrialized communities of the most modern sort. Actually, both kinds of speech communities show more repertoire range (in terms of verbal repertoire and in terms of

FIGURE 3. Speech Communities and Verbal Repertoires (based upon concepts of Gumperz 1964a and elsewhere)

Societal Domain	Speech Community 1	Speech Community 2	Speech Community 3	Speech Community 4
Home	a_1	c_1	c_1	d_1
School and Culture	a_2	b_3/c_2	b_2/c_2	a_2
Work	a_3	c_3	d_2	d_2
Government	a_2	b_1	a_2	a_2
Church	e_1	b_2	b_2	e_1
	(Moscow, 1960)	(Mea Shearim, 1966)	(Ostropol, 1905)	(Ostropol, 1905)
	[Russians]	[Jews]	[Jews]	[Ukrainians]

Some communities have more obviously diversified repertoires than others (e.g., SC1 utilizes three varieties of one language and one of another, whereas SC3 utilizes varieties of four different languages). Varieties that are related to one societal domain in one SC (e.g., b_2 in SC2) may be associated with more or different societal domains in another SC (e.g., b_2 in SC3). All speakers of varieties of a particular language do not necessarily constitute a single speech community.

role repertoire) than is obvious on superficial inspection. Nevertheless, they both tend to have narrower (and less diversified) ranges than are encountered in the stratified speech communities that exist in intermediate societies of the traditional, non-Western world. Whereas the modern, relatively open speech community tends to reveal several varieties of the same language, the more traditional speech community will typically reveal varieties of several languages (see Figure 3).

These two types of speech communities are also quite likely to differ in the extent to which their members have *access* to the roles and to the varieties available in the respective repertoires of their communities. In the more traditional speech communities access to certain roles is severely restricted and is attained, in those cases in which access to new roles *is* available, on the basis of *ascription*. Those whose ancestry is inappropriate cannot attain certain new roles, regardless of their personal achievement. Similarly, access to an expanded verbal repertoire is also severely restricted, most varieties not learned in childhood being available only to those who can afford to devote many years of patient and painstaking formal study to their acquisition. Both of these conditions are not nearly so likely to exist in modern, personal-achievement-oriented societies, although their lack of completely equal and open access is evident to all students of the disadvantaged (including Negro non-standard speech) in the midst of America's plenty.

In more traditional societies in which status is based on ascription there is also likely to be more role *compartmentalization*. Thus, not only are certain individuals barred from enacting certain roles, but in general, the rights and duties that constitute particular roles are more distinct and the transitions from one role to the next, for members of those classes who may enter into them, are ritually governed, as are the roles themselves. Such societies also tend to reveal marked verbal compartmentalization as well (McCormack 1960). When an individual speaks language or variety A he takes great care not to switch into B and not to slip into traces of B, whether phonologically, lexically, or grammatically. Each variety is kept separate and uncontaminated from the other just as is each role. How different such compartmentalization is from the fluidity of modern, democratic speech communities in which there is such frequent change from one role to another and from one variety to another that individuals are frequently father and pal, or teacher and colleague, simultaneously or in rapid succession! The result of such frequent and easy role shifts is often that the roles themselves become more similar and less distinctive or clear-cut. The same occurs in the verbal repertoire as speakers change from one variety (or language) to another with greater frequency and fluidity. The varieties too tend to become more similar as the roles in which they are appropriate become more and more alike. This is particularly likely to occur, as we shall see below, among lower-class speakers whose mastery of the more formal roles and varieties available to their speech communities is likely to be marginal at best.

Thus, just as varieties are characterizable by a small number of attributes and their combinations, so is this true of the attributes that characterize speech communities at the most general level. The interactional basis of speech communities, their symbolic-integrative basis, their size, repertoire range, repertoire access, and repertoire compartmentalization are all concepts that we shall need to refer to again and again in the pages that follow.

INTERACTIONAL SOCIOLOGY
OF LANGUAGE:
MICRO AND MACRO

Boss	Carmen, do you have a minute?
Secretary	Yes, Mr. Gonzalez.
Boss	I have a letter to dictate to you.
Secretary	Fine. Let me get my pen and pad. I'll be right back.
Boss	Okay.
Secretary	Okay.
Boss	Okay, this is addressed to Mr. William Bolger.
Secretary	That's B-o-r-g-e-r?
Boss	B-o-l
Secretary	Oh, oh, I see.
Boss	Okay. His address is in the files.
Secretary	Okay.
Boss	Okay. Dear Bill, Many thanks for telling me about your work with the Science Research Project. The information you gave me ought to prove most helpful.
Secretary	That was "The information you gave me ought to prove most helpful?"

Boss	Correct.
Secretary	Okay.
Boss	Okay, ah. I very much appreciate the time you gave me. Never mind, strike that out. Ah, enclosed are two of the forms that you let me borrow. I'll be sending back the data sheets very soon. Thanks again, I hope that your hospital stay will be as pleasant as possible and that your back will be soon in top shape. Will soon be in top shape. It was nice seeing you again. Sincerely, Louis Gonzalez.
Secretary	Do you have the enclosures for the letter, Mr. Gonzalez?
Boss	Oh yes, here they are.
Secretary	Okay.
Boss	Ah, this man William Bolger got his organization to contribute a lot of money to the Puerto Rican parade. He's very much for it. ¿Tú fuiste a la parada? (Did you go to the parade?)
Secretary	Sí, yo fuí. (Yes, I went.)
Boss	¿Sí? (Yes?)
Secretary	Uh huh.
Boss	¿Y cómo te estuvo? (And how did you like it?)
Secretary	Ay, lo más bonita. (Oh, very pretty.)
Boss	Sí, porque yo fuí y yo nunca había participado en la parada y (Yes, because I went and I had never participated in the parade and

este año me dió curiosidad por ir a ver como
era y estuvo eso
this year I became curious to go and see how it
was and that was

fenómeno. Fuí con mi señora y con mis nenes y
a ellos también
a phenomenon. I went with my wife and my
children and they

le gustó mucho. Eh, y tuve día bien agradable.
Ahora lo que
also liked it very much. And I had a pleasant
day. Now

me molesta a mi es que las personas cuando
viene una cosa así,
what bothers me is that people when something
like this comes along,

la parada Puertorriqueña o la fiesta de San Juan,
corren de la
the Puerto Rican parade, or the festival of San
Juan they run from

casa a participar porque es una actividad festiva,
alegre, y sin
the house to participate because it is a festive
activity, happy, and

embargo, cuando tienen que ir a la iglesia, o la
misa para pedirle . . .
then, when they have to go to church or to
mass, to ask . . .)

Secretary   (Laughter)

Boss   A Diós entonce no van.
             (God then they don't go.)

Secretary   Sí, entonces no van.
             (Yes, then they don't go.)

Boss   Pero, así es la vida, caramba.
            (But that's life, you know.) Do you think that
            you could get this letter out today?
Secretary   Oh yes, I'll have it this afternoon for you.
Boss   Okay, good, fine then.
Secretary   Okay.
Boss   Okay.

If we carefully consider the above conversation it becomes evident that it reveals considerable internal variation. Speaker A does not always speak in the same way nor does his interlocutor, Speaker B. Were it possible for us to listen to the original tapes of this conversation, several *kinds* of variation within each of them would become evident to us: variations in speed of speaking, variations in the extent to which Spanish phonology creeps into English discourse and vice versa, variations in the extent to which English phonology creeps into the Spanish discourse, etc. However, even from the conventionally (orthographically) rendered transcription available to us on the previous pages one kind of variation remains exceedingly clear: that from Spanish to English or from English to Spanish for each speaker. It is precisely because bilingual code switching is often more noticeable than other kinds of sociolinguistic variation that bilingualism is so commonly examined in sociolinguistic theory and research. However, the concepts and findings that derive from such examinations must be provocative and illuminating for the sociology of language more generally. And, indeed, that *is* the case, for the societal patterning of bilingual interaction is merely an instance (hopefully, a more obvious and, therefore, pedagogically useful instance) of the vastly more general phenomenon of societal patterning of variation in verbal interaction.

How shall we describe or measure the phenomenon of interest to us: societal patterning of variation in verbal interaction? Usefully accurate description or measurement is certainly the basic problem of every scientific field of endeavor. Most of mankind has constantly been immersed in a veritable ocean of crosscurrents of talk. Nevertheless, as with most other aspects of everyday social behavior, it is only in very recent days that man has begun to recognize the latent order and regularity in the manifest chaos of verbal interaction that surrounds him.

4.1 HOW SHOULD TALK BE DESCRIBED CONTEXTUALLY?

How should "talk" be contextually described in order to best reveal or discover its social systemization (assuming that its "basic" linguistic description is already available)? Let us begin with some passages of actual "talk," making sure to preserve its verbatim form (preferably, by utilizing sensitive audio and visual recording equipment) rather than merely summarizing the content of such talk. The smallest sociolinguistic unit that will be of interest to us is a *speech act:* a joke, an interjection, an opening remark (Schegloff 1968), a question, in general—a segment of talk that is also societally recognizable and reoccurring. Speech acts are normally parts of somewhat larger *speech events,* such as conversations, introductions, lectures, prayers, arguments, etc. (Hymes 1967b), which, of course, must also be societally recognizable and reoccurring.

If we note that a switch has occurred from variety *a* to variety *b*—perhaps from a kind of Spanish to a kind of English, or from more formal English to less formal English, or from regionally neutral, informal Spanish to Jíbaro (rural) informal Spanish—the first question that presents itself is whether one variety tends to be used (or used more often) in certain kinds of speech acts or events, whereas the other tends to be used (or used more often) in others. Thus, were we aware of the speech acts recognized by bilingual Puerto Rican youngsters in New York, we might venture to explain a switch such as the following:

First Girl Yes, and don't tell me that the United States is the
            only one that has been able to in Puerto Rico. . . .

FERNALD LIBRARY
COLBY-SAWYER COLLEGE
NEW LONDON, N.H. 03257

91064

Boy	Okay so you have a couple of people like Moscoso and Luís Ferrer.
First Girl	¡ Un momento!
Boy	¡ Bueno!
First Girl	¡ Un momento!
Boy	Have you got people capable of starting something like . . . like General Motors?

as being related to the act of interruption or disagreement in the midst of a somewhat specialized argument. There may be a problem, however, when testing this interpretation, in determining the speech acts and speech events that are to be recognized within a speech community.

Certainly, it is not appropriate to simply apply the system of acts and events that has been determined for one speech community in the study of another, without first determining its appropriateness in the second community. Similarly, it is not sufficient for the investigator, no matter how much experience he has had with the verbal behavior of a particular speech community, merely to devise as detailed a listing of speech acts and events as he can. Such a list runs the decided risk of being *etic* rather than *emic,* i.e., of making far too many, as well as behaviorally inconsequential, differentiations, just as was often the case with phon*etic* vs. phon*emic* analysis in linguistics proper. An *emic* set of speech acts and events must be one that is validated as meaningful via final recourse to the native members of a speech community rather than via appeal to the investigator's ingenuity or intuition alone.

An *emic* set of speech acts and speech events is best approximated, perhaps along a never-ending asymptote, by playing back recorded samples of "talk" to native speakers and by encouraging them to react to and comment upon the reasons for the use of variety *a* "here" as contrasted with the use of variety *b* "there." The more the sensitive investigator observes the speech community that he seeks to describe sociolinguistically the more hunches he will have concerning functionally different speech acts and speech events. However, even the best hunches require verification *from within the speech community*. Such verification may take various shapes. The views of both naïve and skilled informants may be cited and tabulated as they comment upon recorded instances of variation in "talk" and as they reply to the investigator's patient probes and queries as to "Why didn't he say 'Just a minute!' instead of '¡Momento!'? Would it have meant something different if he *had* said that instead? When is it appropriate to say '¡Momento!' and when is it appropriate to say 'Just a minute!' (assuming that the persons involved know both languages equally well)?", etc. Once the investigator has *demonstrated* (not merely assumed or argued) the validity of his sets of functionally different speech acts and events, he may then proceed to utilize them in the collection and analysis of samples of talk which are *independent* of those already utilized for validational purposes. Such, at least, is the rationale of research procedure at this microlevel of sociolinguistic analysis, although the field itself is still too young and too linguistically oriented to have produced many instances of such cross-validation of its *social* units selected for purposes of *socio*linguistic analysis.

4.2 MICRO-LEVEL ANALYSIS IN THE SOCIOLOGY OF LANGUAGE

Sociolinguistic description may merely begin—rather than end—with the specification and the utilization of speech acts and events, depending on the purpose of a particular research enterprise. The more linguistically oriented a particular study may be, the more likely it is to remain content with microlevel analysis, since the microlevel in the sociology of language is already a much higher (i.e., a more contextual and complicated) level of analysis than that traditionally employed within linguistics proper. However, the more societally oriented a particular sociolinguistic study may be, the more concerned with investigating social processes and societal organization per se, the more likely it is to seek successively more macrolevel analyses. Microlevel sociology of language (sometimes referred to as ethnomethodological) constitutes one of the levels within sociolinguistic inquiry (Garfinkel 1967; Garfinkel and Sacks in press). The various levels do not differ in the degree to which they are correct or accurate. They differ in purpose, and therefore in method. We can trace only a few of the successive levels in this Section, primarily in order to demonstrate their similarities and their differences.

One of the awarenesses to which an investigator may come after pondering a mountain of sociolinguistic data at the level of speech acts and events is that variation in "talk" is more common and differently proportioned or distributed between certain interlocutors than it is between others (Schegloff 1968). Thus, whereas either the boy or the girl in Conversation 2 may initiate the switch from one language to another, it may seem from Conversation 1 that the boss is the initiator of switching far more frequently than is the secretary. Therefore, while a great deal of switching is functionally *metaphorical*, i.e., it indicates a contrast in emphasis (from humor to seriousness, from agreement to disagreement, from the inessential or secondary to the essential or primary, in any interchange already underway in a particular language variety), interlocutors may vary in the extent to which they may appropriately initiate or engage in such switching, depending on their *role-relationship* to each other. Note, however, that it is necessary for a certain appropriateness to exist between a variety and certain characteristics of the social setting before it is possible to utilize another variety for metaphorical or contrastive purposes.

4.3 ROLE-RELATIONSHIPS

Any two interlocutors within a given speech community (or, more narrowly, within a given speech network within a speech community) must recognize the role-relationship that exists between them at any particular time. Such recognition is part of the communality of norms and behaviors upon which the existence of speech communities depends. Father-son, husband-wife, teacher-pupil, clergyman-layman, em-ployer-employee, friend-friend: these are but some examples of the role relationships that may exist in various (but not in all) speech communities (Goodenough 1965). Role relation-ships are implicitly recognized and accepted sets of mutual rights and obligations between members of the same sociocul-tural system. One of the ways in which members reveal such common membership to each other, as well as their recognition of the rights and obligations that they owe toward each other, is via appropriate variation (which, of course, may include ap-propriate nonvariation) of the way(s) they talk to each other. Perhaps children should generally be seen and not heard, but when they *are* heard most societies insist that they talk dif-ferently to their parents than they do to their friends (Fischer 1958). One of the frequent comments about Ameri-can travelers abroad is that they know (*at most*) only one variety of the language of the country they are visiting. As a result, they speak in the same way to a child, a professor, a bootblack, and a shopkeeper, thus revealing not only their foreignness, but also their ignorance of the appropriate ways of signaling local role relationships.

It is probably not necessary, at this point, to dwell upon the kinds of variation in talk that may be required (or pro-hibited) by certain role-relationships. In addition, and this too should require no extensive discussion at this point, whether the variation required is from one language to another or from one geographic, social, or occupational variety to another, the functionally differential role relation-ships must be *emically* validated rather than merely *etically* enumerated. There are certainly sociolinguistic allo roles in most speech communities. However, two other characteriza-tions of role-relationships do merit mention at this point, particularly because they have proved to be useful in sociolin-guistic description and analysis.

Role-relationships vary in the extent to which their mutual rights and obligations must or must not be *continually stressed*. The king-subject role-relationship may retain more invariant stress than the shopkeeper-customer relationship. If shopkeepers and their customers may also interact with each other as friends, as relatives, as members of the same political party, etc., whereas kings and their subjects (in the same speech community) may not experience a similar degree of role change, access, and fluidity *vis-á-vis each other,* then we would expect to encounter more variation in the "talk" of two individuals who encounter each other as shopkeeper and customer than we would expect between two individuals who encounter each other as king and subject. In addition, a shopkeeper and his customer may be able to set aside their roles entirely and interact entirely on the basis of their individual and momentary needs and inclinations. This may not be permissible for the king and his subjects. Thus, we should say that a shopkeeper and his customer may engage in both *personal* and *transactional* interactions (Gumperz 1964a), whereas the king and his subjects engage only in transactional interactions. Transactional interactions are those which stress the mutual rights and obligations of their participants. Personal interactions are more informal, more fluid, more varied.

In part, speech acts and events are differentially distributed throughout various role relationships because personal and transactional interactions are differentially permitted in various role relationships. The sociology of language is necessarily of interest to those investigators who are concerned with determining the functionally different role relationships that exist within a given community. Microlevel sociology of language, at least, is concerned with the validation of such relationships, via demonstration of differential role access, role range, and role fluidity, as well as via the demonstration of differential proportions of personal and transactional interaction, through the data of "talk." Role-relationships may be used as data-organizing units both with respect to variation in talk as well as with respect to other variations in interpersonal behavior. That is the reason why role-relations are so frequently examined in the sociology of language.

4.4 THE SITUATION: CONGRUENT AND INCONGRUENT

It has probably occurred to the reader that if the shopkeeper and his customer are not to interact only as such, but rather also as friends, lovers, relatives, or party members, that more than their roles are likely to change. After all, neither the *time* nor the *place* of the storekeeper-customer role-relationship is really ideal for any of the other relationships mentioned. Lovers require a time and a place of their own, and the same is true—or, at least, is typical—for other role relationships as well. These three ingredients (the *implementation* of the rights and duties of a particular role-relationship, in the *place* (locale) most appropriate or most typical for that relationship, and at the *time* societally defined as appropriate for that relationship), taken together, constitute a construct that has proven itself to be of great value in the sociology of language: the *social situation* (Bock 1964; see Figure 4).

FIGURE 4. The Social Situation (Bock 1964)

SITUATION: "CLASS"	*Time:* Class Meeting
Space: Classroom	*Roles:* + Teacher + Pupil ± Student-Teacher

+ indicates obligatory occurrence
± indicates optional occurrence

The simplest type of social situation for microlevel sociology of language to describe and analyze is the congruent situation in which all three ingredients "go-together" in the culturally accepted way. This is not to say that the investigator may assume that there is only one place and one time appropriate for the realization of a particular role-relationship. Quite the contrary. As with the wakes studied by Bock on a Micmac Indian Reserve, there may be various times and various places for the appropriate realization of particular role-relationships (see Figure 5). Nevertheless, the

FIGURE 5. Situation-Matrix No. 14: Indian Wake (Bock 1964)

M-14		T-1	T-2	T-3	T-4	T-5
S-1: Bier	s-1.1: nucleus	R-1	R-1	R-1	R-1	R-1
Area	s-1.2: margin	±R-2			±R-2	
S-2: Front Area			R-3	R-4		r-2.1
S-3: Audience Area			R-2	R-2	±R-2 ±R-4	r-2.2 R-4
S-4: Mar-ginal	s-4.1: kitchen				r-2.1	
Area	s-4.2: outside	r-2.2			±r-2.2 ±R-4	

14. SC-A:	Place of Wake—External distribution into 9.S-A.1: House site (usually that occupied by deceased).
S-1:	Bier Area
s-1.1:	nuclus—contains coffin
s-1.2:	margin—area immediately surrounding coffin
S-2:	Front Area—focal region of performances during T-2, -3, and -5.
S-3:	Audience Area—seating area for R-2: Mourner
S-4:	Marginal Area—residual space, including
s-4.1:	kitchen area
s-4.2:	outside of house
14. TC-A:	Time of Wake—External distribution (see discussion above). TC-A = //T-1/T-2//:T-3/T-4://±T-5//:T-3/T-4://
T-1:	Gathering Time—participants arrive at SC-A: Place of Wake
T-2:	Prayer Time—saying of the Rosary by R-3: Prayer Leader
T-3:	Singing Time—several hymns sung with brief pauses in between
T-4:	Intermission—longer pause in singing
T-5:	Meal Time—optional serving of meal (about midnight)
14. RC-A:	Participant Roles—External distribution noted for each:
R-1:	Corpse—from 3: RC-A: Band Member
R-2:	Mourner
r-2.1:	Host—member of 9.RC-A: Household Group (of deceased)
r-2.2:	Other—residual category
R-3:	Prayer Leader
r-3.1:	Priest—from 3.R-B.1.1: Priest
r-3.2:	Other—from 14.R-4
R-4:	Singer—usually from 11.R-A.4: Choir Member

total number of permissible combinations is likely to be small, and small or not, there is likely to be little ambiguity among members of the society or culture under study as to what the situation in question is and what its requirements are with respect to their participation in it. As a result, if there are language usage norms with respect to situations these are likely to be most clearly and uniformly realized in avowedly congruent situations.

However, lovers quarrel. Although they meet in the proper time and place, they do not invariably behave toward each other as lovers should. Similarly, if a secretary and a boss are required to meet in the office at 3:00 A.M. in order to complete an emergency report, it may well be difficult for them to maintain the usual secretary-boss relationship. Finally, if priest and parishioner meet at the Yonkers Raceway during the time normally set aside for confessions, this must have some impact on the normal priest-parishioner role relationship. However, in all such instances of initial incongruency (wrong behavior, wrong time, or wrong place) the resulting interaction—whether sociolinguistic or otherwise—is normally far from random or chaotic. One party to the interaction of another, if not both, reinterprets the seeming incongruency so as to yield a congruent situation, at least phenomenologically, for that particular encounter, where one does not exist socioculturally.

Because of incongruent behavior toward each other lovers may reinterpret each other as employer and employee and the date situation is reinterpreted as a dispassionate work situation. Because of the incongruent time, secretary and boss may view the work situation as more akin to a date than is their usual custom. Because of the incongruent place priest and parishioner may pretend not to recognize each other, or to treat each other as "old pals." In short, after a bit of "fumbling around" in which various and varying tentative re-definitions may be tried out, a new congruent situation is interpreted as existing and *its* behavioral and sociolinguistic requirements are implemented (Blom and Gumperz 1968; Fishman 1968b). Thus, whereas bilingual Puerto Rican parents and their children in New York are most likely to talk to each other in Spanish at home when conversing about family matters, they will probably speak in English to each other in the public school building (Fishman, Cooper, and Ma 1968). As far as they are concerned these are two different situations, perhaps calling for two different role relationships and requiring the utilization of two different languages or varieties.

Situational contrasts need not be as discontinuous as most of our examples have thus far implied. Furthermore, within a basically Spanish-speaking situation one or another member of a bilingual speech community may still switch to English (or, in Paraguay, to Guarani) in the midst of a speech event for purely metaphorical (i.e., for emphatic or contrastive) purposes. Such *metaphorical switching* would not be possible, however, if there were no general norm assigning the particular situation, as one of a class of such situations, to one language rather than to the other. However, in contrast to the frequently unilateral and fluid back-and-forth nature of metaphorical switching (perhaps to indicate a personal interlude in a basically transactional interaction) there stands the frequently more reciprocal and undirectional nature of *situational* switching.

More generally put, *situational switching is governed by common allocation*, i.e., by widespread normative views and regulations that commonly allocate a particular variety to a particular cluster of topics, places, persons, and purposes. *Metaphorical switching, on the other hand, is governed by uncommon or contrastive allocation.* It is operative as a departure from the common allocations that are normally operative. Without well-established normative views and regulations relative to the functional allocation of varieties within the repertoire of a speech community neither situational nor metaphorical switching could effectively obtain. A switch to cockney where Received Pronunciation (and grammar) is called for may elicit a brief raising of eyebrows or a pause in the conversation—until it is clear from the speaker's demeanor and from the fact that he has reverted to *RP* that no change in situation was intended. However, such metaphorical switching can be risky. Someone might feel that for the situation at hand cockney is in poor taste. Metaphorical switching is a luxury that can be afforded only by those that comfortably share not only the same *set* of situational norms but also *the same view as to their inviolability*. Since most of us are members of several speech networks, each with somewhat different sociolinguistic norms, the chances that situational shifting and metaphorical switching will be misunderstood and conflicted—particularly where the norms pertaining to variety selection have few or insufficiently powerful guardians—are obviously great.

4.5 THE TRANSITION TO MACRO-LEVEL SOCIOLOGY OF LANGUAGE

The situational analysis of language and behavior represents the boundary area between microlevel and macrolevel sociology of language. The very fact that a baseball conversation "belongs" to one speech variety and an electrical engineering lecture "belongs" to another speech variety is a major key to an even more generalized description of sociolinguistic variation. The very fact that humor during a formal lecture is realized through a metaphorical switch to another variety must be indicative of an underlying sociolinguistic regularity, perhaps of the view that lecturelike or formal situations are generally associated with one language or variety whereas levity or intimacy is tied to another (Joos 1959). The large-scale aggregative regularities that obtain between varieties and societally recognized functions are examined via the construct termed *domain* (Fishman 1965d; Fishman in press).

Sociolinguistic domains are societal constructs derived from painstaking analysis and summarization of patently congruent situations (see Fishman, Cooper, and Ma 1968, for many examples of the extraction of *emic* domains via factor analysis as well as for examples of the validation of initially *etic* domains). The macrosociologist or social psychologist may well inquire: What is the significance of the fact that school situations and "schoolish" situations (the latter being initially incongruent situations reinterpreted in the direction of their most salient component) are related to variety *a*? Frequently, it is helpful to recognize a number of behaviorally separate domains (behaviorally separate in that they are derived from discontinuous social situations), all of which are commonly associated with a particular variety or language. Thus, in many bilingual speech communities such domains as school, church, professional work sphere, and government have been verified and found to be congruent with a language or variety that we will refer to as *H* (although for purely labeling purposes we might refer to it as *a* or *X* or *1*). Similarly, such domains as family, neighborhood, and lower work sphere have been validated and found to be congruent with a language or variety that we will refer to as *L* (or *b*, or *Y* or *2*). All in all, the fact that a complex speech community contains various superposed varieties—in some cases, various languages, and in others, various varieties of the same language—is now well documented. The existence of complementary varieties for intragroup purposes is known as *diglossia* (Ferguson 1959a) and the communities in which diglossia is encountered are referred to as *diglossic*. Domains are particularly useful constructs for the macrolevel (i.e., community-wide) functional description of societally patterned variation in "talk" within large and complex diglossic speech communities, about which more will be said in Section 7, below.

Some members of diglossic speech communities can verbalize the relationship between certain broad categories of behavior and certain broad categories of "talk." More educated and verbally fluent members of speech communities can tell an investigator about such relationships at great length and in great detail. Less educated and verbally limited members can only grope to express a regularity which they vaguely realize to exist. However, the fact that the formulation of a regular association between language (variety) and large-scale situational behaviors may be difficult to come by is no more indicative of a dubious relationship than the fact that grammatical regularities can rarely be explicitly formulated by native speakers is to be considered as calling the abstracted rules themselves into question.

As with all constructs (including situations, role-relation-ships, and speech events), domains originate in the integrative intuition of the investigator. If the investigator notes that student-teacher interactions in classrooms, school corridors, school auditoriums, and school laboratories of elementary schools, high schools, colleges, and universities are all realized via H as long as these interactions are focused upon educational technicality and specialization, he may begin to suspect that these hypothetically congruent situations all belong to a single (educational) domain. If he further finds that hypothetically incongruent situations involving an educational and a noneducational ingredient are, by and large, predictably resolved in terms of H rather than L if the third ingredient is an educational time, place, or role relationship, he may feel further justified in positing an educational domain. Finally, if informants tell him that the predicted language or variety would be appropriate in all of the examples he can think of that derive from his notion of the educational domain, whereas they proclaim that it would not be appropriate for examples that he draws from a contrasted domain, then the construct is as usefully validated as is that of situation or event—with one major difference.

Whereas particular speech acts (and speech excerpts of an even briefer nature) can be apportioned to the speech events and social situations in which they occurred, the same cannot be done with respect to such acts or excerpts in relationship to societal domains. Domains are extrapolated from the *data* of "talk" rather than being an actual component of the *process* of talk. However, domains are as real as the very social institutions of a speech community, and indeed they show a marked paralleling with such major social institutions (Barker 1947). There is an undeniable difference between the social institution, "the family," and any particular family, but there is no doubt that the societal norms concerning the former must be derived from data on many instances of the latter. Once such societal norms are formulated they can be utilized to test predictions concerning the distributions of societally patterned variations in talk across all instances of one domain vs. all instances of another.

Thus, domains and social situations reveal the links that exist between microlevel and macrolevel sociology of language. The members of diglossic speech communities can come to have certain views concerning their varieties or languages because these varieties are associated (in behavior and in attitude) with particular domains. The *H* variety (or language) is considered to reflect certain values and relationships within the speech community, whereas the *L* variety is considered to reflect others. Certain individuals and groups may come to advocate the expansion of the functions of *L* into additional domains. Others may advocate the displacement of *L* entirely and the use of *H* solely. Neither of these revisionist views could be held or advocated without recognition of the reality of domains of language-and-behavior in the existing norms of communicative appropriateness. The high culture values with which certain varieties are associated and the intimacy and folksiness values with which others are congruent are both derivable from domain-appropriate norms governing characteristic verbal interaction.

4.6 ON THE REALITY OF SOCIOLINGUISTIC COMPOSITING

So little (if, indeed, any) microsociolinguistic data has been subjected to rigorous quantitative analysis or obtained via experimentally controlled variation that it is fitting that we pause to examine a study that has attempted to do so, even if it deals only with sociolinguistic normative views and claims. The study in question (Fishman and Greenfield 1970) is concerned with the relative importance of persons, places, and topics in the perception of congruent and incongruent situations and with the impact of perceived congruence or incongruence on claimed language use in different domains. Since domains are a higher order generalization from *congruent situations* (i.e., from situations in which individuals interact in appropriate role relationships with each other, in the appropriate locales for these role relationships, and discuss topics appropriate to their role relationships) it was first necessary to test intuitive and rather clinical estimates of the widespread congruences that were felt to obtain. After more than a year of participant observation and other data-gathering experiences it seemed to Greenfield (1968) that five domains could be generalized from the innumerable situations that he had encountered. He tentatively labeled these "family," "friendship," "religion," "education," and "employment" and proceeded to determine whether a typical *situation* could be presented for each domain as a means of collecting self-report data on language choice. As indicated below each domain was represented by a congruent person (interlocutor), place, and topic in the self-report instrument that Greenfield constructed for high school students.

DOMAIN	INTERLOCUTOR	PLACE	TOPIC
Family	Parent	Home	How to be a good son or daughter.
Friendship	Friend	Beach	How to play a certain game
Religion	Priest	Church	How to be a good Christian
Education	Teacher	School	How to solve an algebra problem
Employment	Employer	Workplace	How to do your job more efficiently

Greenfield's hypothesis was that within the Puerto Rican speech community, among individuals who knew Spanish and English equally well, Spanish was primarily associated with family and with friendship (the two, family and friendship constituting the intimacy value cluster), while English was primarily associated with religion, work, and education (the three constituting the status-stressing value cluster). In order to test this hypothesis he first presented two seemingly congruent situational components and requested his subjects (a) to select a third component in order to complete the situation, as well as (b) to indicate their likelihood of using Spanish or English if they were involved in such a situation and if they and their Puerto Rican interlocutors knew Spanish and English equally well. Section I of Table 1 shows that Greenfield's predictions were uniformly confirmed among those subjects who selected congruent third components. Spanish was decreasingly reported for family, friendship, religion, employment, and education, regardless of whether the third component selected was a person, place, or topic.

TABLE 1. Spanish and English Usage Self-Ratings in Various Situations for Components Selected

I.   *Congruent Situations:* Two "congruent" components presented; S selects third congruent component and language appropriate to situation. 1=all Spanish, 5=all English.

Congruent Persons Selected

	Parent	Friend	Total		Priest	Teacher	Employer	Tot
Mean	2.77	3.60	3.27		4.69	4.92	4.79	4.8
S.D.	1.48	1.20	1.12		.61	.27	.41	.3
N	13	15	15		13	13	14	15

Congruent Places Selected

	Home	Beach	Total		Church	School	Work-place	Tot
Mean	2.33	3.50	2.60		3.80	4.79	4.27	4.2
S.D.	1.07	1.26	1.10		1.51	.58	1.34	.9
N	15	6	15		15	14	15	1

Congruent Topics Selected

	Family	Friend-ship	Total		Reli-gion	Edu-cation	Employ-ment	Tot
Mean	1.69	3.30	2.64		3.80	4.78	4.44	4.3
S.D.	.92	1.20	.95		1.47	1.53	1.12	.7
N	16	18	18		15	18	18	1

II.   *Incongruent Situations:* Two "incongruent" components presented; S selects third component and language appropriate to situation. 1=all Spanish, 5=all English.

Persons Selected

	Parent	Friend	Total		Priest	Teacher	Employer	To
Mean	2.90	3.92	3.60		4.68	4.77	4.44	4.7
S.D.	1.20	.64	.70		.59	.48	.68	.5
N	16	16	16		14	15	9	1

Places Selected

	Home	Beach	Total		Church	School	Work-place	To
Mean	2.63	3.86	2.77		3.71	4.39	4.42	4.1
S.D.	.77	.94	.70		1.32	1.90	.96	.8
N	15	5	15		15	15	15	1

Topics Selected

	Family	Friend-ship	Total		Reli-gion	Edu-cation	Employ-ment	To
Mean	2.83	3.81	3.26		3.07	3.66	3.81	3.4
S.D.	1.04	1.13	1.02		1.00	1.20	.85	.7
N	18	16	18		18	17	18	1

However, as Blom and Gumperz (in press), Fishman (1968b), and others have indicated, seemingly incongruent situations frequently occur and are rendered understandable and acceptable (just as are the seemingly ungrammatical sentences that we hear in most spontaneous speech). Interlocutors reinterpret incongruences in order to salvage some semblance of the congruency in terms of which they understand and function within their social order. Were this not the case then no seemingly congruent domains could arise and be maintained out of the incongruences of daily life. In order to test this assumption Greenfield proceeded to present his subjects with two incongruent components (e.g., with a person from one hypothetical domain and with a place from another hypothetical domain) and asked them to select a third component in order to complete the situation as well as to indicate their likelihood of using Spanish or English in a situation so constituted. Greenfield found that the third component was overwhelmingly selected from either one or the other of any two domains from which he had selected the first two components. Furthermore, in their attempts to render a seemingly incongruous situation somewhat more congruent his subject's language preferences left the relationship between domains and language choice substantially unaltered (directionally), regardless of whether persons, places, or topics were involved. Nevertheless, all domains became somewhat less different from each other than they had been in the fully congruent situations. Apparently, both individual indecisiveness as well as sociolinguistic norms governing domain regularity must be combined and compromised when incongruences appear. Language choice is much more clear-cut and polarized in "usual" situations governed neatly by sociolinguistic norms of communicative appropriateness than they are in "unusual" situations which must be resolved by individual interpretation.

Yet another (and for this presentation, final) indication of the construct validity of domains as analytic parameters for the study of large-scale sociolinguistic patterns is yielded by Edelman's data (1968). Here we note that when the word-naming responses of bilingual Puerto Rican children in Jersey City were analyzed in accord with the domains derived from Greenfield's and Fishman's data reported above significant and instructive findings were obtained. The most Spanish domain for all children was "family" (Table 2A). The most English domain for all children was "education." The analysis of variance (Table 2B) indicates that not only

TABLE 2A. Mean Number of Words Named by Young Schoolchildren (Edelman 1968)

(N=34)

Age	Language	Family	Education	Domain Religion	Friendship	Total
6-8	English	6.2	8.2	6.6	8.3	7.3
	Spanish	7.6	6.2	5.8	6.4	6.5
	Total	6.9	7.2	6.2	7.4	6.9
9-11	English	11.7	12.8	8.7	10.9	11.0
	Spanish	10.5	9.4	7.2	9.7	9.2
	Total	11.1	11.1	7.9	10.3	10.1
Total	English	9.0	10.5	7.7	9.6	9.2
	Apanish	9.0	7.8	6.5	8.0	7.8
	Total	9.0	9.1	7.1	9.0	8.5

TABLE 2B. Analysis of Variance of Young Schoolchildren's Word-Naming Scores

Source	Sum of Squares	df	Mean Square	F	F_{95}	F_{99}
Between Subjects	1844.12	33				
C (age)	689.30	1	689.30	19.67*	4.17	7.56
D (sex)	15.54	1	15.54	.44	4.17	7.56
CD	87.87	1	87.87	2.51	4.17	7.56
error (b)	1051.41	30	35.05			
Within Subjects	1795.88	238				
A (language)	123.13	1	123.13	9.73*	4.17	7.56
B (domain)	192.54	3	64.18	8.51*	2.71	4.00
AB	65.12	3	21.71	11.67*	2.71	4.00
AC	16.50	1	16.50	1.30	4.17	7.56
AD	42.08	1	42.08	3.32	4.17	7.56
BC	61.54	3	20.51	2.72	2.71	4.00
BD	2.89	3	.96	.13	2.71	4.00
ABC	23.99	3	8.00	4.30*	2.71	4.00
ABD	6.70	3	2.23	1.20	2.71	4.00
ACD	14.62	1	14.62	1.15	4.17	7.56
BCD	13.53	3	4.51	.60	2.71	4.00
ABCD	7.98	3	2.66	1.43	2.71	4.00
error (w)	1225.26	210				
$error_1$ (w)	379.88	30	12.66			
$error_2$ (w)	678.31	90	7.54			
$error_3$ (w)	167.07	90	1.86			
Total	3640.00	271				

*Significant at or above the .01 level.

did the children's responses differ significantly by age (older children giving more responses in both languages than did younger children), by language (English yielding more responses than does Spanish), and by domain (church yielding fewer responses than does any other domain), but that these three variables *interact significantly* as well. This means that one language is much more associated with certain domains than is the other and that this is differentially so by age. This is exactly the kind of finding for which domain analysis is particularly suited. Its utility for inter-society comparisons and for gauging language shift would seem to be quite promising, but its major value should be in describing and demonstrating the dependence of communicative appropriateness on the compositing appropriateness of members of speech communities, whether monolingual or bilingual.

One thing appears to be clear from the theoretical and empirical work cited: there are classes of events recognized by each speech network or community in which several seemingly different situations are classed as being of the same kind. No speech network has a linguistic repertoire that is as differentiated as the complete list of apparently different role relations, topics, and locales in which its members are involved. Just *where the boundaries come* that do differentiate between the *class of situations* generally requiring one variety and another class of situations generally requiring another variety must be empiracally determined by the investigator, and constitutes one of the major tasks of descriptive sociology of language. The various domains and the appropriate usage in each domain must be discovered from the data of numerous discrete situations and the shifting or nonshifting which they reveal. This is a central task of descriptive sociology of language, and it can only be accomplished by painstaking research—utilizing *all* the available social science methods: participant observation, interviews, surveys, and experiments too. The compositing concerns of some researchers in the sociology of language are thus far from being research strategies alone. Ultimately they also seek to reveal the behavioral parsimony of members of speech communities, all of whom inevitably come to rely on a relatively functional sociolinguistic typology to guide them through the infinite encounters of daily interaction.

4.7 SOCIOLOGY OF LANGUAGE:
MULTILEVEL AND MULTIMETHOD

The list of constructs utilized in the sociolinguistic description and analysis of samples of "talk" is far from exhausted. We have not mentioned several of the social units long advocated by Hymes (1962), such as participant vs. audience roles, the purposes and the outcomes of speech events, the tone or manner of communication, the channel of communication employed (oral, written, telegraphic), or all the various parameters and components for the analysis of talk data that he has more recently advanced (Hymes 1967b; see Figure 6A); we have not discussed such social psychological

FIGURE 6A

COMPONENTS OF SPEECH EVENTS:
A heuristic schema (Hymes 1967b)

(S) SETTING or SCENE: time and place; also, psychological setting and cultural definition as a *type* of scene

(P) PARTICIPANTS or PERSONNEL: e.g., addressor-addressee-audience

(E) ENDS: ends in view (goals, purposes) and ends as outcomes

(A) ART CHARACTERISTICS: the form *and* the content of what is said

(K) KEY: the tone, manner or spirit in which an act is done

(I) INSTRUMENTALITIES: channel (the choice or oral, written, telegraphic, or other medium) and code (Spanish, English, etc.) or subcode (dialect, sociolect)

(N) NORMS OF INTERACTION and of INTERPRETATION: specific behaviors and properties that may accompany acts of speech, as well as shared rules for understanding what occurs in speech acts

(G) GENRES: categories or types of speech acts and speech events: e.g., conversation, curse, prayer, lecture, etc.

parameters as the saliency of individual vs. collective needs (Herman 1961), or the several functions of speech so revealingly discussed by Ervin-Tripp. Suffice it to say that there are several levels and approaches to sociolinguistic description and a host of linguistic, sociopsychological, and societal constructs within each (see Figure 6B). One's choice from among them depends on the particular problem at hand (Ervin-Tripp 1964). This is necessarily so. The sociology of language is of interest to students of small societies as well as to students of national and international integration. It must help clarify the change from one face-to-face situation to another. It must also help clarify the different language-related beliefs and behaviors of entire social sectors and classes. In some cases the variation between closely related varieties must be highlighted. In other cases the variation between obviously unrelated languages is of concern.

It would be foolhardy to demand that one and the same method of data collection and data analysis be utilized for such a variety of problems and purposes. It is one of the hallmarks of scientific social inquiry that methods are selected as a *result* of problem specifications rather than independently of them. The sociology of language is neither methodologically nor theoretically uniform. Nevertheless, it is gratifying to note that for those who seek such ties the links between micro- and macroconstructs and methods exist (as do a number of constructs and methods that have wide applicability through the entire range of the sociology of language). Just as there is no societally unencumbered verbal interaction, so are there no large-scale relationships between language and society that do not depend on individual interaction for their realization. Although there is no mechanical part-whole relationship between them, microlevel and macrolevel sociology of language are both conceptually and methodologically complementary.

FIGURE 6B. Relationships among Some Constructs Employed in Sociolinguistic Analysis*

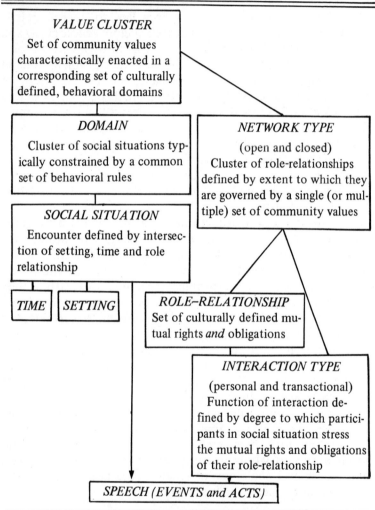

*From: Robert L. Cooper, "How Can We Measure the Roles Which a Bilingual's Languages Play in His Everyday Behavior?", in L. G. KELLY (ed.), *The Description and Measurement of Bilingualism.* Toronto University Press, Toronto, 1969, p. 202.

SOCIETAL DIFFERENTIATION
AND
REPERTOIRE RANGE

Speech communities—particularly those at the city-wide, regional, or national levels—obviously vary in the degrees and kinds of language diversity that they reveal. What do such differences imply with respect to the social differentiation and organization of the communities and networks to which they apply? If we examine the varieties of Javanese required by linguistic etiquette in the communities described by Geertz (1960), the varieties of Baghdadi Arabic described by Blanc (1964), the varieties of Hindi or Kannada described by Gumperz (1958) or McCormack (1960), and the varieties of Indonesian described by Tanner (1967), it is clear that these compose quite different kinds of repertoires than do the varieties of Norwegian described by Haugen (1961), or the varieties of American English described by Labov (1963, 1964, 1965), or by Levine and Crockett (1966). In addition, the types of speech communities in which these varieties are encountered also differ strikingly, as do the larger national or regional units in which the communities are imbedded. To put it very briefly, the speech communities in the first cluster seem to be much more stratified socially and to employ much more diversified repertoires linguistically than do those in the second. The documented co-occurrence of linguistic heterogeneity and societal heterogeneity—when both are examined in intragroup perspective—is a major contribution of the sociology of language to the study of social organization and social change.

5.1 THE SIGNIFICANCE OF PERVASIVE LINGUISTIC DISCONTINUITY

Prior to the development of the sociology of language per se, area dialectology had already clearly indicated that discontinuous populations (i.e., populations that lived at some distance from each other or that were impeded in their communication with each other by physical or political barriers) frequently revealed substantial phonological and morphological differences between their language systems (see, e.g., Herzog 1965 and Kandori 1968 for examples of such work today). Where such differences did not obtain despite the absence of communicational frequency and sociocultural unity, recency of settlement from a single source or other similar unifying factors (conquest, religious conversion, etc.) were assumed and encountered. Indeed, if we view the entire world as a single geographic area we tend to find similar (i.e., genetically related) languages clustered contiguously or closely to each other ("language families" are normally clustered geographically, except for the confounding fact of colonization and distant migration). Some parts of the world, of course, are famous for their concentration of highly diversified languages found in close proximity to each other. However, these same areas are also noted for their mountains, jungles, deserts, and rivers, i.e., for barriers that have limited travel, commerce, and common endeavor.

More difficult to explain are those variations in language and behavior that are *coterritorial*. In such instances sheer physical distance cannot be invoked as either a causal or a maintenance variable for the variations encountered. In such cases cultural and social factors alone must be examined, and they alone must be meaningfully related to the *degree* and *kind* of language differences noted. In reviewing coterritorial linguistic diversity throughout history it becomes clear that it can be maintained in an extremely stable manner. Through-out the world—but particularly throughout the ancient and traditional world—populations have lived side by side for centuries without learning each other's languages and without significantly modifying or giving up their distinctly discontinuous repertoires. Except for the relatively few middle-men that connect them (merchants, translators, etc.) such populations represent distinct speech communities, although they may be citizens of the same country, of the same city, and, indeed, of the same neighborhood. However, the mainte-nance of such well-nigh complete linguistic and sociocultural cleavage—equal in degree and kind to that encountered between territorially discontinuous populations—is usually indicative of population relocation some time in the past that has subsequently been buttressed and maintained by socio-cultural (including ethnic and religious) differences. The *former* differences are responsible for the origin of the differences noted by Blanc (1964) between the Moslem Arabic, Christian Arabic, and Jewish Arabic of Baghdad. The *latter* differences are responsible for the *maintenance* of these cleavages in as sharp a manner, or nearly so, as initially established.

While it may often be relatively difficult to overcome the cleavage between separate but coterritorial speech communities, it is not impossible to do so. The forced conversion of various Jewish and Christian communities during certain periods of Islamic rule, the urban-industrial assimilation of hitherto rural or small town immigrants and their children in the United States (Nahirny and Fishman 1965, Fishman 1965a, 1965e, 1966c), the very similar assimilation of tribal populations moving to Wolof-speaking Dakar (Tabouret-Keller 1968), the Hellenization and Roman-ization of many "barbarian" elites in ancient Rome and Alexandria, the convergence between illiterate speakers of Marathi and Kannada in India (Gumperz 1967)—these are all examples of the fusing into one of populations that originally functioned as largely separate though coterritorial speech communities. Conversely, the mutual alienation of popula-tions that originally considered themselves to be united can create fargoing linguistic differences between them where none, or few, existed previously. In general, the more

SOCIAL CLASS DIFFERENCES IN JAVANESE LINGUISTIC REPERTOIRES (GEERTZ, 1960)

FIGURE 7A. Dialect of Non-Prijaji, Urbanized, Somewhat Educated Persons

Level	are	you	going	to eat	rice	and	cassava	now	Complete sentence
3a	menapa	pandjenengan	badé	dahar	sekul	kalijan		samenika	Menapa pandjenengan badé dahar sekul kalijan kaspé samenika?
3				neda			kaspé		Menapa sampéjan badé neda sekul kalijan kaspé samenika?
2	napa	sampéjan	adjeng			lan		saniki	Napa sampéjan adjeng neda sekul lan kaspé saniki?
1a	apa		arep		sega			saiki	Apa sampéjan arep neda sega lan kaspé saiki?
1		kowé		mangan					Apa kowé arep mangan sega lan kaspé saiki?

FIGURE 7B. CONTINUED

FIGURE 7B. Dialect of Peasants and Uneducated Townspeople

Level	are	you	going	to eat	rice	and	cassava	now	Complete sentence
2	*napa*	*sampéjan*	*adjeng*	*neda*	*sekul*	*lan*	*kaspé*	*saniki*	*Napa sampéjan adjeng neda sekul lan kaspé saniki?*
1a	*apa*	*sampéjan*	*arep*	*neda*	*sega*	*lan*	*kaspé*	*saiki*	*Apa sampéjan arep neda sega lan kaspé saiki?*
1	*apa*	*kowé*	*arep*	*mangan*	*sega*	*lan*	*kaspé*	*saiki*	*Apa kowé arep mangan sega lan kaspé saiki?*

FIGURE 7C. Dialect of the Prijajis

Level	are	you	going	to eat	rice	and	cassava	now	Complete sentence
3a	menapa	pandjenengan	badé	dahar	sekul	kalijan	kaspé	samenika	*Menapa pandjenengan badé dahar sekul kalijan kaspé samenika?*
3		sampéjan		neda					*Menapa sampéjan badé neda sekul kalijan kaspé samenika?*

Level	are	you	going	to eat	rice	and	cassava	now	Complete sentence
1b	apa	pandjenengan	arep	dahar	sega	lan	kaspé	saiki	*Apa pandjenengan arep dahar sega lan kaspé saiki?*
1a		kowé		neda					*Apa sampéjan arep neda sega lan kaspé saiki?*
1		sampéjan		mangan					*Apa kowé arep mangan sega lan kaspé saiki?*

fargoing the linguistic differences between any two co-territorial populations (i.e., the more the differences are basically grammatical—syntactic and morphological—rather than primarily phonological or lexical), the more their linguistic repertoires are compartmentalized from each other so as to reveal little if any interference, and the more they reveal functionally different verbal repertoires in terms of the sociolinguistic parameters reviewed in Section 4, above—then the greater the interactional and sociocultural gap between the speech communities involved.

Geertz's data (see Figures 7A, 7B, and 7C) might well be examined in the light of the above generalization concerning the social significance of marked grammatical discontinuity between the repertoires of coterritorial speech communities. In Geertz's case we are dealing with coterritorial speech networks that differ greatly in verbal repertoires, but that cannot be considered to be either of separate geographic origin or of separate cultural or religious self-definition. Here we find three different social classes or strata within Java, each differing in repertoire range and each lacking entirely one or more speech varieties available to at least one of the others. While the intranetwork variation shown by Geertz is probably less than that which actually exists (thus, we may assume that metaphorical switching also occurs in Java, and if it does, level 2, for example, may be employed on occasions which are normatively viewed and regulated as being more appropriate for level 1b or 1a), let us consider this to be merely an artifact of the data model that Geertz employs and ask ourselves (a) what *kind(s) of variations* does it reveal, and (b) what kind(s) of repertoire differences does it reveal.

Geertz's data clearly indicate that social-class differences exist (or existed at the time his field work was done) in Javanese verbal behavior. In addition, however, the data also indicate that contextual-situational variation also exists in Javanese verbal behavior. The very fact that both of these types of variation regularly co-occur is an indication that although stratificational differences involved are rigid and deep, nevertheless the strata constitute a single integrated speech community with shared normative expectations and regulations vis-à-vis intrastrata and interstrata communication.

FIGURE 8. Verbal and Behavioral Discontinuity

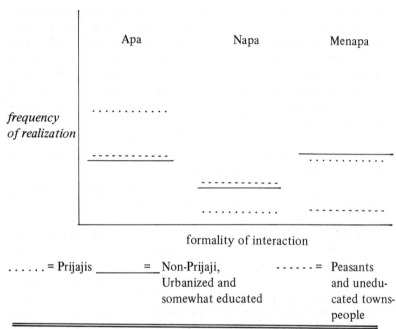

...... = Prijajis _____ = Non-Prijaji,   - - - - - = Peasants
                        Urbanized and   and unedu-
                        somewhat educated   cated towns-
                                                     people

The fact that networks in each stratum lack at least one variety available to networks drawn from the other strata is a sign of fargoing discontinuity also in their respective behavioral repertoires. Networks from certain strata are not expected to engage in certain role relationships and as a result, lack entirely certain morphosyntactic co-occurrences available to networks from other strata. Thus, in these latter respects, the variation that occurs is *stratificational only* and not contextual at all. This stratificational discontinuity in morphosyntactic co-occurrences is shown graphically in Figure 8 for the forms *apa, napa,* and *menapa.* The strata that do possess these forms use them for identical contexts of interaction and with apparently equal frequency of realization. However, there is in each case also a stratum that lacks these forms. The graphic representation of social and verbal discontinuity should be kept in mind for comparison with other graphs presented further below (e.g., Figures 9A and 9B).

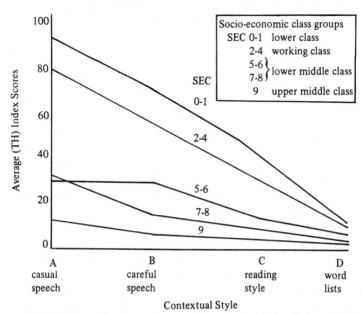

FIGURE 9A. Class Stratification Diagram for (th). (Labov 1964)

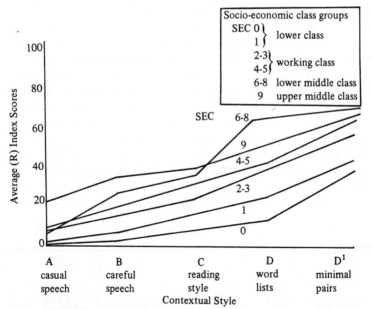

FIGURE 9B. Class Stratification Diagram for (r). (Labov 1964)

5.2 MORE MARGINAL BUT SYSTEMATIC LINGUISTIC DIFFERENCES BETWEEN SOCIAL STRATA

However, most coterritorial populations that differ in verbal repertoire cannot be considered fully separate speech communities, even if the differences between them can be considered as basically geographic in origin. There are very many areas today, primarily urban in nature, where sub-populations that differ in social class, religion, or ethnic affiliation, nevertheless view themselves as sharing many common norms and standards and where these sub-populations interact sufficiently (or are sufficiently exposed to common educational institutions and media) to be termed a single speech community. It is hardly surprising, therefore, that the linguistic differences between such sociocultural subpopulations (or networks) within the same speech community are more linguistically marginal (i.e., lexical, and to a lesser degree, morpho- and phonological) rather than syntactic and all-embracing. It is clear that the social class variation that exists in New York City English is of this kind rather than of the kind that develops between clearly separate, noninteracting, and mutually alienated speech communities. One of the surest indications of this is the fact that (if we delete features attributable to Southern Negro, Puerto Rican, and other recent geographically derived differences) few of the characteristic phonological features of lower-class speech in New York are entirely absent from the speech of other classes in New York City, just as few of the characteristic phonological features of its upper-class speech are entirely lacking from the lower-class speech of that city. What does differentiate between the social classes in New York is the degree to which certain phonological *variables* are realized in *certain ways* on *particular occasions*, rather than their complete absence from the repertoire of any particular class.

Labov's studies of the phonological correlates of social stratification (1964, 1965, 1966a, 1966b, 1966c, 1968a and b) illustrate this point. In one of his studies (1964) Labov gathered four different samples of speech (each by a different method calculated to elicit material approximating a different kind of speech situation) from four different social classes of informants. Studying such variables as *th* (as in thing, through), *eh* (the height of the vowel in bad, ask, half, dance), *r* (the presence or absence of final and preconsonantal /r/) and *oh* (the height of the vowel in off, chocolate, all, coffee), Labov found that *all* social classes yielded some values of each variable in nearly every speech situation (see Figure 9). However, the differences between the social classes remained clear enough. Lower class speakers were less likely to pronounce the fricative form of the [θ] when saying 'thing' or 'through' than were working class speakers; working class speakers less likely to pronounce it than lower middle-class speakers; lower middle-class speakers less likely to yield it than upper middle-class speakers. Speakers of all classes were more likely to pronounce the standard fricative form (rather than the substandard affricate [t θ] or lenis stop [t]) in reading word lists than they were when reading passages; more likely to pronounce it when reading passages than when being interviewed (=careful speech); more likely to pronounce it when being interviewed than when recounting "a situation where you thought you were in serious danger of being killed" (=casual speech).

This may be considered a hallmark of social class differences in speech where the classes as a whole share *continuous* experiences, goals, and expectations, i.e., neither their role repertoires nor role access have been fully compartmentalized. As long as individuals in each class can differ in repertoire, depending on their personal opportunities and experiences with respect to interaction with various speech networks, there can be no complete discontinuity in repertoires, no complete freezing of social class position, and no overriding alienation into separate religious, ethnic, or other relatively fixed and immutable speech communities.

Of course, not all variables yield such dramatic and clear-cut social-class differences as those found iin connection with *th* in New York. With respect to *r*, *eh*, and *oh* Labov's data reveal much more *similarity* between the several social classes, although the differences between contexts and between classes remain quite clear. Labov's data also reveal a recurring *reversal* with respect to the lower middle-class performance on word and passage reading lists. This reversal, dubbed *hypercorrection*, shows the lower middle class to be more "correct" (more careful, more inclined to use the standard or cultured pronunciation) than is the upper middle class at its most correct or careful. Such a reversal may well indicate a variable that has become a stereotype rather than merely a marker of class position. As such it tends to be used (or overused) by those who are insecure about their social position, i.e., by those who are striving to create a more advantageous social position for themselves in a speech community in which upward social mobility seems to be possible. This explanation is not dissimilar from that which Labov utilized to explain observed differences in centralization of /ai/ and /au/ in Martha's Vineyard (1963). Such centralization was most common among minority group members (of Portuguese and Indian extraction) who sought to *stress their positive orientation to Martha's Vineyard*, rather than among the old Yankees whose feelings toward the Vineyard were more low-keyed and required no linguistic underscoring. Whether consciously employed or not, the "Pygmalion effect" in language is a striking indicator of reference group behavior and of social aspirations more generally (Ross 1956).

Similar results to Labov's (in the sense that the proportional realizations of particular variables were found to differ regularly and smoothly both between *social classes* and between *contexts*) have been reported by Lindenfeld, 1969. Examining syntactic variation in French, Lindenfeld found that nominalization, relativization, and sentence length (but not subordination) showed both types of variation, although upper middle-class speakers were much more likely to reveal contextual variation than were lower-class speakers (Figure 10). This may be taken as a sign that the socioeconomically more favored subjects had more of a real repertoire range behaviorally so that the difference between formal and informal interactions was very real for them. For lower-class speakers, on the other hand, this difference may be quite hypothetical in that it tends to have much less functional reality associated with it.

The demographic differentials observed in usage are as related to the societal allocation of codes as are the more directly contextual or functional differentials. The fact that

FIGURE 10. The Social Conditioning of Syntactic Variation in French (Lindenfeld 1969)

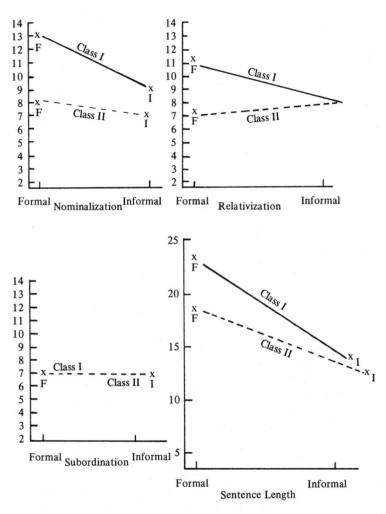

an extensive cluster of phonological, lexical, and grammatical realizations is more widely or characteristically employed by one particular social class than by another is commonly related to the fact that the social class in question is also more likely or characteristically engaged in particular pursuits or involved in particular situations. Demographic and contextual variations are particularly likely to be redundant in relatively closed societies in which role access is restricted and in which roles tend to be ascribed and compartmentalized. However, the awareness of verbal and behavioral repertoires—a central awareness indeed in the sociology of language—should not keep us from realizing that even in relatively open societies there is often appreciable redundancy between demographic and contextual differentials in usage. Both Labov's and Lindenfeld's data referred to previously reveal this redundancy when they show that for most levels of formality one social class is much more likely to yield a particular variant than are the others, even though repertoire continuity exists. This redundancy strengthens the normative sense of members of speech communities and, indeed, enables them to guide their own speech behavior more appropriately, as well as to comment upon it validly to one another and to outside investigators and to do so over and above the metaphorical variation that undoubtedly obtains round about them.

5.3 THE IMPLICATIONS OF EITHER CONTEXTUAL-SITUATIONAL OR DEMOGRAPHIC VARIATION

The foregoing comparisons of social class differences and contextual-situational differences in language usage suffer in at least two ways. Neither Geertz nor Labov nor Lindenfeld have been able to indicate which of these two sources of language variation is the stronger for their data. In order to answer this question a more quantitative approach is needed to the study of social-class or other demographic-group variation in usage. In addition, neither Geertz nor Labov nor Lindenfeld has asked the question "what could it mean—in so far as the over-all societal organization of language behavior—if only *one or another* of these two sources of usage variation obtained?" In order to answer these two questions let us take another look at data obtained in the study of *Bilingualism in the Barrio* (Fishman, Cooper, Ma, et al. 1968).

The data we will review were obtained as part of an interdisciplinary project on the measurement and description of widespread and relatively stable bilingualism in a Puerto Rican neighborhood in the Greater New York City area. The neighborhood studied by a team of linguists, psychologists, and sociologists included 431 Puerto Ricans (or individuals of Puerto Rican parentage) living in ninety households. All these individuals were covered in a language census that obtained the demographic data utilized for the purposes of this report at the same time that it obtained detailed self-reports on bilingual usage and ability (Fishman 1969d). The linguistic data utilized for this report were obtained in the course of two to four-hour interviews and testing sessions with a random-stratified sample of those Puerto Ricans living in the study neighborhood who were over the age of 12.

SPEECH CONTEXTS

The interviews and testing sessions were designed to elicit speech data in five different contexts that form a continuum from most formal or careful to most informal or casual as follows:

Context D: Word Reading.   Subjects were asked to read two different lists of separate words, one in English and one in Spanish. The speech data obtained in this fashion were considered to be representative of the most careful pronunciation available to the subjects.

Context C: Paragraph Reading.   Subjects were asked to read four different paragraphs, two in English and two in Spanish. The speech data obtained in this fashion were considered to be representative of somewhat less careful pronunciation.

Context WN: Word Naming.   Subjects were asked to "name as many words as come to mind that have to do with (domain-locales)." This task was performed separately in English and in Spanish for each of the following domain-locales: home, neighborhood, school, work, church. The speech data obtained in this fashion was considered to be representative of intermediate pronunciation (neither markedly careful nor casual).

Context B: Careful Conversation. Subjects were asked factual questions concerning five taped "playlets" to which they had just listened. Ideally, half of the questions were asked (and answered) in Spanish and half were asked and answered in English. The speech data obtained in this fashion were considered to be representative of somewhat (but not completely) casual pronunciation.

Context A: Casual Conversation. Subjects were asked their personal opinions and preferences with respect to the problems that figured in the "playlets" to which they had just listened. The speech data obtained in this fashion were considered to be representative of the most informal pronunciation that could be elicited by an interviewer.

Only the last three contexts (WN, B, A) will be examined in the discussion that follows in view of the restricted corpora obtained in the two reading contexts in the study population.

LINGUISTIC VARIABLES

The taped speech samples obtained for the above-mentioned five contexts were independently scored by two linguists on seven Spanish and ten English variables. The reliability of scoring varied only slightly and irregularly from context to context and from one language to the other; the reliability coefficients obtained ranged from 0.73 to 0.94, with a median of 0.90. A full report on the contextual variation encountered for each variable as well as on the factorial relationship between all variables is available elsewhere (Ma and Herasimchuk 1968). The present discussion deals only with selected values on one Spanish and one English variable in order to illustrate a method of analysis hitherto not utilized in sociolinguistic research. The particular linguistic values selected for presentation in this study are further explained in the Results subsection below.

DEMOGRAPHIC VARIABLES

Four demographic factors (sex, age, education, and birthplace) are included in the analyses presented in this report.

Social class, a variable frequently utilized in other socio-linguistic research on phonological variables, was not utilized in the present research because of the severe restriction in range that our overwhelmingly lower-class Puerto Rican subjects revealed in this connection. An extensive analysis of the demographic variation encountered in our study neighborhood is available elsewhere (Fishman 1968c). The reliability coefficients for the various items of obtained demographic information are all 0.90 or higher.

Sex has consistently proved to be a nonsignificant demographic variable in accounting for phonological variation in Puerto Rican Spanish. It was included in the present study merely in order to provide a comparison with prior studies.

Age was categorized in two separate ways. As a three-category variable the categories employed were < 25, 25-34, > 34. As a two-category variable the categories utilized were < 25 and > 25. By categorizing age in two different ways we will be able to tell whether one categorization is more related to linguistic variation than the other, and at the same time, sum both age categorizations into one age variable.

Education was categorized in three different ways. As a four-category variable the categories were < 7 years, all in Puerto Rico; 7 or more years, all in Puerto Rico; partially in Puerto Rico and partially in continental United States; all in continental United States. As a two-category variable education was categorized in two different ways: first, all in Puerto Rico vs. all or part in continental United States, and, second, all United States vs. all or part in Puerto Rico. Once again our analytic technique enabled us to sum these three different ways of categorizing education as well as to tell whether there is any difference between them in explaining linguistic variation.

Birthplace was categorized in two different ways. As a four-category variable the categories used were highland Puerto Rico, coastal Puerto Rico other than San Juan and suburbs, San Juan and suburbs, and continental United States. As a two-category variable the categories utilized were highland Puerto Rico vs. all other birthplaces. As in the other two instances of multiple categorization of demographic variables, we will be able both to compare the effectiveness of these two categorizations of birthplace in explaining linguistic variation and to sum them into one birthplace variable.

STATISTICAL ANALYSIS

The statistical technique utilized in this report is that of analysis of variance via multiple regression analysis. Analysis of variance is a technique designed to answer questions concerning the separate significance as well as the interactional significance of several simultaneous effects. In the context of the present study, analyses of variance can tell us whether context, age, education, or birthplace are separately significant in explaining variation in the production of a particular linguistic variant or whether the interaction between any two of them, e.g., between context and birthplace, has explanatory significance. Multiple regression analysis is a technique designed to answer questions concerning the value of utilizing additional explanatory parameters beyond those already utilized at any given stage in the explanatory process (Bottenberg and Ward 1963; Cohen 1965, 1968a, 1968b). In the context of the present study multiple regression analysis can tell us whether or not certain explanatory parameters (e.g., context plus age) are already so powerful in explaining variation in the production of a particular linguistic variant that it is not necessary or productive to add other explanatory parameters even if the latter too are significantly related per se to the variation in question.

HYPOTHESES

Spanish Variables

Our general hypothesis regarding linguistic variation in Puerto Rican Spanish (PRS) in the speech community under study is that it will consist of contextual variation primarily and demographic variation only secondarily. Except for regionally related differences between speakers of highland origin and speakers of coastal origin we consider our subjects as constituting a single speech community. Our subjects have all learned the norms of Spanish communicative competence pretty much in the same way and at the same developmental period of their lives. These norms incorporate contextual variation. Too few of our subjects have had too little exposure to formal, educated Spanish to constitute an educated network of the speech community. Such a network might develop speech norms of its own that could significantly modify (i.e., raise or lower) the contextual variation norms that exist for the speech community as a whole.

Our general hypothesis is that beyond a highland-coastal difference in a few variables no significant demographic factors will be encountered in explaining any linguistic variation that may exist in Puerto Rican Spanish above and beyond contextual variation. This hypothesis will be tested here against one illustrative Spanish variant where a variant is described as one of the realizations that a variable can assume.

English Variables

With respect to linguistic variation in Puerto Rican English in the speech community under study our general hypothesis is that it will exist of demographic variation primarily and contextual variation secondarily (if at all). We do not view our subjects as constituting a unitary English speech community with its own contextual norms of communicative competence in that language. In general, the English-speaking horizons and experiences of most of our subjects are still too limited for contextual varieties of English to have developed (or to have been adopted) and to have been stabilized. On the other hand, there are within the speech community those whose English has been significantly modified by substantial influences stemming from outside the community, such as those that derive from American education in particular and increased time in the continental United States in general. We would expect their English to differ from those with other demographic characteristics who have not had these experiences. We expect these differences between demographic groups to be pervasive in their use of English rather than contextualized along a casualness-carefulness dimension for intragroup purposes. This hypothesis will be tested here against one illustrative English variant.

RESULTS

Spanish Variant SpC-0

SpC-0 refers to the dropping of the plural marker *s* when the following word begins with a consonant. An example of this realization is *(los) muchacho comen* as opposed to the standard realization *(los) muchachos comen* (SpC-1) or the common PRS variation *(los) muchachoh comen* (SpC-2). This variable (SpC) had a very high number of occurrences, and the realization in question showed considerable contextual variation, accounting for just 17 per cent of the cases of SpC in the most formal context but 62 per cent in the least formal context (Ma and Herasimchuk 1968). *S* in this morphophonemic environment was realized quite differently from *s* in other environments. For instance, *s* before a consonant within a word showed zero realization only 11 per cent of the time in the least formal context. Similarly, *s* marking a plural article preceding a word beginning with a consonant was realized as zero only 23 per cent of the time in the least formal context. In these environments S-2 or [h] was the preferred realization 81 per cent and 70 per cent of all times respectively in style A. Thus SpC is definitely a favorable environment for zero realization of *s*, with the further advantage, for our present purposes, that there was substantial variation in the realization of SpC-0 across contexts. Under these circumstances, then, we decided to ask whether other parameters of a directly demographic nature might also be significantly related to differential production of SpC-0.

If we examine the first column in Table 3 (labeled r), we will note that only context, in each of its aspects, correlates significantly with differential use of SpC-0. The second aspect of context (that which differentiates between word naming and B + A) correlates with SpC-0 as well (0.423) as do both aspects taken together (column 3, R = 0.424).

The fact that only the two aspects of context correlate significantly with SpC-0 is corroborated in column 8, where only the two aspects of context yield significant F ratios. Thus we can safely conclude that in the speech community under study demographic differences are not significantly

TABLE 3. Analysis of Variance via Multiple Regression Analysis of Puerto Rican Spanish SpC-O (n=34)

Source	(1) r	(2) r^2	(3) R	(4) R^2	(5) Cum R	(6) Cum R^2	(7) ΔR^2	(8) F_{r^2}	(9) F_{R^2}	(10) $F_{\Delta R^2}$
1. Context: WN vs. B vs. A	0.380*	0.144	0.424	0.180	0.424	0.180		5.4*	3.0	
2. Context: WN vs. all other	−0.423*	0.180	0.240	0.058	0.494	0.244	0.064	7.0*	2.5	<1
3. Sex	−0.240	0.058						2.0		
4. Age: <25 vs. 25-34 vs >	−0.055	0.003						<1		
5. Age: <25 vs. all other	−0.021	0.000						<1		
6. Educ: <7 yrs. PR vs. 7+ yrs. PR vs. PR and US vs. US only	−0.116	0.013	0.156	0.024	0.509	0.259	0.015	<1	<1	<1
7. Educ: all PR vs. other	0.111	0.012	0.193	0.037	0.535	0.286	0.037	<1	<1	<1
8. Educ: all USA vs. other	−0.022	0.001						<1		
9. Birthplace: Highland vs. Coastal vs. San Juan vs. USA	0.063	0.004						<1		
10. Birthplace: Highland vs. all other	−0.163	0.027	0.216	0.047	0.585	0.342	0.056	<1	<1	<1
11. Context × Birthplace	0.239	0.057	0.239		0.602	0.362	0.020	2.0	2.0	<1

*Significant at 0.05 level.

related to differential use of SpC-0, whereas contextual differences are so related. However, if we are to stop our prediction of SpC-0 with context alone, we will have accounted for only 18 per cent of the casual variance (see column 6). If we add sex of speaker to the prediction of SpC-0, we can account for 24.4 per cent of the casual variance. This increase is due to the fact that there is a slight tendency (column 1: $r = -0.240$) for males to use SpC-0 more frequently than females.

If we continue to add successive demographic variables, our multiple prediction of SpC-0 continues to rise (see column 5) and finally reaches the appreciable figure of 0.602. A multiple correlation of this magnitude accounts for 36.2 per cent of the casual variance in SpC-0, a substantial increase beyond that accounted for by context alone.

Although none of the demographic variables is significantly related to differential use of SpC-0, sex of speaker approaches such significance. This, however, is due to the fact that in the speech community under study more women than men are of highland origin in Puerto Rico. The context by birthplace interaction, therefore, also approaches significance, which indicates that some birthplace groups show more contextual variation than do others.

Table 4 reveals the mean number of occurrences of SpC-0 in the three different contexts for our sample as a whole and for two different birthplace subsamples. This table confirms that the effective contextual difference comes between WN and the two conversational styles. Table 2 also confirms the greater contextual sensitivity of highland-born subjects, for whom we find greater average contextual differences than those found for other subjects.

English Variant EH-2

EH-2 represents the Standard American English sound [æ], as in cat, bad, ham. Two other variants of this EH variable were recognized: EH-1, as in New York City [kɛət, bɛəd, hɛəm], and EH-3, as in accented English cah'nt, bahd, hahm. EH-2 serves fairly effectively to differentiate accented from native English speakers, as the sound is not available in Spanish phonology. Mastery of this phone seems to imply mastery of

TABLE 4. Contextual Differences in Mean Number of Occurrences
of SpC-O, for Total Sample and for Birthplace Groups

Birthplace groups	Contexts			Total
	WN	B	A	
Highland	27.13	57.27	66.58	49.17
Other	30.38	53.29	57.05	56.09
Total	29.13	54.17	59.87	54.39

a number of other typically English sounds not available in
Spanish.

Use of the three variants of EH changed but slightly and
irregularly with context (Ma and Herasimchuk 1968), which
supports the hypothesis of more or less fixed usage of one
sound by any given speaker. EH-2 showed an overall higher
incidence of occurrence, and for this reason, was chosen over
EH-1 for testing. It is also less ambiguously American; EH-1
can be approximately by the Spanish $[\xi]$ or $[e]$, so a score
of EH-1 does not clearly isolate the sound as English but
rather marks some form or other of dialect realization. For
reasons both of numerical frequency and of phonological
exclusiveness then, EH-2 is a very good variant for the
statistical testing of relationships between differential use of
sounds and the characteristics of their users.

Table 5 reveals quite a different picture from that shown
in Table 3. The values in column 1 indicate that neither of
the two aspects of context are significantly related to
differential use of EH-2. Indeed even when both aspects of
context are taken together, it is still the least important
multiple predictor of EH-2 except for sex of speaker (column
3). If we utilize context alone, we are able to account for
only 3.6 per cent of the causal variance pertaining to
differential use of EH-2 (column 6). If we add sex of speaker
to context, our prediction rises only to 5.8 per cent.
However, as soon as we consider such demographic variables

TABLE 5. Analysis of Variance Via Multiple Regression Analysis of Puerto Rican English EH-2 (n=26)

Source	(1) r	(2) r^2	(3) R	(4) R^2	(5) Cum R	(6) Cum R^2	(7) ΔR^2	(8) F_{r^2}	(9) F_{R^2}	(10) $F_{\Delta R^2}$
1. Context: WN vs. B vs. A	0.174	0.030						<1		
2. Context: WN vs. all other	−0.112	0.013	0.189	0.036	0.189	0.036		<1	<1	
3. Sex	−0.136	0.018	0.136		0.241	0.058	0.022	<1		<1
4. Age: <25 vs. 25-34 vs.> 34	−0.524	0.275						9.1†		
5. Age: <25 vs. all other	0.555	0.308	0.556	0.309	0.582	0.338	0.280	10.7†	5.17*	4.2*
6. Educ: <7 yrs. PR vs. 7+yrs. PR vs. PR and US vs. US only	−0.717	0.514						25.2†		
7. Educ: all PR vs. other	−0.722	0.521						26.1†		
8. Educ: all USA vs. other	0.589	0.347	0.753	0.567	0.785	0.616	0.278	12.8†	9.45†	4.1*
9. Birthplace: Highland vs. Coastal vs. San Juan vs. USA	0.446	0.199						6.0*		
10. Birthplace: Highland vs. all other	−0.309	0.095	0.491	0.241	0.810	0.656	0.040	2.5	3.67	<1
11. Context×Birthplace	0.428	0.183	0.428	0.183	0.815	0.664	0.008	5.4*	5.4*	<1

* Significant at 0.05 level.   † Significant at 0.01 level.

as age, education, and birthplace the picture changes
radically.

Of the three major demographic variables related to
differential use of EH-2, the most important is clearly
education (column 1). If we combine all three aspects of
education, we obtain a multiple correlation of 0.753 (column
3), which itself accounts for 56.7 per cent of the causal
variance (column 4).

Those of our subjects who were partly or entirely
educated in the United States are more likely to utilize EH-2
than those entirely educated in Puerto Rico (note minus
correlations in column 1). This relationship between differential use of EH-2 and education is further clarified in Table
6, which reveals it to be consistent for each speech context.

TABLE 6. Contextual Differences in Mean Number of Occurrences of
EH-2 for Total Sample and for Educational Groups

Educational groups	Contexts			Total
	WN	B	A	
Educated entirely in Puerto Rico	15.75	16.43	19.40	16.46
Educated partially or entirely in USA	60.71	64.43	65.17	63.35
Total	35.79	38.57	51.71	40.20

If education is now combined with the variables that
precede it in Table 5 (context, sex of speaker, and age), then
the resulting cumulative multiple correlation with EH-2 rises
to 0.785 (column 5), and we have accounted for 61.6 per
cent of the causal variance in differential use of EH-2
(column 6).

Although neither age nor birthplace is as strongly related to EH-2 as is education, their independent correlations with EH-2 are clearly significant (columns 1 and 8). When all three of them are added to context and sex of speaker, we arrive at a cumulative correlation of 0.810 (column 5), which indicates that we have accounted for 65.6 per cent of the causal variance in differential use of EH-2 (column 6).

Although context itself is not significantly related to differential use of EH-2, the interaction between context and birthplace is significantly related to such use. This implies that certain birthplace groups show more contextual variation than do others. Whereas our sample as a whole increasingly uses EH-2 as it proceeds from *WN* (35.79) to *B* (38.57) to *A* (51.71), this variation occurs primarily between *B* and *A* for our highland-born subjects and between *WN* and *B* for 'other subjects, with the latter using EH-2 more frequently in all contexts.

Incremental Prediction of EH-2

Not only are age and education significant variables in accounting for differential use of EH-2, but they are also incrementally significant in this respect. Column 10 of Table 5 reveals that it pays to add age as a predictor of differential use of EH-2 when one has previously used only context and sex of speaker in this connection. Another way of saying this is that 0.338 (column 6), the cumulative prediction of EH-2 based on three variables (context, sex of speaker, and age), is significantly better than the cumulative prediction based on only the first two (0.058). Similarly, Table 5 indicates that it pays to add education as well to our prediction of differential use of EH-2, even after context, sex of speaker, and age have been used cumulatively in this connection. The cumulative prediction of EH-2 based upon these four variables (0.616) is significantly greater than that based on the first three (0.338).

The same cannot be said, however, with respect to birthplace or the interaction between birthplace and context. Although it is true that their cumulative addition to the prediction of differential use of EH-2 (after context, sex of speaker, age, and education have been cumulatively utilized for this purpose) does increase the multiple prediction of EH-2 from 0.616 to 0.656 to 0.664, these increases, though welcome, are not statistically significant. Thus, if birthplace were an expensive or difficult measure to obtain, we would be justified in deciding to forego it because it does not produce a significant increment in our efforts to account for differential use of EH-2.

There have recently been several other studies of the importance of demographic factors in accounting for the variability of usage (see, e.g., Ellis 1967, Huffine 1966, Jernudd 1968, McCormack 1968). The study just reported gains considerably from the fact that it sought to compare demographic with contextual variation, and to do so in quantitative terms, as well as to do so separately for each of the languages used in a functioning community (rather than by a random sample of speakers).

Conclusions

The foregoing analysis of SpC-0 shows that its variable realization was primarily attributable to contextual-situational variation along a continuum of formality-informality. Whereas demographic factors (not social class in this case since our subjects were so uniformly of the lower class) added to the over-all prediction of this variable—as did the interaction between demographic factors and speech context—it is clear that these are of lesser importance than the speech-community-wide norms relating SpC-0 to informality rather than to formality. Scores of other Spanish phonological variables behave in this same way in the Puerto Rican neighborhood under study. As a result we may consider it a single, relatively homogeneous speech network as far as Spanish phonology is concerned, i.e., one in which experiential differences have not resulted in the formation of significantly different groups within the population with substantially unique speech norms of their own. Our Puerto Rican subjects are behaving more like Labov's Lower East Siders than like Geertz's Javanese in this respect.

Just the opposite seems to be true vis-à-vis variability in the realization of English phonology. In connection with

EH-2—and scores of other English variables—no neighbor-hood-wide contextual-situational variation has as yet developed. Those individuals who have spent larger proportions of their lives in the United States and who have obtained more formal education in the United States have an English phonology different from that of their more recently arrived and less American-educated neighbors. Instead of a single set of speech community norms with respect to English phonology there are several different demographic subgroups (social classes if you like), each with its own substantially different English phonologies used consistently in all contexts (by and large). Our Puerto Rican subjects are behaving more like Geertz's Javanese than like Labov's Lower East Siders in this respect. Without common contextual norms vis-à-vis English phonology they are fragmented into more and less advantaged discontinuous strata in so far as English phonology is concerned.

More generally stated in conclusion, the existence of societally shared contextual variation is a sure indication of the existence of a speech community or speech network. Societally shared contextual variation is indicative of social interaction governed by common normative regulations. On the other hand, demographic variation alone is not necessarily indicative of the existence of a speech community or speech network. Indeed, demographic variation in usage is, in and of itself, ambiguous in this very respect. On the one hand, it may be merely indicative of separate experiential groups (e.g., separate castes, social classes, regional origin groups, etc.) that are required to interact in marginal or limited ways. On the other hand, demographic variation may be indicative of realtively pervasive, inflexible, and compartmentalized role relationships within a speech community, such that members of network X always utilize variety x, members of network Y always utilize variety y, etc. Sorenson (1967) has described multilingual speech communities of this kind in the northwest Amazon region.

The co-occurrence of contextual and demographic variations must not, therefore, be considered a necessary feature of speech communities. It reflects a degree of interaction, a degree of complexity of stratification, and a

degree of shared open-network access and repertoire fluidity
that are by no means encountered everywhere.

5.4 NONPROLETARIANS OF ALL REGIONS, UNITE!

In a relatively open and fluid society there will be few
characteristics of lower-class speech that are not also present
(albeit to a lesser extent) in the speech of the working and
lower middle classes. Whether we look to phonological
features such as those examined by Labov or to morphological units such as those reported by Fischer (1958)
(Fischer studied the variation between -*in'* and -*ing* for the
present participle ending, i.e., runnin' vs. running—and found
that the former realization was more common when children
were talking to each other than when they were talking to
him, more common among boys than among girls and more
common among "typical boys" than among "model boys"),
we find not a clearcut cleavage between the social classes, but
a difference in rate of realization of particular variants of
particular variables for particular contexts. Even the widely
publicized distinction between the "restricted code" of
lower-class speakers and the "elaborated code" of middle-
class speakers (Bernstein 1964, 1966) is of this type, since
Bernstein includes the cocktail party and the religious service
among the social situations in which restricted codes are
realized. Thus, even in the somewhat more stratified British
setting the middle class is found to share some of the features
of what is considered to be "typically" lower-class speech.
Obviously then, "typicality," if it has any meaning at all in
relatively open societies, must refer largely to repertoire
range rather than primarily to unique features of the
repertoire.

This is the most suitable point at which to observe that
between Bernstein's view that lower-class speech is typically
more restricted and Labov's view that lower-class speech is
typically more informal there is an implied contradiction, if
"restricted" is defined as *more* predictable and informal as
less predictable. Actually, the contradiction is more apparent
than real. In terms of speech repertoire range both investigators would agree that the range of the lower class is

typically narrower than that of the middle and upper middle classes. This is what Bernstein is reacting to when he considers lower class speech more restricted, and therefore more predictable. On the other hand, both investigators would certainly agree that the phonological, lexical, or grammatical markers of lower class speech more commonly resemble those of informal usage within the larger speech community. However, as far as redundancy of speech is concerned, one must distinguish between predictability *between* varieties and predictability *within* any of them. Lower-class usage may well be more predictable or redundant when *between*-variety variation is considered, as Bernstein claims, and yet be more eliptical and incomplete than middle or upper middle-class usage when *within*-variety variation is considered. When Joos and others point to the greater redundancy (ritualization, predictability) of frozen and other more formal styles they are reacting to within-variety rather than between-variety variation. Thus, rather than being in conflict, Bernstein and Labov, taken together, sensitize us additionally to two different but equally important types of variation in the speech behavior of socially variegated speech communities.

Those speech networks with the widest range of experiences, interactions, and interests are also those that have the greatest linguistic repertoire range. In many speech communities these networks are likely to be in one or another of the middle classes since some networks within these classes are most likely to maintain direct contact with the lower and working classes below them (in employer-employee, teacher-pupil, and other role relationships), as well as with the upper class above them (in educational, recreational, and cultural interactions). However, whereas the repertoire ranges of the upper and lower classes are likely to be equally discontinuous (even if not equally restricted), there is likely to be a very major distinction between them if the larger speech community (the region, the country) is considered. Lower classes tend to be regionally and occupationally separated from each other to a far greater extent than do upper and middle classes (Gumperz 1958). Thus, there may well be several different lower-class varieties in a country (depending on regional and on occupational or other specializations), while at the same time upper- and upper middle-class speech may attain greater uniformity and greater regional neutrality. The more advantaged classes travel more frequently, engage in joint enterprises more frequently, and control the agencies of language uni-formation (schools, media, language planning agencies, and government itself). They more quickly arrive at a common standard, at least for formal occasions, than do the lower classes, who remain fragmented and parochial. Differences such as these are illustrated in Nancy Tanner's case study of an Indonesian elite group (1967; see Figure 11). Whereas the lower classes speak only their local ethnic language, the middle and upper classes also speak several varieties of Indonesian (including a regionally neutral variety that is least influenced by local characteristics), and the elites speak English and Dutch as well. One can predict that as these elites lose their local ties and affiliations and assume Pan-Indonesian roles, establishing speech communities of their own in Djakarta and in a few other large cities, their need for local languages and for locally influenced and informal Indonesian will lessen and their stylistic variation will

FIGURE 11. Functional Specialization of Codes in Indonesia and Among the Case Study Group

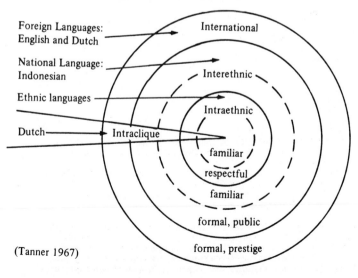

(Tanner 1967)

proceed, as it has with elites in England, France, Germany, Russia, and elsewhere in the world, via contrasts with foreign tongues.

Another way of arriving at the conclusions indicated above concerning the greater discontinuity between the lower-class varieties than between upper or middle-class varieties in most relatively open societies is to consider the differences referred to in Figure 12. Here we note that when all other factors are held constant, coterritorial groups of diverse regional origin may frequently be expected to differ most profoundly linguistically. The lower classes are exactly those whose regional origins are most diversified in most cities the world over. Indeed, the lower classes are likely to

FIGURE 12. Extent of Linguistic Differences and Extent of Sociocultural Differences within Various Kinds of Speech Networks (as Judged by Stanford Students Native to the Lower Peninsula)*

NETWORKS DRAWN FROM DIVERSE**	Lexical Differences	Phonoligical Differences	Grammatical Differences
EXTRA-REGIONAL-Origin Groups	++	++	++
RACIAL Groups	++	++	++
ETHNIC Groups	++	+	+
OCCUPATIONAL Groups	++	+	+
RELIGIOUS Groups	+	+	+
AGE Groups	++	-	-
SEX Groups	++	-	-

*Legend: ++=Substantial differences are judged to exist between categories (e.g., between different age groups) on the diversity parameter in question.
    += Moderate differences are judged to exist between categories on the diversity parameter in question.
    -= Negligible or no differences are judged to exist between categories on the diversity parameter in question.

** Categories are compared on the assumption that all other bases of group-functioning are held constant when networks are selected at the level of any given diversity parameter. Thus, when considering networks drawn from diverse occupational groups judges were asked to assume that racial, ethnic, religious, and other diversity parameters were held constant.

be more heterogeneous than the upper classes in exactly those factors—whether they be diversity of origin or diversity of experience—that are associated with more than peripheral lexical differences between coterritorial populations. They are far more likely to be regionally, socially, culturally, occupationally, and religiously diverse than are the upper classes, whose self-uniformizing tendencies and capacities have already been mentioned. Indeed, it is only in connection with sex and age variationability that the lower classes are often more homogeneous than the upper, but these generally tend to be associated only with the more marginal linguistic differences.

As a result of the differential experiences and opportunities vis-à-vis uniformation to which they are exposed, social class differences in relatively open societies have commonly arrived at the following state of affairs: (a) the middle and upper middle classes have larger repertoires in language and in social behavior than do the lower classes; (b) the lower classes tend to remain more diverse—regionally, ethnically, religiously, racially, etc.—than the upper classes, and therefore there are preserved more· and more discontinuous varieties of lower-class speech than of upper-class speech. These two tendencies are not in conflict with each other, except as social conflict itself may exist, and therefore come to disturb whatever societal and usage patterns have been stabilized. They are both due to societal differentials in normal social class role ranges and in exposure to the uniformizing institutions of the larger polity.

5.5 DIVERSIFICATION VS. MASSIFICATION

One further consideration deserves at least brief attention in our review of societal differentiation and language variation; namely, the common view that there is a trend toward over-all uniformation, in language and in other social behavior, as industrialization progresses (Bell 1961; Boulding 1963; Hertzler 1965; Hodges 1964). It is undeniable that life in urbanized and industrial countries is in some ways more uniform than it is in countries where local and regional particularisms remain relatively untouched. Nevertheless, it seems to be erroneous to think of preindustrial rural heterogeneity and industrial urban homogeneity as either accurate or mutually exclusive designations. Both stages of development seem to foster as well as to inhibit certain kinds of uniformation and differentiation in language as well as in other aspects of behavior.

Certainly, the preindustrial rural society is not as internally heterogeneous as is the urban society with its variety of classes, religions, ethnic groups, and interest groups. Thus, the supposedly uniformizing effect of urbanization and industrialization must pertain to interregional or interurban comparisons rather than to intraurban or intralocal ones. Nevertheless, the best available evidence indicates that no trend toward interregional homogeneity in religion, politics, or other generalized behaviors is apparent in the United States (Glenn 1966, 1967a, 1967b), nor are such trends apparent in other countries, such as England, France, Holland, or Belgium that have been industrialized or urbanized for the greatest length of time. There the differences in values, tastes, and social and political orientations between manual and nonmanual workers seem to be as great or greater than they are today in the United States (Hamilton 1965; Bonjean 1966; Schnore 1966; Broom and Glenn 1966, etc.).

At the language level both uniformation and differentiation are found to go on simultaneously, indicative of the fact that the traditional and the modern are frequently *combined* into new constellations rather than *displaced* one by the other. Uniformation pressures seem to be strongest in conjunction with only certain varieties within a speech community's verbal repertoire as well as in conjunction with only some of the interaction networks of that community. The language variety associated with school, government, and industry tends to be adopted differentially, the degree of its adoption varying with the degree of interaction in these domains. Not only need such adoption not be displacive (particularly when populations remain in their former places of residence), but even though the adoption may be quite uniform and official for an entire country, it may remain an entirely passive rather than active component in the repertoire of many interaction networks. Thus, even though television viewing and radio listening are most frequent and prolonged among the lower classes, their overt repertoires seem to be little influenced by such viewing or listening.

Finally, it should be recognized that urbanization may also foster certain kinds of differentiation. Whereas the number of different ethnic groups (and therefore the number of mutually exclusive language groups) may decline, new social differentiations and new occupational and interest groups normally follow in the wake of industrialization. These latter commonly develop sociolects and specialized usages of their own, thus expanding the repertoires of many speakers. Even the rise of languages of wider communication frequently results in differentiation rather than in uniformation. The spread of English as a second language in the past fifty years has resulted in there being more varieties of English today (including Indian English, East African English, Franglais, Spanglish, and others) rather than less. It is, of course, true that certain languages, now as in the past, are in danger of dying out. Nevertheless, others frequently regarded as "mere varieties" rather than as full-fledged languages are constantly being "born" in terms of differentiating themselves within the linguistic repertoires of certain interaction networks, and, at times, of entire speech communities. Modernization is a complex phenomenon. While it depresses the status and decreases the number of speakers of certain varieties (e.g., in recent years: Frisian, Romansch, Landsmal, Yiddish) it raises the status and increases the speakers of others (Macedonian, Neo-Melanesian, Indonesian, Swahili, etc.).

Our own American environment is an atypical example. It reveals the uniformation that results from the rapid urbanization and industrialization of *dislocated* populations. We must not confuse the American experience with that of the rest of the world (Greenberg 1965). In addition, we must come to recognize that American uniformation, whether in speech or in diet, is at times a surface phenomenon. It is an added variety to the repertoires that are still there and that are still substantial if we will but scratch a little deeper (Fishman 1967a).

SOCIETAL BILINGUALISM:
STABLE AND TRANSITIONAL

Societal bilingualism has been referred to so many times in the previous pages that it is time to consider it in its own right rather than as a means of illustrating more general sociolinguistic phenomena. The psychological literature on bilingualism is so much more extensive than its sociological counterpart that workers in the former field have often failed to establish contact with those in the latter. It is the purpose of this section to relate these two research traditions to each other by tracing the interaction between their two major constructs: bilingualism (on the part of psychologists and psycholinguists) and diglossia (on the part of sociologists and sociolinguists).

6.1 DIGLOSSIA

In the few years that have elapsed since Ferguson (1959a) first advanced it, the term diglossia has not only become widely accepted by sociolinguists and sociologists of language, but it has been further extended and refined. Initially it was used in connection with a *society* that

recognized two (or more) languages or varieties for intrasocietal communication. The use within a single society of
several separate codes (and their stable maintenance rather
than the displacement of one by the other over time) was
found to be dependent on each code's serving functions
distinct from those considered appropriate for the other
code. Whereas one set of behaviors, attitudes, and values
supported, and was expressed in, one language, another set of
behaviors, attitudes, and values supported and was expressed
in the other. Both sets of behaviors, attitudes, and values
were fully accepted as culturally legitimate and complementary (i.e., nonconflictual), and indeed little if any
conflict between them was possible in view of the functional
separation between them. This separation was most often
along the lines of a H(igh) language, on the one hand, utilized
in conjunction with religion, education, and other aspects of
high culture, and an L(ow) language, on the other hand,
utilized in conjunction with everyday pursuits of hearth,
home, and lower work sphere. Ferguson spoke of H as
"superposed" because it is normally learned later and in a
more formal setting than L and is thereby superposed upon
it.

To this original edifice others have added several significant considerations. Gumperz (1961, 1962, 1964a, 1964b,
1966) is primarily responsible for our greater awareness that
diglossia exists not only in multilingual societies which
officially recognize several "languages," and not only in
societies that utilize vernacular and classical varieties, but also
in societies which employ separate dialects, registers, or
*functionally differentiated language varieties of whatever
kind*. He has also done the lion's share of the work in
providing the conceptual apparatus by means of which
investigators of multilingual speech communities seek to
discern the societal patterns that govern the use of one
variety rather than another, particularly at the level of small
group interaction. Fishman (1964, 1965a, 1965c, 1965d,
1965e, 1966a, 1968c), on the other hand, has attempted to
tract the maintenance of diglossia as well as its disruption at
the national or societal level. In addition he has attempted to
relate diglossia to psychologically pertinent considerations
such as compound and co-ordinate bilingualism (1965b).

Finally, Kaye (1970) has indicated that diglossia is often a far more flexible, changeable, and even ill-defined status, particularly in its linguistic aspects, than has often been presumed. The present section represents an extension and integration of these several previous attempts.

For purposes of simplicity it seems best to represent the possible relationships between bilingualism and diglossia by means of a four-fold table such as shown in Figure 13.

FIGURE 13. The Relationships Between Bilingualism and Diglossia

BILINGUALISM	*DIGLOSSIA*	
	+	−
+	1. Both diglossia and bilingualism	2. Bilingualism without diglossia
−	3. Diglossia without bilingualism	4. Neither diglossia nor bilingualism

6.2 SPEECH COMMUNITIES CHARACTERIZED BY BOTH DIGLOSSIA AND BILINGUALISM

The first quadrant of Figure 13 refers to those speech communities in which both diglossia and bilingualism are widespread. At times such communities comprise an entire nation, but of course this requires extremely widespread (if not all-pervasive) bilingualism, and as a result there are really few nations that are fully bilingual and diglossic. An approximation to such a nation is Paraguay, where more than half of the population speaks both Spanish and Guarani (Rubin 1962, 1968). A substantial proportion of the formerly monolingual rural population has added Spanish to its linguistic repertoire in connection with matters of education, religion, government, and high culture (although in the rural areas social distance or status stressing more generally may still be expressed in Guarani). On the other hand, the vast majority of city dwellers (being relatively new from the country) maintain Guarani for matters of intimacy and primary group solidarity, even in the midst of their more newly acquired Spanish urbanism (see Figure 14). Note that

FIGURE 14. National Bilingualism in Paraguay: Ordered Dimensions in the Choice of Language in a Diglossic Society *(Joan Rubin 1968)*

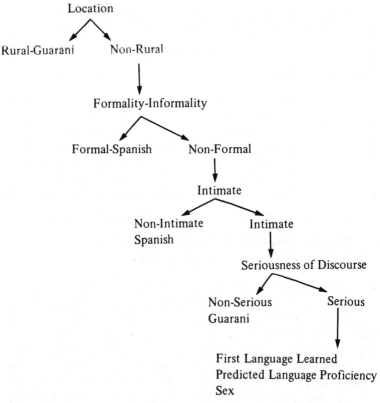

Guarani is not an "official" language (i.e., recognized and utilized for purposes of government, formal education, the courts, etc.) in Paraguay, although it was finally recognized as a "national language" at the 1967 constitutional convention. It is not uncommon for the H variety alone to be recognized as "official" in diglossic settings without this fact threatening the acceptance or the stability of the L variety within the speech community. However, the existence of a particular "official" or "main" language should not divert the investigator from recognizing the fact of widespread and stable multilingualism at the levels of societal and interpersonal functioning (see Table 7).

TABLE 7. Linguistic Unity and Diversity, by World Region

REGION	No. of Countries by Percent of Population Speaking Main Language									
	90-100	80-89	70-79	60-69	50-59	40-49	30-39	20-29	10-19	Total 10-100%
Europe	17	4	2	2	2	–	–	–	–	27
East and South Asia	5	3	4	3	1	4	–	1	–	21
Oceania*	2	–	–	–	–	–	–	–	–	2
Middle East and Northern Africa	8	6	2	3	1	2	–	–	–	22
Tropical and Southern Africa	3	–	–	2	5	8	7	5	3	33
The Americas	15	6	–	–	2	2	1	–	–	26
World Total	50	19	8	10	11	16	8	6	3	131

Source: Table 1 (Rustow, D. 1967).
*Not including New Guinea, for which no breakdown by individual languages was available.

Below the level of nationwide functioning there are many more examples of stable diglossia co-occurring with widespread bilingualism. The Swiss-German cantons may be mentioned since their entire population of school age and older alternates between High German (H) and Swiss German (L), each with its own firmly established and highly valued functions (Ferguson 1959a; Weinreich, U. 1951, 1953a). Hughes (1970) has demonstrated how English (H) and French (L) diglossia-and-bilingualism are peripheral and external in many Montreal agencies and businesses in which clients (or customers) and management (or owners) must interact although coming from different origins. On the other hand, in plants (where no customers/clients are present) the communication between workers and management reveals bilingualism-and-diglossia of a hierarchical and internal nature. Traditional (pre-World War I) Eastern European Jewish males communicated with each other in Hebrew (H) and Yiddish (L). In more recent days many of their descendants have continued to do so in various countries of resettlement, even while adding to their repertoire a Western language (notably English) in certain domains of *intragroup* communication as well as for broader *intergroup* contacts (Fishman 1965a, 1965e; Weinreich, U. 1953a; Weinreich, M. 1953). This development differs significantly from the traditional Eastern European Jewish pattern in which males whose occupational activities brought them into regular contact with various strata of the non-Jewish coterritorial population utilized one or more coterritorial languages (which involved H and L varieties of their own, such as Russian, German, or Polish on the one hand, and Ukrainian, Byelorussian, or "Baltic" varieties, on the other), but did so primarily for *intergroup* purposes. A similar example is that of upper and upper middle-class males throughout the Arabic world who use classical (Koranic) Arabic for traditional Islamic studies, vernacular (Egyptian, Syrian, Lebanese, Iraqui, etc.) Arabic for informal conversation, and not infrequently, also a Western language (French or English, most usually) for purposes of *intragroup* scientific or technological communication (Blanc 1964; Ferguson 1959a; Nader 1962).

All of the foregoing examples have in common the existence of such a fairly large and complex speech community that its members have available to them both a range of *compartmentalized* roles as well as ready *access* to these roles. If the *role repertoires* of these speech communities were of lesser range, then their *linguistic repertoires* would also become more restricted in range, with the result that one or more separate languages or varieties would become superfluous. In addition, were the rules not compartmentalized, i.e., were they not *kept separate* by dint of association with quite separate (though complementary) values, domains of activity, and everyday situations, one language (or variety) would displace the other as role and value distinctions merged and became blurred. Finally, were widespread access not available to the range of compartmentalized roles (and compartmentalized languages or varieties) then the bilingual population would be a small, privileged caste or class (as it is or was throughout most of traditional India or China) rather than a broadly based population segment.

These observations must lead us to the conclusion that many modern speech communities that are normally thought of as monolingual are rather marked by both diglossia and bilingualism, if their several registers are viewed as separate varieties or languages in the same sense as the examples listed above. Wherever speech communities exist whose speakers engage in a considerable range of roles (and this is coming to be the case for all but the extremely upper and lower levels of complex societies), wherever the access to several roles is encouraged or facilitated by powerful social institutions and processes, and finally, wherever the roles are clearly differentiated (in terms of when, where, and with whom they are felt to be appropriate), both diglossia and bilingualism may be said to exist. The benefit of this approach to the topic at hand is that it provides a single theoretical framework for viewing bilingual speech communities and speech communities whose linguistic diversity is realized through varieties not yet recognized as constituting separate "languages." Thus, rather than becoming fewer in modern times, the number of speech communities characterized by diglossia and the widespread command of diversified linguistic repertoires has increased greatly as a consequence of modernization and growing social complexity (Fishman 1966b). In such communities each generation begins anew on a monolingual or restricted repertoire base of hearth and home and must be rendered bilingual or provided with a fuller repertoire by the formal institutions of education, religion, government, or work sphere. In diglossic-bilingual speech communities children do *not* attain their full repertoires at home or in their neighborhood play groups. Indeed, those who most commonly remain at home or in the home neighborhood (the preschool young and the postwork old) are most likely to be functionally monolingual, as Lieberson's tables on French-English bilingualism in Montreal amply reveal (see Table 8). Once established, and in the absence of rapid and extensive social change, bilingualism under circumstances of diglossia becomes an ingredient in the situational and metaphorical switching patterns available for the purposes of intra-communal communicative appropriateness. Many conversations and utterances demonstrably "mean something else," depending on the language in which they are expressed (Table 9), even when all other factors are kept constant (Kimple et al. 1969).

6.3 DIGLOSSIA WITHOUT BILINGUALISM

Departing from the co-occurrence of bilingualism and diglossia we come first to polities in which diglossia obtains whereas bilingualism is generally absent (quadrant 3). Here we find two or more speech communities united politically, religiously, and/or economically into a single functioning unit notwithstanding the sociocultural cleavages that separate them. At the level of this larger (but not always voluntary) unity, two or more languages or varieties must be recognized as obtaining. However, one or both of the speech communities involved are marked by relatively impermeable group boundaries such that for "outsiders" (and this may well mean those not born into the speech community, i.e., an emphasis on ascribed rather than on achieved status) role access and linguistic access are severely restricted. At the same time linguistic repertoires in one or both groups are limited due to role specialization.

Examples of such situations are not hard to find (see, e.g., the many instances listed by Kloss 1966a). Pre-World War I European elites often stood in this relationship with their countrymen, the elites speaking French or some other fashionable H tongue for their *intragroup* purposes (at various times and in various places: Danish, Salish, Provencal, Russian, etc.) and the masses speaking another, not necessarily linguistically related, language for their intragroup purposes. Since the majority of elites and the majority of the masses never interacted with one another they *did not form a single speech community* (i.e., their linguistic repertoires were discontinuous) and their intercommunications were via

TABLE 8. Percentage Bilingual, by Age and Sex, Montreal Area, 1931-61.

| | MALES | | | | | FEMALES | | | | |
| | Montreal-Verdun | | Montreal-Outremont-Verdun | | | Montreal-Verdun | | Montreal-Outremont-Verdun | | |
Age	1931 (1)	1941 (2)	1941 (3)	1951 (4)	1961 (5)	1931 (6)	1941 (7)	1941 (8)	1951 (9)	1961 (10)
0- 4 ...	4.1	5.7	5.7	3.3	2.5	4.0	5.6	5.7	3.4	2.5
5- 9 ...	18.2	11.3	11.5	9.7	9.9	18.0	11.5	11.8	9.7	9.6
10-14 ...	43.4	22.2	22.6	20.5	22.4	41.4	21.9	22.3	20.1	21.9
15-19 ...	62.4	51.4	51.7	50.6	49.6	54.7	43.1	43.5	44.5	46.7
20-24 ...	67.2	67.1	67.2	64.9	59.4	53.3	51.5	51.7	48.2	44.4
25-34 ...	61.9	68.8	68.8	68.8	59.7	49.0	47.8	48.1	47.8	41.1
35-44 ...	62.2	63.6	63.7	68.1	65.3	44.5	40.9	41.2	45.2	45.5
45-54 ...	59.3	60.3	60.3	62.7	63.6	41.6	35.6	36.0	37.4	42.6
55-64 ...	57.4	53.7	53.8	57.3	57.2	37.1	31.2	31.6	30.8	34.5
65-69 ...	56.4	49.4	49.6	49.7	52.0	34.3	28.0	28.5	26.5	28.5
70+ ...	51.2	42.9	43.3	42.2	44.0	31.2	24.4	24.7	23.5	24.5

(Lieberson 1965).

TABLES 9A and 9B. The Interpretation of Language Switching (English-Spanish) given both Bilingualism and Diglossia (Kimple et al 1969)

Analysis of variance for items requiring
subjective judgment: conversation 1 (boy calls girl for date)

Item no.	Source	df	MS	F
10 (Length of family's residence in N.Y.C.)	Treatments Within	3 45	4.13 1.18	3.50*
11 (Length of boy's residence in N.Y.C.)	Treatments Within	3 45	11.70 1.75	6.69**
12 (Kind of job held by girl's father)	Treatments Within	3 45	2.46 .62	3.97*
13	Treatments Within	3 45	.17 .73	.23
14	Treatments Within	3 45	.18 .35	.51
15	Treatments Within	3 45	.32 .42	.76
16 (Naturalness of conversation between boy & girl)	Treatments Within	3 45	2.32 .33	7.03**
17 (Naturalness of conversation between mother & girl)	Treatments Within	3 45	2.19 .56	3.91*
18	Treatments Within	3 45	.67 .46	1.45

*$p < .05$
**$p < .01$

Analysis of variance for items requiring
subjective judgment: conversation 2 (invitation to stay for dinner)

Item no.	Source	df	MS	F
9	Treatments Within	3 45	.37 .51	.73
10	Treatments Within	3 45	3.33 2.58	1.29
11	Treatments Within	3 45	1.42 .75	1.89
12	Treatments Within	3 45	.06 .93	.65
13 (Naturalness of conversation between mother & guest)	Treatments Within	3 45	2.97 .51	5.82**
14 (Naturalness of conversation between boy & guest)	Treatments Within	3 45	3.96 .48	8.25**

**$p < .01$

translators or interpretors (a certain sign of *intragroup* monolingualism). Since the majority of the elites and the majority of the masses led lives characterized by extremely narrow role repertoires, their linguistic repertoires too were too narrow to permit widespread societal bilingualism to develop. Nevertheless, the body politic in all of its economic and national manifestations tied these two groups together into a "unity" that revealed an upper and a lower class, each with a language appropriate to its own restricted concerns. Some have suggested that the modicum of direct interaction that does occur between servants and masters who differ in mother tongue contributes to bringing into being the marginal languages (pidgins) for which such settings are known (Grimshaw in press).

Thus, the existence of national diglossia does *not* imply widespread bilingualism amongst rural or recently urbanized African groups (as distinguished from somewhat more westernized populations in those settings); nor amongst most lower-caste Hindus, as distinguished from their more fortunate compatriots the Brahmins, nor amongst most lower-class French Canadians, as distinguished from their upper and upper middle-class city cousins, etc. In general, this pattern is characteristic of polities that are economically underdeveloped and unmobilized, combining groups that are locked into opposite extremes of the social spectrum, and therefore groups that operate within extremely restricted and discontinuous linguistic repertoires (Friederich 1962, Fishman 1969a, Pool 1969). Obviously such polities are bound to experience language problems as their social patterns alter as a result of industrialization, widespread literacy and education, democratization, and modernization more generally. Since few polities that exhibit diglossia without bilingualism developed out of prior sociocultural consensus or unity, rapid educational, political, or economic development experienced by their disadvantaged groups or classes is very likely to lead to demands for secessionism or for equality for their submerged languages. The linguistic states of Eastern Europe and India, and the language problems of Wales and Belgium stem from origins such as these. This is the pattern of development that may yet convulse many African and Asian nations if their de-ethnicized and westernized elites continue to fail to foster widespread and stable bilingual speech communities that incorporate the masses and that recognize both the official languages of wider communication and the local languages of hearth and home (Figure 15).

6.4 BILINGUALISM WITHOUT DIGLOSSIA

We turn next to those situations in which bilingualism obtains, whereas diglossia is generally absent (quadrant 2). Here we see more clearly than before that bilingualism is essentially a characterization of *individual* linguistic versatility, whereas *diglossia is a characterization of the social allocation of functions* to different languages or varieties. Under what circumstances do bilinguals function without the benefit of a well-understood and widely accepted social consensus as to *which* language is to be used between which interlocutors, for communication concerning *what* topics or for *what* purposes? Under what circumstances do the varieties or languages involved lack well-defined or protected separate functions? Briefly put, these are circumstances of rapid social change, of great social unrest, of widespread abandonment of prior norms before the consolidation of new ones. Children typically become bilingual at a very early age, when they are still largely confined to home and neighborhood, since their elders (both adult and school age) carry into the domains of intimacy a language learned outside its confines. Formal institutions tend to make individuals increasingly monolingual in a language other than that of hearth and home. Ultimately, the language of school and government replaces the language of home and neighborhood, precisely because it comes to provide status in the latter domains as well as in the former, due to the extensive social change to which home and neighborhood have been exposed (see Section 7, below).

Many studies of bilingualism and intelligence or of bilingualism and school achievement have been conducted

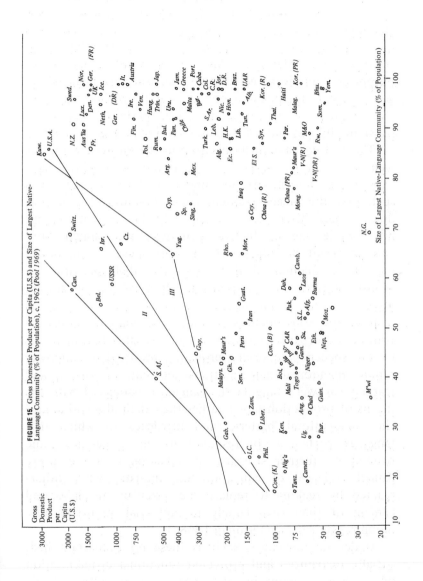

FIGURE 15. Gross Domestic Product per Capita (U.S.$) and Size of Largest Native-Language Community (% of Population), c. 1962 (Pool 1969)

within the context of bilingualism without diglossia (for a review see Macnamara 1966), often without sufficient understanding on the part of the investigators that this was but one of several possible contexts for the study of bilingualism (Corpas 1969, Metraux 1965). As a result many of the purported "disadvantages" of bilingualism have been falsely generalized to the phenomenon at large rather than related to the absence or presence of social patterns that reach substantially beyond bilingualism (Fishman 1965b, 1966a).

The history of industrialization in the Western world (as well as in those parts of Africa and Asia which have experienced industrialization under Western "auspices") is such that the means (capital, plant, organization) of production have often been controlled by one speech community, while the productive manpower was drawn from another (Deutsch 1966). Initially, both speech communities may have maintained their separate diglossia-with-bilingualism patterns or, alternatively, that of an overarching diglossia without bilingualism. In either case, the needs as well as the consequences of rapid and massive industrialization and urbanization were frequently such that members of the speech community providing productive manpower rapidly abandoned their traditional sociocultural patterns and learned (or were taught) the language associated with the means of production much earlier than their absorption into the sociocultural patterns and privileges to which that language pertained. In response to this imbalance some reacted by further stressing the advantages of the newly gained language of education and industry while others reacted by seeking to replace the latter by an elaborated version of their own largely preindustrial, preurban, premobilization tongue (Fishman 1968c).

Under circumstances such as these no well-established, socially recognized and protected functional differentiation of languages obtains in many speech communities of the lower and lower middle classes. Dislocated immigrants and their children (for whom a separate "political solution" is seldom possible) are particularly inclined to use their mother tongue and other tongue for intragroup communication in *seemingly* random fashion (Fishman, Cooper, and Ma 1968; Nahirny and Fishman 1965; Herman 1961). Since the formerly separate roles of the home domain, the school domain, and the work domain are all disturbed by the massive dislocation of values and norms that result from simultaneous immigration and industrialization, the language of work (and of the school) comes to be used at home. As role compartmentalization and value complementarity decrease under the impact of foreign models and massive change, the linguistic repertoire also becomes less compartmentalized. Languages and varieties formerly kept apart come to influence each other phonetically, lexically, semantically, and even grammatically much more than before. Instead of two (or more) carefully separated languages each under the eye of caretaker groups of teachers, preachers, and writers, several intervening varieties may obtain differing in degree of interpenetration. Under these circumstances the languages of immigrants may come to be ridiculed as "debased" and "broken" while at the same time their standard varieties are given no language maintenance support.

Thus, bilingualism without diglossia tends to be transitional both in terms of the linguistic repertoires of speech communities as well as in terms of the speech varieties involved per se. Without separate though complementary norms and values to establish and maintain functional separation of the speech varieties, that language or variety which is fortunate enough to be associated with the predominant drift of social forces tends to displace the others. Furthermore, pidginization (the crystallization of new fusion languages or varieties) is likely to set in when members of the "work force" are so dislocated as not to be able to maintain or develop significantly compartmentalized, limited-access roles (in which they might be able to safeguard a stable mother tongue variety), on one hand, and when social change stops short of permitting them to interact sufficiently with those members of the "power class" who might serve as standard other-tongue models, on the other hand.

6.5 NEITHER DIGLOSSIA NOR BILINGUALISM

Only very small, isolated, and undifferentiated speech communities may be said to reveal neither diglossia nor bilingualism (Gumperz 1962; Fishman 1965c). Given little role differentiation or compartmentalization and frequent face-to-face interaction between all members of the speech community, no fully differentiated registers or varieties may establish themselves. Given self-sufficiency, no regular or significant contacts with other speech communities may be maintained. Nevertheless, such groups—be they bands or clans—are easier to hypothesize than to find (Owens 1965; Sorensen 1967). All speech communities seem to have certain ceremonies or pursuits to which access is limited, if only on an age basis. Thus, all linguistic repertoires contain certain terms that are unknown to certain members of the speech community, and certain terms that are used differently by different subsets of speakers. In addition, metaphorical switching for purposes of emphasis, humor, satire, or criticism must be available in some form even in relatively undifferentiated communities. Finally, such factors as exogamy, warfare, expansion of population, economic growth, and contact with others all lead to internal diversification and consequently to repertoire diversification. Such diversification is the beginning of bilingualism. Its societal normalization is the hallmark of diglossia. Quadrant four tends to be self-liquidating.

Many efforts are now underway to bring to pass a rapprochement between psychological, linguistic, and sociological work on bilingualism (Fishman and Terry 1969). The student of bilingualism, most particularly the student of bilingualism in the context of social issues and social change, should benefit from an awareness of the various possible relationships between individual bilingualism and societal diglossia illustrated in this section. One of the fruits of such awareness will be that problems of transition and dislocation will not be mistaken for the entire gamut of societal bilingualism.

LANGUAGE MAINTENANCE
AND
LANGUAGE SHIFT

Modern history reveals at least five major instances of language shift, i.e., instances when huge populations adopted a new language or variety into their repertoires, whether or not at the same time they also gave up a language or variety that they had previously used. The instances referred to are (a) the vernacularization of European governmental, technical, educational, cultural activity, (b) the Anglification/ Hispanization of the populations of North/South America respectively (Table 10), (c) the adoption of English and French as languages of elitist wider communication throughout much of the world, but particularly in Africa and Asia, (d) the Russification of Soviet-controlled populations, and most recently (e) the growing displacement of imported languages of wider communication and the parallel vernacularization of governmental, technical, educational, and cultural efforts in many parts of Africa and Asia. Having previously noted (Section 5) that divergence and

TABLE 10. 1940-1960 Totals for 23 Non-English Mother Tongues in the USA (Fishman 1966c).

Language	1940 Total	1960 Total	Total Change	
			n	%
Norwegian	658,220	321,774	−336,446	−51.1%
Swedish	830,900	415,597	−415,303	−50.0%
Danish	226,740	147,619	− 79,121	−65.1%
Dutch/Flemish	289,580	321,613	+ 32,033	+11.1%
French	1,412,060	1,043,220	−368,840	−26.1%
German	4,949,780	3,145,772	−1,804,008	−36.4%
Polish	2,416,320	2,184,936	−231,384	−9.6%
Czech	520,440	217,771	−302,669	−58.2%
Slovak	484,360	260,000	−224,360	−46.3%
Hungarian	453,000	404,114	−48,886	−10.8%
Serbo-Croatian	153,080	184,094	+31,014	+20.3%
Slovenian	178,640	67,108	−111,532	−62.4%
Russian	585,080	460,834	−124,246	−21.2%
Ukrainian	83,600	252,974	+169,374	+202.6%
Lithuanian	272,680	206,043	−66,637	−24.4%
Finnish	230,420	110,168	−120,252	−52.2%
Rumanian	65,520	58,019	−7,501	−11.4%
Yiddish	1,751,100	964,605	−786,495	−44.9%
Greek	273,520	292,031	+18,511	+6.8%
Italian	3,766,820	3,673,141	−93,679	−2.5%
Spanish	1,861,400	3,335,961	+1,474,561	+79.2%
Portuguese	215,660	181,109	−34,551	−16.0%
Arabic	107,420	103,908	−3,512	−3.3%
Total	21,786,540	18,352,351	−3,434,189	−15.8%

In 1940 the numerically strongest mother tongues in the United States were German, Italian, Polish, Spanish, Yiddish, and French, in that order. Each of these languages was claimed by approximately a million and a half or more individuals. In 1960 these same languages remained the "big six" although their order had changed to Italian, Spanish, German, Polish, French, and Yiddish. Among them, only Spanish registered gains (and substantial gains at that) in this 20-year interval. The losses among the "big six" varied from a low of 2.5% for Italian to a high of 44.9% for Yiddish. The only other languages to gain in overall number of claimants during this period (disregarding the generational distribution of such gains) were Ukrainian, Serbo-Croatian, "Dutch"/ Flemish, and Greek. The greatest gain of all was that of Ukrainian

(202.6%!). Most mother tongues, including five of the "big six", suffered substantial losses during this period, the sharpest being that of Danish (65.1%). All in all, the 23 non-English mother tongues for which a 1940-1960 comparison is possible lost approximately one-sixth of their claimants during this interval. Yet the total number of claimants of non-English mother tongues in the United States is still quite substantial, encompassing nearly 11% of the total 1960 population (and an appreciably higher proportion of the white population).[6]

[6]The 1940 and 1960 totals shown in Table 9 must not be taken as the totals for *all* non-English mother tongue claimants in those years. Figures for Armenian were reported in 1940 but not in 1960. Figures for Chinese and Japanese were reported in 1960 but not in 1940. Total figures for "All other" languages were reported in both years. None of these inconsistent or non-specific listings are included in Table 2.4. Adding in these figures as well as the necessary generational estimates based upon them, the two totals would become 1940: 22,036,240; 1960: 19,381,786.

---

differentiation of the verbal repertoire are reflections of societal distance and segmentation, we must now point out that the sociocultural changes that carry with them changes in verbal repertoires are themselves differentially associated with the various speech communities and speech networks of any polity. As a result, not only are the verbal repertoires of communities and networks that experience the greatest sociocultural change the most likely to be altered, but the repertoires of those who gain most in economic, political, or other sociocultural status are the most likely to be adopted or copied by others who see opportunities for desirable changes in their own status by so doing.

The study of language maintenance and language shift focuses upon cell 2 of Figure 13 above and is basically concerned with the relationship between degree of change (or degree of stability) in language usage patterns, on one hand, and ongoing psychological, cultural, or social processes, on the other hand, in populations that utilize more than one speech variety for intragroup or for intergroup purposes. That languages (or language varieties) *sometimes* displace each other, among *some* speakers, particularly in *certain* interpersonal or system-wide interactions, has long aroused curiosity and comment. However, it is only in quite recent years that this topic has been recognized as a field of systematic inquiry among professional students of language behavior. It is suggested here that the three major topical subdivisions of this field are: (a) habitual language use at more than one point in time or space; (b) antecedent, concurrent, or consequent psychological, social, and cultural processes and their relationship to stability or change in habitual language use; and (c) behavior toward language, including directed maintenance or shift efforts. It is the purpose of this Section to discuss each of these three topical subdivisions briefly, to indicate their current stage of development, and to offer suggestions for their further development.

7.1 HABITUAL LANGUAGE USE AT MORE THAN ONE POINT IN TIME

The basic datum of the study of language maintenance and language shift is that some demonstrable change has occurred in the pattern of habitual language use. The consequences that are of *primary* concern to the student of language maintenance and language shift are *not* interference phenomena per se, but rather degrees of maintenance or displacement in conjunction with several sources and domains of variance in language behavior. Thus, the very first requirement of inquiry in this field is a conceptualization of variance in language behavior whereby language maintenance and language displacement can be accurately and appropriately ascertained. In the course of their labors linguists, psychologists, anthropologists, and other specialists have developed a large number of quantitative and qualitative characterizations of variance in language behavior. By choosing from among them and adding to them judiciously, it may be possible to arrive at provocative insights into more sociolinguistic concerns as well. Whether those aspects of variance in language behavior that have, in the past, been conceived of as *qualitative* can be rendered ultimately commensurable with those that have more frequently been considered *quantitative* is a topic to which we will return, after first considering the two aspects separately.

7.1.1 Degree of Bilingualism

For the student of language maintenance and language shift the *quantification* of habitual language use is related to the much older question of ascertaining *degree of bilingualism*. This question, in turn, has been tackled by a great number of investigators from different disciplines, each being concerned with a somewhat different nuance. Linguists have been most concerned with the analysis of bilingualism from the point of view of *switching or interference*. The measures that they have proposed from their disciplinary point of departure distinguish between phonetic, lexical, and grammatical proficiency and intactness (Mackey 1962). At the other extreme stand educators who are concerned with bilingualism in terms of *total performance contrasts* in very complex contexts such as the school or even the society (Manuel 1963). Psychologists have usually studied degrees of bilingualism in terms of speed, automaticity, or habit strength (Macnamara 1966). Sociologists have relied upon relative frequencies of use in *different settings* (Hayden 1964, Hofman 1966a, 1966b, Nahirny and Fishman 1966). Thus, since a great number of different kinds of bilingualism scores or quotients are already available, the sociolinguistically oriented student of language maintenance and language shift must decide which, if any, are appropriate to his own concerns. Since the study of this topic cannot be reduced to or equated with the concerns of any particular discipline, it seems highly likely that a *combination or organization of approaches* to the measurement and description of bilingualism will uniquely characterize the study of language maintenance and language shift.

7.1.2 *The Need for a Combination of Interrelated Measures*

It would seem that the linguist's interest in itemizing examples of interference and switching introduces an outside criterion into the study of language maintenance and language shift which may not at all correspond to that utilized by speech communities or speech networks under study. The linguist's distinction between what is English and what is French and the distinction made by English-French bilinguals may differ so widely that the linguist's *conclusions* about the drift of shift, based upon interference and switch data, may be seriously in error.

However, even where a linguist is obviously interested only in a carefully delimited question about the relative frequency of a particular instance or class of interferences or shifts, it is clear that it may be far easier to answer this question in some cases than in others (e.g., it may be easier to answer in connection with encoding than in connection with inner speech; it may be easier to answer in connection with writing than in connection with speaking; it may be easier to answer in connection with formal and technical communication than in connection with intimate communication), for the "density," stability, and clarity of interference and switching varies for the same individual from occasion to occasion and from situation to situation. Although interference and switching are lawful behaviors, there are advanced cases of language shift in which even linguists will be hard pressed to determine the answer to "Which language is being used?", particularly if a single supralevel answer is required.

Similarly, concern with relative proficiency, relative ease and automaticity, and relative frequency of language use in a contact setting are also not necessarily indicative of over-all language maintenance or shift. Conclusions based on such measures may be particularly far off the mark in bilingualism-plus-diglossia settings in which most speakers use both languages equally well (correctly), effortlessly, and frequently, but differ *primarily* in connection with the topics, persons, and places (or, more generally, the *situations* and situation types or domains) in which these languages are used. Thus, in conclusion, the contribution that the student of language maintenace and language shift can make to the measurement of bilingualism is precisely his awareness (a) that *various* measures are needed if the social realities of multilingual settings are to be reflected, and (b) that the measures *can be organized* in terms of relatively *general variance considerations.* Of the many approaches to variance in language use that have been suggested the following is both simple enough for easy presentation as well as sufficiently involved to imply that even greater complexity exists not too far below the surface.

7.1.3 Media Variance: Written, Read, and Spoken Language

Degree of maintenance and shift may be quite different in these very different media. Where literacy has been attained prior to interaction with an "other tongue," reading and writing in the mother tongue may resist shift longer than speaking. Where literacy is attained subsequent to (or as a result of) such interaction the reverse may hold true (Fishman 1965e). More generally, the linguist's disinclination to be concerned with the written language is a luxury that cannot be afforded in the study of language maintenance and language shift, where the contrasts involved are so frequently between languages that vary greatly in the extent to which they have literacy or other "higher"functions for the speech networks under study.

7.1.4 Overtness Variance

Degree of maintenance and shift·may be quite different in connection with *inner speech* (in which ego is both source and target), *comprehension* (decoding, in which ego is target), and *production* (encoding, in which ego is the source). Where language shift is unconscious or resisted, inner speech may be most resistant to interference, switching, and disuse of the mother tongue. Where language shift is conscious and desired, this may less frequently be the case (Fishman 1965f).

7.1.5 Location of Bilingualism: The Domains of Language Behavior

The *qualitative* aspects of bilingualism are most easily illustrated in connection with the *location* of language maintenance and language shift in terms of *domains* of language behavior. What is of concern to us here is the most parsimonious and fruitful designation of the societally or institutionally clusterable occasions in which one language (variant, dialect, style, etc.) is habitually employed and normatively expected rather than (or in addition to) another.

7.1.5.1 The Domains of Language Behavior and the Compound-Coordinate Distinction

If the concept of *domains of language behavior* proves to be as fruitful and as manageable a one as seems to be likely on the basis of recent empirical evidence, it may also yield beneficial results in connection with other areas of research on bilingualism, e.g., in connection with the distinction between *co-ordinate* and *compound* bilingualism (Ervin and Osgood 1954, p. 140). The latter distinction arose out of an awareness (mentioned by several investigators over the years) that there are at least two major types of bilingual functioning," one (the compound type) being "characteristic of bilingualism acquired by a child who grows up in a home where two languages are spoken more or less interchangeably by the same people and in the same situations" and the other (the co-ordinate) being "typical of the 'true' bilingual, who has learned to speak one language with his parents, for example, and the other language in school and at work. The total situations, both external and emotional, and the total behaviors occurring when one language is being used will differ from those occurring with the other." From our previous discussion of domains of language behavior it is clear that these two types of bilingual functioning (more accurately put, two extremes of a continuum of psychoneurological organization) have been distinguished on the bases of some awareness, however rudimentary, that *bilinguals vary with respect to the number and overlap of domains in which they habitually employ each of their languages.* However, this is true not only initially, in the acquisition of bilingualism (with which the compound-co-ordinate distinction is primarily concerned) but also subsequently, *throughout* life. Initially co-ordinate bilinguals may become exposed to widespread bilingualism in which both languages are used rather freely over a larger set of overlapping domains. Similarly, compound bilinguals may become exposed to a more restrictive or dichotomized environment in which each language is assigned to very specific and nonoverlapping domains.

Going one step further it appears that the domain concept may facilitate a number of worthwhile contributions to the understanding of the compound-co-ordinate distinction in conjunction with language maintenance and language shift per se. Thus, domain analysis may help organize and clarify the previously unstructured awareness that language maintenance and language shift proceed quite unevenly across the several sources and domains of variance in habitual language use. Certain domains may well appear to be more maintenance-prone than others (e.g., the family domain in comparison to the occupational domain) across all multi-lingual settings characterized by urbanization and economic development, regardless of whether immigrant-host or coindigenous populations are involved. Under the impact of these same sociocultural processes other domains (e.g., religion) may be found to be strongly maintenance oriented during the early stages of interaction and strongly shift oriented once an authoritative decision is reached that their organizational base can be better secured via shift. Certain interactions between domains and other sources of variance may remain protective of contextually "disadvantaged" languages (e.g., family domain: internal speech, husband-wife role relations), even when language shift has advanced so far that a given domain as such has been engulfed. On the other hand, if a strict domain separation becomes institutionalized so that each language is associated with a number of

FIGURE 16. Type of Bilingual Functioning and Domain Overlap during Successive Stages of Immigrant Acculturation

BILINGUAL FUNCTIONING TYPE	DOMAIN OVERLAP TYPE	
	Overlapping Domains	Nonoverlapping Domains
Compound ("Interdependent" or fused)	2. Second Stage: More immigrants know more English and therefore can speak to each other either in mother tongue or in English (still mediated by the mother tongue) in several domains of behavior. Increased interference.	1. Initial Stage: The immigrant learns English via his mother tongue. English is used only in those few domains (work sphere, governmental sphere) in which mother tongue cannot be used. Minimal interference. Only a few immigrants know a little English.
Coordinate ("Independent")	3. Third Stage: The languages function independently of each other. The number of bilinguals is at its maximum. Domain overlap is at its maximum. The second generation during childhood. Stabilized interference.	4. Fourth Stage: English has displaced the mother tongue from all but the most private or restricted domains. Interference declines. In most cases both languages function independently; in others the mother tongue is mediated by English (reverse direction of Stage 1, but same type).

important but distinct domains, bilingualism may well become both universal and stabilized even though an entire population consists of bilinguals interacting with other bilinguals. Finally, in conjunction with language maintenance and language shift among American immigrant groups, the interaction between domain analysis and the compound-co-ordinate distinction may prove to be particularly edifying.

As suggested by Figure 16, most late nineteenth and early twentieth century immigrants to America from Eastern and Southern Europe began as compound bilinguals, with English assigned to quite specific and restricted domains. With the passage of time (involving increased interaction with English-speaking Americans, social mobility, and acculturation with respect to other-than-language behaviors as well) their bilingualism became characterized, first, by far greater domain overlap (and by far greater interference) and then by progressively greater co-ordinate functioning. Finally, language displacement advanced so far that the mother tongue remained only in a few restricted and nonoverlapping domains. Indeed, in some cases, compound bilingualism once more became the rule, except that the ethnic mother tongue came to be utilized via English (rather than vice versa, as was the case in early immigrant days). Thus the domain concept may help place the compound-co-ordinate distinction in sociocultural perspective, in much the same way as it may well serve the entire area of language maintenance and language shift.

7.1.5.2 The Dominance Configuration   Subsection 7.1.5.1 above clearly indicates the need for basic tools of a complex and sophisticated sort. Precise measurement of *degree of maintenance or displacement* will be possible only when more diversified measures of degree of bilingualism (including attention to media and overtness variance) are at hand. Precise measurement of *domains of maintenance or displacement* will be possible only after concerted attention is given to the construction of instruments that are based upon a careful consideration of the various domains of language behavior (and the role relations, topics, and locales—these being the three components of situational variation)

mentioned in a scattered international literature. The availability of such instruments will also facilitate work in several
related fields of study, such as the success of intensive
second-languge learning programs, accurate current language
facility censuses, applied "language reinforcement" efforts,
etc. Given such instruments, the intercorrelations between
the several components of variance in degree of bilingualism
will become amenable to study, as will the variation of such
intercorrelations with age or with varying degrees of language
ability, opportunity, and motivation. The relationship
between maintenance or displacement in the various domains
of language will also become subject to scrutiny. Speculation
concerning the relationship between shifts in degree and
direction of bilingualism and shifts in the domains of
bilingualism will finally become subject to investigation.
Finally, out of all the foregoing, it will become possible to
speak much more meaningfully about the *dominance
configurations* of bilinguals and of changes in these
configurations in language maintenance-language shift
contexts.

7.1.5.3 Some Preliminary Suggestions Figures 17 and 18 are
primarily intended to serve as possible presentation formats
for dominance configurations based upon several *domains*
and *sources of variance* in language behavior mentioned
earlier in this discussion. The types of language use data
favored by linguists, psychologists, and educators have been
set aside temporarily in favor of grosser "frequency use"
data. However, of primary interest at this time are the
suggested parameters rather than the rough data presented.
An inspection of these figures refeals several general
characteristics of the dominance configuration: (a) the
dominance configuration summarizes multilingual language
use data for a particular population studied at two points in
time and space; (b) a complete cross-tabulation of all
theoretically possible sources and domains of variance in
language behavior does not actually exist. In some instances,
logical difficulties arise. In others, occurences are logically
possible, but either necessarily rare or rare for the particular
populations under study; (c) each cell in the dominance

FIGURE 17. Intragroup Yiddish-English Maintenance and Shift in the United States: 1940-1970 Summary Comparisons for Immigrant Generation "Secularists" Arriving Prior to World War I ("Dummy Table" for Dominance Configuration).

Sources of Variance					
		Family role-rels.	Neighb. role-rels.	Work role-rels.	Jew Rel/Cult role-rels.
Media	Overtness	1 2 3	1 2	1 2 3	1 2
Speaking	Production				
	Comprehension				
	Inner				
Reading	Production				
	Comprehension				
Writing	Production				
	Comprehension				

FIGURE 18. Part of "Dummy Table" in Greater Detail

Media	Overtness	Domains	Role Relations	Summary Ratings 1940	1970
Speaking	Production	Family	Husband-Wife	Y	Y
			Parent-Child	Y	E
			Grandparent-Grandchild	–	E
			Other: same generation	Y	Y
			Other: younger generation	E	E
		Neighborhood	Friends	Y	E
			Acquaintances	Y	E
		Work	Employer-Employer	E	E
			Employer-Employee	E	E
			Employee-Employee	E	E
		Jewish Rel./Cult	Supporter-Writer, Teacher, etc.	Y	Y
			Supporter-Supporter	Y	Y

configuration summarizes detailed process data pertaining to the particular role relation (parent-child, teacher-pupil, etc.) pertinent to it and the situations, network types (open and closed), and/or transaction types (interactional and personal) encountered; (d) some of the domains utilized do not correspond to those listed in subsection 7.2 above, nor are all of the domains previously listed utilized here. This should sensitize us further to the probability that no invariant set of domains can prove to be maximally revealing, notwithstanding the efforts expended in pursuit of such a set (Dohrenwend and Smith 1962, Jones and Lambert 1959, Mackey 1962, Schermerhorn 1964); (e) an exhaustive analysis of the data of dominance configurations may well require sophisticated pattern analysis or other mathematical techniques which do not necessarily assume equal weight and simple additivity for each entry in each cell; (f) a much more refined presentation of language maintenance or language shift becomes possible than that which is provided by means of mother-tongue census statistics (Kloss 1929, Nelson 1947). Word naming scores, self-ratings of frequency of usage, observed occurrences of various phonological, lexical, or grammatical realizations, all of these and many other types of scores or indices can be utilized for dominance configuration analysis of speech communities or networks. The need to *summarize* and *group* language-usage data necessarily leads to some loss of refinement when proceeding from specific instances of actual speech in face-to-face interaction to grouped or categorized data. However, such summarization or simplification is an inevitable aspect of the scientific process of discovering meaning in continuous multivariate data by attending to differential relationships, central tendencies, relative variabilities, and other similar characterizations. Moreover, the ultimate "summary" nature of the dominance configuration and the further possibilities of collapsing domains according to higher order psychological or sociological similarities (e.g., "public" vs. "private" language use) obviates the proliferation of atomized findings.

All in all, the dominance configuration represents a great and difficult challenge to students of bilingualism and of language maintenance or language shift. It is possible that once this challenge is recognized, serious problems of

TABLE 11. Frequency of Mother Tongue Use in Conversations by Oldest and Youngest Children of Four Ethnic Backgrounds.* (Fishman 1966c)

In Conversation with:	German			Jewish			Polish			Ukrainian		
	Almost Always (N %)	Frequently (N %)	Almost Never (N %)	Almost Always (N %)	Frequently (N %)	Almost Never (N %)	Almost Always (N %)	Frequently (N %)	Almost Never (N %)	Almost Always (N %)	Frequently (N %)	Almost Never (N %)
Grandparents	6 26.1	6 26.1	11 47.8	6 20.0	9 30.0	15 50.0	15 57.6	5 19.2	6 23.2	26 96.3	—	1 3.7
Father	7 18.4	10 26.4	21 55.2	5 15.0	23 34.3	34 50.7	22 38.3	17 26.7	21 35.0	42 84.0	6 12.0	2 4.0
Mother	5 16.1	4 12.9	22 71.0	5 9.8	19 37.4	27 52.9	16 29.1	14 25.4	25 45.5	41 89.1	5 10.9	—
Brothers and Sisters	2 8.7	2 8.7	19 82.6	—	7 18.9	30 81.1	7 19.4	5 13.8	24 66.7	20 50.0	18 45.0	2 5.0
Friends	3 10.0	7 23.3	20 66.7	—	10 22.7	34 77.3	4 9.8	9 21.9	28 68.3	15 27.3	20 36.4	20 36.4
Husband and Wife	2 11.1	1 5.6	15 83.3	—	1 4.5	21 95.5	3 15.0	—	17 85.0	4 36.4	3 27.3	4 36.4
Own Child	1 5.6	3 16.7	14 77.8	—	1 5.3	18 94.7	3 20.0	—	12 80.0	4 50.0	3 37.5	1 12.5

*Data reported by parents. The German and Polish parents studied were primarily second-generation individuals. The Jewish and Ukrainian parents studied were primarily first-generation individuals. All parents were ethnic cultural or organizational "leaders."

configurational analysis will also arise, as they have in other substantive areas requiring attention to *patterns* of quantitative or qualitative measures. However, it is unnecessary to prejudge this matter. It does seem fitting to conclude that the dominance configuration—if it is to have maximal analytic value—might best be limited to those aspects of *degree of bilingualism* and of *location of bilingualism* which further inquiry may reveal to be of greatest relative *importance* and *independence*. Focused attention on the study of spoken production (as initially suggested by Table 11) has amply demonstrated the rich yield that a self-imposed limitation of this kind can produce in appropriately selected speech communities. (Fishman, Cooper, Ma, et al. 1968).

7.2 PSYCHOLOGICAL, SOCIAL, AND CULTURAL PROCESSES RELATED TO STABILITY OR CHANGE IN HABITUAL LANGUAGE USE

The second major topical subdivision of the study of language maintenance and language shift deals with the psychological, social, and cultural processes associated with habitual language use. Under certain conditions of interaction the relative incidence and configuration of bilingualism stabilizes and remains fairly constant over time within various bilingual-diglossic speech communities. However, under other circumstances one variety or another may continue to gain speakers with the result that bilingualism initially increases and then decreases as the variety in question becomes the predominant language of the old and the mother tongue of the young. The second subdivision of the study of language maintenance and language shift seeks to determine the processes that distinguish between such obviously different conditions of interaction as well as processes whereby one condition is transformed into the other. The processes pertaining to this topical subdivision may be conceived of either as antecedent, concurrent (contextual), or consequent variables, depending on the design of particular studies. Their major common characteristic is that they are primarily *outside* of language per se.

7.2.1 The Paucity of Cross-Cultural and Diachronic
Regularities

Just as an understanding of social-behavior-through-language must depend upon a general theory of society so the understanding of language maintenance or language shift must depend on a theory of sociocultural contact and sociocultural change. Furthermore, it would seem that since we are concerned with the possibility of stability or change in language behavior on one hand, we must be equally concerned with all of the forces contributing to stability or to change in societal behavior more generally, on the other. Thus the selection of psychological, social, and cultural variables for the study of language maintenance and language shift may well be guided not only by impressions of what seem to be the most relevant processes in a particular contact situation but also by more general theories of personal, social, and cultural change. This is not to imply that all forces leading to *change* in other-than-language behaviors *necessarily* also lead to language *shift*. Indeed, whether or not this is the case (or, put more precisely, a determination of the circumstances under which language and nonlanguage behaviors change concurrently, consecutively, or independently) constitutes one of the major intellectual challenges currently facing this field of inquiry. If this challenge is to be met, it will be necessary for the study of language maintenance and language shift to be conducted within the context of studies of intergroup contacts that attend to important other-than-language processes as well: urbanization (ruralization), industrialization (or its abandonment), nationalism (or de-ethnization), nativism (or cosmopolitanization), religious revitalization (or secularization), etc.

Our current state of generalizable knowledge in the area of language maintenance and language shift is insufficient for the positing of relationships of cross-cultural or diachronic validity. Indeed, many of the most popularly cited factors purportedly influencing maintenance and shift have actually been found to "cut both ways" in different contexts or to have no general significance when viewed in broader perspective. Thus, Kloss illustrates that no uniform consequences for language maintenance or language shift are derivable from (a) absence or presence of higher education in the mother tongue, (b) larger or smaller numbers of speakers, (c) greater or lesser between-group similarity, and (d) positive or hostile attitudes of the majority toward the minority (Kloss 1966b, pp. 9-13). The presence of so many ambivalent factors is a clear indication that complex interactions between partially contributory factors (rather than a single overpowering factor) must frequently be involved and that a typology of *contact situations* (as well as a theory of sociocultural change) may be required before greater regularity among such factors can be recognized.

Although debunking represents a rather primitive level of scientific development, it may be a necessary stage on the path to greater maturity. Although we *cannot* currently formulate universally applicable regularities in our area of inquiry, we *can* indicate that several attempts along these lines fall somewhat short of their mark:

7.2.1.2   A Few Questionable Generalizations   Among the evidence pointing to the need for refining or justifying this view is that which reveals that the Guayqueries of Venezuela preserved their groupness by preserving their property relations while giving up their language and religion (Hohenthal and McCorkle 1955), that lower-caste groups in India pursue Sanskritization (emulation) rather than solidarity as a means of *group* mobility, that "the Raetoromans, like the Italian Swiss, cultivate the fullest possible loyalty to their language without aspiring to such nationalistic goals as political independence" (Weinreich 1953a, p. 100), that the "Yiddishist" movement in Eastern Europe before and after World War I similarly concentrated on a language program rather than on political organization (Weinreich 1953a, p. 100), that second and third generation Americans frequently maintain "cultural [refinement] bilingualism" after ethnic group loyalty disappears at any functional level, and vice versa, that vestiges of behavioral ethnicity often remain generations after language facility has been lost (Fishman and Nahirny 1964); that many Auslandsdeutsche maintained their self identification as Germans in the midst of Polish or Ukrainian majorities, long after completely giving up their German mother tongue (Kuhn 1930, 1934); that language loyalty is low in many newly developing and highly nationalistic African states (Brosnahan 1963b, Spencer 1963), etc. Thus it would seem, on one hand, that language maintenance has continued under various and highly different forms of group membership, some of which have involved significant changes in traditional social relationships and in pre-established role-relations. On the other hand, it appears that group loyalty can be similarly (if not more) ubiquitous, continuing both with and without language maintenance. The American readiness to use language as an index of acculturation may, in itself, be quite culture bound (Samora and Dean 1956). Hymes's observation that "some languages do not enjoy the status of a symbol crucial to group identity" (Hymes 1962, p. 30) and Weinreich's observation that "the connection [between language maintenance and group maintenance] is thus at least flexible and cannot be taken entirely for granted" (Weinreich 1953a, p. 100) really represent important intellectual challenges for the study of language maintenance and language shift. We very much need a more refined understanding of the circumstances under which behaviors toward language and behaviors toward the group are related to each other in particular ways. We can recognize today that the pre-World War II views of many German students of language maintenance and language shift (as to whether language and language consciousness create—or are derived from—race, peoplehood, and consciousness of kind) were too simplified and too colored by then current political considerations. However, the fact remains that the relationship between language saliency and group saliency is almost as speculative today as it was at that time, although it seems clear that a language undergoing massive displacement may be retained most fully by increasingly atypical and self-consciously mobilized populations as displacement progresses. Nevertheless, it is also clear that ideologies normally mobilize only a relatively younger, more active, and perhaps more alienated or dislocated segment of any large population. Language maintenance may depend *most* on nationalist ideologies in populations whose lives have otherwise been *greatly dislocated*, and it may also depend *least* on such ideologies in those populations that have best preserved their total social context against the winds of change (Fishman, 1969d).

The nationalism of several African and Asian countries seems to be much more characterized by *nationism* than by the nationalistic elaboration of ethnicity per se. It is much more concerned with the instrumental political and economic conditions of *nationhood* than with the sociocultural content of *peoplehood*. The political and administrative limits of new nations are now usually defined in advance of their formation rather than in the process of their formation. The new nations are less frequently formed as the result of the "painful but glorious" unification of hitherto particularistics who have groped to define the language, the history, the customs, and the missions that unite them and set them apart from others. They are formed along supraethnic lines that normally follow colonial demarcations which depended on the fortunes of conquest and the skills of treaty making. Political and economic self-determination are much more prominent considerations in the new nations that is cultural self-determination of the European pre- and post-World War I variety. Political leadership is much more evident than cultural leadership. The Western experience has typically been that industrialization preceded urbanization and (particularly in Eastern Europe) that nationalism preceded nationism and that the first set of phenomena preceded the second. In the new nations, the reverse sequences seem to be more common, and these may be among the major sociocultural determinants de-emphasizing language issues in connection with local or regional languages on one hand, and which favor continued use of supraregional and colonial languages on the other. Indeed, it may be that language concerns are most noticeable today where we find sociocultural distinctions remaining (even after the attainment of considerably more politico-operational integration than has currently been attained in most new nations), particularly when hitherto backward, exploited, or disadvantaged groups begin to experience great and rapid economic and cultural development in their own areas of primary population concentration (as, e.g., the French Canadians, Flemings, Jura-regionists, etc.). The displacement of Western languages of wider communication in Africa and Asia is coming—particularly in connection with mass education and governmental operations and services—and it is coming on sociocultural integrative grounds, but it is still just coming, rather than having arrived together with independence.

7.2.1.2   Urban Dwellers Are More Inclined to Shift; Rural Dwellers (More Conversative and More Isolated) Are Less Inclined to Shift. This is one of the most reasonable and best documented generalizations in the study of language maintenance and language shift. Nevertheless, it runs counter to the first-mentioned generalization above, in that *consciousness* of ethnicity and the *espousal* of nationalism have been primarily urban phenomena. Language revival movements, language loyalty movements, and organized language maintenance efforts have commonly originated and had their greatest impact in the cities. Intelligentsia and middle-class elements, both of which are almost exclusively urban, have frequently been the prime movers of language maintenance in those societies which possess both rural and urban populations. Indeed, urban groups have been "prime movers," organizers or mobilizers more generally, that is in connection with other than language matters as well as in connection with language behavior and behavior toward language. Thus, whereas small rural groups may have been more successful in establishing relatively self-contained traditional interaction patterns and social structures, urban groups, exposed to interaction in more fragmented and specialized networks, may reveal more conscious, organized, and novel attempts to preserve or revive or change their traditional language. The urban environment does facilitate change. However, the *direction of such change* has not always favored language shift at the expense of language maintenance. *When* it has favored one and *when* the other (and when urban-inspired language shift has actually signified a return to a languishing ancestral language) represents a further challenge to this field of study.

Discussions of rurality-urbanness in relation to language maintenance have often unwittingly combined two related but importantly separate factors: separation and concentration. Thus, rurality is often not so much significant for language maintenance because of a higher relative concentration of own-mother-tongue population as because rural populations can isolate themselves consciously—or are more isolated even without particularly wanting to be—from differently speaking populations. Data from several countries illustrate this aspect of rurality. In the United States in 1940 the "second generation foreign white stock" (that is native-born individuals of foreign-born parents) was regularly more retentive of its ethnic mother tongues—regardless of whether this stock was derived from less retentive old-immigrant (Scandinavian and German) or from more retentive new-immigrant (Southern and Eastern European) groups—if living in rural than if living in urban areas (Table 12, Haugen 1953). Seemingly, at that time, it was more possible to hand on more traditional ways of life, including the traditional mother tongue, in rural areas, particularly in those that were populated largely by others of the same language background. Such separation no longer made much difference in the United States in 1960 (Fishman 1966c).

Similarly, nonrurality in India (as well as a more advanced level of education which accompanies nonrurality) is positively related to claiming English as a subsidiary language in contemporary India (Table 13), but it is negatively related to the claiming of Hindi as a subsidiary language (Table 14). Seemingly, the acquisition of English depends on institutions, higher schools, government bureaus, organizations, and media (newspapers, motion pictures) not readily available in the rural areas. However, the acquisition of Hindi (in non-Hindi mother-tongue areas) depends more on lower schools, on radio broadcasts, and on federal governmental agricultural demonstration and assistance programs and these *are* available in rural areas. Thus, rurality in India means well-nigh full separation from English-acquisition opportunities, and therefore a relative intensification of Hindi-acquisition opportunities. Language shift is occurring in both settings, but in different directions as a result of the differential separations that rurality represents for English and for Hindi (Das Gupta and Fishman, in press). Of course, separation need not depend on rurality and can occur—although less readily—in urban areas as well. Lieberson (in press) has shown that "separating occupations" can serve

TABLE 12. Mother Tongue of Second Generation Foreign White Stock for Urban and Rural Population in U. S. and Selected States (1940) (Haugen 1953)

		Norway	Sweden	Denmark	Neth.	Germany	Austria	Poland	Finland	Italy
U.S. Urban	Stock...	312,980	538,500	164,480	143,100	2,570,740	596,360	1,608,600	85,000	2,612,740
	Language	127,160	222,860	44,600	48,020	1,397,260		1,176,580	54,480	1,832,000
	Retention	40.7	41.4	27.1	33.6	42.6*		73.3	64.0	70.2
U.S. Rural Non-farm	Stock...	134,660	148,360	64,380	48,120	651,360	125,680	186,000	35,140	283,100
	Language	72,080	63,100	19,120	18,320	412,380		151,420	24,420	193,300
	Retention	53.5	42.4	29.7	38.2	50.5		81.4	69.8	68.3
U.S. Rural	Stock...	214,960	169,460	76,780	70,100	776,740	59,300	117,780	46,940	75,360
	Language	145,000	88,080	31,740	36,900	626,060		100,820	39,560	55,380
	Retention	67.5	52.5	41.3	52.6	70.7		85.6	84.3	73.6
Wis. Urban	Stock...	30,600	14,680	12,820	8,520	214,080	17,040	60,980	2,460	18,260
	Language	14,900	6,260	5,100	3,480	145,120		53,600	1,460	13,800
	Retention	48.6	42.7	39.7	40.9	61.3		83.2	59.3	75.7
Wis. Rural Non-farm	Stock...	17,980	6,920	4,860	2,840	63,640	4,200	7,740	1,480	2,440
	Language	11,500	3,020	1,620	1,700	46,220		7,200	1,180	1,820
	Retention	64.0	43.7	33.4	59.9	64.5		93.5	79.8	74.6
Wis. Rural	Stock...	33,820	12,360	6,800	6,140	103,100	6,400	18,080	3,780	1,380
	Language	24,660	6,540	2,960	3,840	81,880		17,660	2,980	960
	Retention	72.9	52.9	43.5	62.6	70.7		97.8	79.8	69.6

TABLE 12 (Continued)

		Norway	Sweden	Denmark	Neth.	Germany	Austria	Poland	Finland	Italy
Minn. Urban	Stock...	73,720	87,880	13,380	2,920	91,340	10,880	19,180	12,540	8,760
	Language	37,320	44,000	4,380	760	58,840		13,840	9,240	5,460
	Retention	50.7	50.2	32.7	26.0	55.7		72.3	73.6	62.4
Minn. Rural Non-farm	Stock...	33,980	24,260	5,320	2,340	42,820	1,920	2,540	5,680	1,720
	Language	22,640	13,260	2,120	960	32,380		2,420	4,300	1,240
	Retention	66.8	54.6	39.2	41.0	70.7		95.3	75.8	72.2
Minn. Rural	Stock...	69,240	49,820	10,860	7,760	90,500	3,560	6,920	15,880	380
	Language	52,660	32,020	4,580	4,440	69,560		7,400	14,300	200
	Retention	76.2	64.4	42.2	57.2	72.4		?	90.2	—
N.Y. Urban	Stock...	27,700	44,380	12,160	12,380	433,180	207,960	365,220	7,500	952,440
	Language	9,620	17,260	2,000	2,440	210,780		196,580	3,500	664,760
	Retention	34.8	38.9	16.4	19.7	32.1		53.8	46.7	69.8
N.Y. Rural Non-farm	Stock...	3,280	7,980	2,660	4,000	62,320	10,280	27,420	1,240	52,140
	Language	660	2,560	500	1,200	25,180		21,440	520	33,340
	Retention	20.1	32.1	18.8	30.0	33.4		78.3	41.9	63.8
N.Y. Rural	Stock...	680	2,560	900	3,430	22,620	3,880	14,920	880	8,240
	Language	160	1,180	200	1,680	12,100		13,260	640	5,720
	Retention	—	46.2	—	49.0	42.5		88.9	—	69.6

*Figures for Switzerland have everywhere been added to the German stock.

TABLE 13. Ten Best Predictors of District Variation in English Claiming (N = 129) (Das Gupta and Fishman 1971)

CUMULATIVE PREDICTOR	r	Cum R	Cum R²	ΔR²	FΔR²
% Male Pri + Jr	-.336**	.336	.113	—	—
% Male Matric +	.176*	.497	.247	.134	22.3***
Rural Pop/Total Pop	-.054	.649	.421	.174	37.8***
% Immigrants	.038	.659	.434	.013	2.8
% Female Matric	.057	.670	.448	.014	3.1
Crude Literacy	-.067	.672	.452	.004	<1
% Female Pri + Jr	-.146	.678	.459	.007	1.6
Agricult/% Rural	-.122	.679	.461	.002	<1
Workers in retail	.039	.679	.462	.001	<1
Persons/sq. mile	.056	.680	.463	.001	<1
Workers in manuf	-.005	.681	.463	.000	0.0
Scheduled caste	.021	.681	.464	.001	<1

* Significant at .05 level
** Significant at .01 level
*** Significant at .001 level

TABLE 14. Ten Best Predictors of District Variation in Hindi Claiming (N = 75) (Das Gupta and Fishman 1971)

CUMULATIVE PREDICTOR	r	Cum R	Cum R²	ΔR²	FΔR²
% Male Pri + Jr.	.425**	.425	.181	—	—
Crude Literacy	-.167	.619	.384	.203	23.6***
% Female Matric +	-.019	.635	.403	.019	2.2
% Male Matric +	-.163	.680	.462	.059	7.7
Agricult/% Rural	.303**	.719	.518	.056	8.0**
% Immigrants	-.086	.736	.542	.024	3.6
% Female Pri + Jr.	.055	.744	.553	.011	1.6
Rural Pop/Total Pop	.030	.746	.556	.003	<1
Persons/sq. mile	-.120	.747	.558	.002	<1
Scheduled caste	.046	.748	.559	.001	<1
Workers in Manuf.	-.051	.752	.565	.006	<1
Workers in retail	-.142	.753	.566	.001	<1

* Significant at .05 level
** Significant at .01 level
*** Significant at .001 level

language maintenance quite as well as does the separation factor in rurality (Table 15).

TABLE 15. Foreign Born White Males Unable to Speak English, By Occupation, 1890 (Lieberson and Curry 1971)

Occupation	Per Cent Unable to Speak English
All	23
Agricultutal Laborers	28
Miners (coal)	55
Stock Raisers, Herders	52
Professional Service	8
Dentists	4
Lawyers	2
Bartenders	6
Launderers	30
Auctioneers	4
Clerks and Copyists	6
Salesmen	5
Artifical Flower Makers	30
Brick and Tile Makers	46
Harness and Saddle Makers	10
Iron and Steel Workers	33
Printers, Lithographers	8
Tailors	29
Tobacco and Cigar Factory Operatives	44

Note: Persons born in England, Ireland, Scotland, and Canada (English) are excluded since it is assumed that virtually all could speak English prior to migration.

The impact of population concentration, i.e., the proportion that speakers of language X are of the total coterritorial population of a particular administrative unit, is quite another matter from rurality per se. Of course, rurality *is* related to population concentration in general, but as we have used it here, concentration is a proportional matter rather than merely an absolute one. Once again, there is much evidence that population concentration is important in language maintenance, but this is true in urban rather than in rural settings. Thus, Lieberson (in press) has shown that in cities in which the proportions of non-English-speaking immigrants were higher in 1900, the proportion of second-generation Americans unable to speak English was also higher (Table 16). Sixty years later, those non-English mother

TABLE 16. Proportion Unable to Speak English in Cities, Second Generation Cross-Tablulated by Foreign Born, 1900. (Lieberson and Curry 1971)

Cities Classified by Proportion of Foreign Born Unable to Speak English	Mean Proportion Unable to Speak English Among	
	Foreign Born	Second Generation
.10+	.1957	.0065
.05 to .09	.0682	.0005
.04 or less	.0267	.0003

Data based on 20% sample of cities with 25,000 or more population. "Foreign born" refers to Foreign Born Whites; "Second Generation" refers to Native Whites of Foreign Parentage.

tongues that were numerically in the strongest position in the United States were exactly those that constituted the highest relative proportions of the total populations of the states in which their claimants were concentrated (Table 17). Seemingly, a relatively large community of speakers is necessary, in many immigrant settings at least, in order for language maintenance to be most useful as well as most likely in the increasingly urban context with which it is faced. Under circumstances of high relative concentration non-English schools, publications, broadcasting, organization activity, and, above all, non-English family patterns can more readily be maintained in interactional American urban environments. Thus, not only is an intergroup diglossia fostered in urban centers with a high relative concentration on non-English speakers, but in addition, intragroup diglossia, in terms of the separate societal allocation of functions, becomes more of a possibility. Soviet developments during the past few decades also seem to reveal similar processes with respect to the coexistence of Russian and the languages of at least the major Soviet minorities (Table 18).

7.2.1.3 The More Prestigious Language Displaces the Less Prestigious Language. Our earlier discussions of *sources of variance* and *domains of language behavior* may have pre-

TABLE 17. External Concentration (In Selected States), Internal Concentration and Urbanness (In the United States) of Foreign Born Claimants of 23 Non-English Mother Tongues (Fishman 1966c)

Composite Ranking of Language Overall Strength: 1960	Foreign Born Claimants In Selected States:* 1960	Total Population In Selected States:* 1960	"External" Concentration	Rank	% Urban	Rank	"Internal" Concentration: No. of States
1. Spanish	467,147	25,296,881	.01846	2	.848	12	2
2. German	694,824	53,900,032	.01196	3	.837	13	4
3. Italian	692,155	34,168,452	.02026	1	.932	5	3
4. French	173,775	40,183,320	.00432	6	.836	14	4
5. Polish	340,347	46,006,022	.00739	5	.905	8	4
6. Dutch/Flemish	72,823	46,389,484	.00157	15	.787	20	4
7. Hungarian	110,170	32,555,483	.00338	8	.900	9	3
8. Yiddish	295,308	16,782,304	.00760	4	.982	1	1
9. Ukranian	58,678	34,168,452	.00172	14	.910	7	3
10. Russian	157,917	43,818,874	.00360	7	.927	6	3
11. Greek	89,429	47,729,244	.00185	13	.944	2	4
12. Norwegian	76,492	38,766,586	.00197	11	.765	21	4
13. Swedish	109,102	45,994,530	.00237	10	.806	17	4
14. Slovak	85,925	43,874,849	.00196	12	.831	16	3
15. Slovenian	16,692	31,106,921	.00054	21	.825	18	4
16. Serbo-Croatian	47,577	46,824,125	.00102	17	.880	11	4
17. Lithuanian	60,203	43,331,406	.00139	16	.899	10	2
18. Portuguese	56,257	20,865,782	.00270	9	.834	15	4
19. Czech	45,376	52,287,063	.00087	18	.803	19	5
20. Arabic	26,630	55,177,677	.00048	22	.937	4	4
21. Danish	37,415	45,338,203	.00083	19	.764	22	3
22. Rumanian	12,946	33,246,795	.00039	23	.739	3	5
23. Finnish	32,242	48,838,144	.00066	20	.669	23	
U.S.A.					.699		

*"Selected States" = least number of states required in order to include 50% of claimants.

TABLE 18. Proportions of Russians in Populations of Union Republics in 1926 and 1959, and Percentage of Migrant and Non-Migrant Populations Using Russian as Native Language   (Lewis 1971)

Republic	% of Russians in Population			% Using Russian 1959	
	1926	1959			
		Total	Urban	Non-Migrant	Migrant
Russia	78	83.0	87.2	—	—
Ukraine	9	16.9	29.9	12.0	23.0
Belorussia	8	8.2	19.4	15.0	28.0
Uzbekistan	6	13.5	33.4	0.3	12.6
Kazakhistan	20	42.7	57.6	1.2	4.3
Azerbaidjhan	10	13.6	24.9	1.2	9.3
Armenia	2	3.2	4.5	8.0	15.0
Georgia	4	10.1	18.8	0.4	8.0
Lithuania	—				
Lithuania	—	8.5	17.0	0.1	3.5
Moldavia	9	10.2	30.8	3.0	15.0
Latvia	—	26.6	34.5	1.4	25.0
Tadzhikstan	5	13.3	35.3	0.5	18.0
Turkmenia	8	17.5	35.4	0.6	6.7
Estonia	—	20.1	30.8	0.5	25.0
Kirgisia	12	30.1	51.8	0.3	16.0

Sources - a)   Figures for 1926 and 1959 are drawn from the respective Census returns.
        b)   Volova, N.G. Voprosy Dvuyazychaya na Severnom Kaụkasa, Sovetskaya Etnografiya, 1967, No. 1, 27-40.

pared us for the realization that language prestige is not a unit trait or tag that can be associated with a given language under all circumstances. Indeed, our earlier discussion was necessary precisely *because* the prestige of languages can vary noticeably from one context to another for the same interlocutors, as well as from one speech network to another within the same speech community. It is for this very reason that Weinreich recommends that "as a technical term ... 'prestige' had better be restricted to a language's value in social advance," (Weinreich 1953a, p. 79). However, even this limitation does not make the concept "prestige" any more useful for research purposes, since social advance itself is relative to various reference groups. Advance in family and neighborhood standing may require a different language than advance in occupational or governmental standing. The fact that an over-all hierarchy of reference groups may exist does not mean that the topmost reference group will be dominant in each face-to-face situation.

It may be precisely because "prestige" obscures so many different considerations and has been used with so many different connotations that the relationship between prestige data and language maintenance or language shift data has been more uneven than might otherwise be expected. Thus, whereas Hall claims that "it is hard to think of any modern instance in which an entire speech community is under pressure to learn a substandard variety of a second language" (Hall 1952, p. 19), it is really not very hard to do so: A Low German dialect displaced Lithuanian in East Prussia before World War I, although many Lithuanians there were highly conversant with Standard German (Gerullis 1932). Unstandardized Schwyzertutsch is replacing Romansh, although several generations of Raetoromans have known Standard German as well (Weinreich 1951, pp. 284-286). Standard German completely displaced Danish in a trilingual area of Schleswig, but it was itself then increasingly displaced by the local Low German dialect (Selk 1937). Obviously, Schwyzertutsch maintains itself quite successfully in competition with Standard German, Landsmaal achieved considerable success (into the 1930's, at the very least) in competition with Dano-Norwegian; Yiddish won speakers and adherents among Russified, Polonized, and Germanized Jewish elites in Eastern Europe before and after World War I; Castillian-speaking workers settling in more industrialized Catalonia tend to shift to Catalan, etc. Indeed, the entire process whereby a few classical languages were displaced by "lowly" vernaculars and whereby some of the latter, in turn, were later displaced by still other and even less prestigious vernaculars (Deutsch 1942; the latter varieties are still referred to as "dialects" in many popular (as well as in all too many sociolinguistically insensitive though scholarly) publications, e.g., Yiddish, Ukrainian, Byelo-Russian, Flemish, Afrikaans, Macedonian, to mention only European derivatives) indicates that the prestige notion is easily discredited unless serious qualifications and contextual redefinitions are attempted. This too may be an appropriate task for the study of language maintenance and language shift.

Quite clearly it is not some mystically invariant prestige of a language or variety that need concern us, but rather the highly variant fates and fortunes of its speakers. The triumphs of English, Spanish, and Portuguese in the New World are a triumph of physical might, of economic control, and of ideological power. None of these language factors per se, but languages that happen to be associated with such powerful forces and developments can open up advantages to their speakers far beyond those available to nonspeakers of these languages. Under circumstances in which desired sociocultural change follows from verbal repertoire change, schools and media and organizations and programs have no difficulty facilitating shift (as e.g., in Israel, see Figure 19). Without such circumstances—and they are usually differentially available to various population segments—neither better pedagogic approaches nor more intense exhortation can have major impact on language shift.

7.2.2 *Toward More General Theory and a More Inclusive Comparative Approach*

When bilingual speech networks are in touch with each other on one hand, as well as with monolingual speech networks on the other, they are *differentially* involved in the crucial sociocultural processes that influence or regulate their interaction. These processes serve to increase or decrease interaction between populations or subpopulations in question, to either detach them from or to confirm them in their accustomed sources of authority, to either lead them to influence others or to be particularly receptive to influence from others, to either emphasize or minimize their own groupness and its various manifestations, to either rise or fall in relative power or control over their own and each other's welfare, to either view with positiveness or negativeness the drift of the interaction between them and to react toward this drift on the basis of such views. We must look to these engulfing sociocultural processes, and particularly to indices of individual and group involvement in them, in our efforts to explain the direction or rate of language maintenance and language shift.

However, after having appropriately selected and specified one or more variables from among the endless subleties that make up the "process" of sociocultural change, it may still be found that their cross-cultural and diachronic study reveals inconsistent results. The "same" process (e.g., "urbanization," as measured by constant indices such as those selected and cross-culturally applied by Reissman (1964) may result in language shift away from hitherto traditional languages in some cases, in language shift *back* to traditional languages in other cases, while revealing significantly unaltered maintenance of the status quo in still others. Under such circumstances a typology of contact situations might serve to control or regularize a number of group or contextual characteristics, in the manner of moderator variables, and by so doing, reveal greater order in the data.

We all have an intuitive impression that the "American immigrant case" is different from the "Brazilian immigrant case" (Willems 1943); that the "Spanish conquest case" (Bright 1960; Dozier 1951) is different from the "Anglo-American conquest case" (Cook 1943; Gulick 1958); that the "immigrant case," in general, is different from the "conquest case" in general; that the "Yiddish speaking immigrant to America case" (Fishman 1965f) is different from "German speaking immigrant to America case" (Kloss 1966b), etc. The question remains how best to systematize these intuitive impressions, i.e., what variables or attributes to utilize in order that contact situations might be classified in accord with the differences between them that we sense to exist. In the terms of R. A. Schermerhorn's recently formulated typology (1964) the "American immigrant case" immediately prior to World War I would be characterized as revealing (i) sharply unequal power configurations between non-English-speaking immigrants and English-speaking "old-Americans"; (ii) incorporation (rather than extrusion or colonization) as the *type of control* exercised by American core society over the immigrants; (iii) marked plurality and recent immigration (rather than duality, intermediate plurality without recent immigration, or any other of a continuum of patterns) as the *plurality pattern;* (iv) intermediate stratification and substantial mobility within the *stratification pattern;* (v) widespread mutual legitimization of acculturation and de-ethnization as the *interpretation of contact* in philosophical or group-image terms; and (vi) growing industrialization, mass culture, and social participation as *major social forces.*

Given the above typological framework, it has proved possible to summarize the current status of language maintenance and language shift among pre-World War I immigrants in terms of a very few *precontact factors, host factors,* and *product factors.* Unfortunately, Schermerhorn's typology for intergroup contacts is so recent that it has not yet been widely *tested* on either practical or theoretical grounds, whether in conjunction with language maintenance-language shift or in conjunction with other topics in the area of intergroup relations. While it may be expected that any typology based upon six parameters, each with several subdivisions, is likely to be somewhat unwieldy and require simplification, it is clear that Schermerhorn's system has at least heuristic value for the sociology of language from Verdoodt's efforts to put it to use in such fashion (in press).

At the opposite extreme of complexity from Schermerhorn's typology is one which is derivable from an intensive review of the extensive literature on Auslandsdeutschtum (Kuhn 1934). One of the major differentiations among the German settlers seems to have been the *original legitimization and concentration of their settlements.* A three-way break is recognizable here: *Stammsiedlungen* (settlements founded as a result of official invitation and assistance from non-German governments), *Tochtersiedlungen* (settlements founded by those who left the earlier Stammsiedlungen and who settled elsewhere as *groups,* but without governmental invitation or assistance), and *Einsiedlungen* (the inmigration of German individuals or of small occupationally homogeneous groups into non-German communities). Another related distinction is that between the relative "cultural development" of the settlers and their hosts. During the decade before the Second World War the two most frequently recognized co-occurrences were (a) *Einsiedlungen* of "culturally more mature" Germans living in the midst of a "culturally less developed" population, as opposed to (b) *Stamm- and Tochtersiedlungen* of "culturally younger" Germans surrounded by a "more mature, nation-oriented" population. Thus, although only two diagonal cells of a theoretically complete two-by-two typology are extensively discussed, it is possible to find examples of the remaining cells as well. Even when limited to the two co-occurrences mentioned above, very interesting and consistent differences appear both in rate and in stages of language shift and acculturation. The implications of this rough typology and of the regularities that it has suggested deserve consideration in connection with quite different intergroup contact settings.

Although the study of language maintenance or language shift *need* not be completely limited to the comparison of separate cases, it is nevertheless undeniably true that the comparative method is quite central to inquiry within this topic area. Certainly the comparative method is indispensable in our pursuit of cross-cultural and diachronic regularities. Assuming that a relatively uniform set of appropriate sociocultural process measures could be selected and applied, and assuming that a recognizably superior typology of contact situations were available it would then become possible to study:

(i) The same language group in two separate interaction contexts that are judged to be highly similar (with respect to primary sociocultural processes and contact type), e.g., two separate German *Stammsiedlungen* in rural Poland.

(ii) The same language group in two separate interaction contexts judged to be quite dissimilar (with respect to major sociocultural processes and contact type, e.g., one German-Swiss community in contact with Swiss Raetoromans and another German-Swiss community in Cincinnati, Ohio.

(iii) Different language groups in two separate interaction contexts judged to be highly similar (with respect to major sociocultural processes and contact type), e.g., a Polish-speaking and a Slovak-speaking community, both of rural origin, in Cincinnati, Ohio.

(iv) Different language groups in two separate interaction contexts judged to be quite dissimilar (with respect to major sociocultural processes and contact type), e.g., a German *Stammsiedlung* in rural Poland and a Slovak community in Cincinnati, Ohio.

Thus, by judiciously contrasting groups, socioculturaly processes, and types of contact situations (*not* necessarily taken two at a time, if higher level interaction designs prove to be feasible) it should become possible to more meaningfully apportion the variance in language-maintenance or language-shift outcomes. Furthermore, the greater our insight with respect to sociocultural processes and the more appropriate our typology of intergroup contact situations, the more possible it becomes to meaningfully assemble and analyze language maintenance and language shift files. Such files would permit both cross-cultural and diachronic analysis, of primary as well as of secondary data, based upon comparable data, collected and organized in accord with uniform sets of sociocultrual processes and contact categories. This state of affairs is still far off, but it is the goal toward which we might attempt to move within this second topical subdivision of the study of language maintenance and language shift, once more basic methodological and conceptual questions reach a somewhat more advanced level of clarification.

7.3 BEHAVIOR TOWARD LANGUAGE

The third (and final) major topical subdivision of the study of language maintenance and language shift is concerned with behavior toward language (rather than with language behavior or behavior through language), particularly with more focused and conscious behaviors on behalf of either maintenance or shift per se. Strictly speaking, this subdivision may properly be considered a subtopic under 7.2, above. However, it is of such central significance to this entire field of inquiry that it may appropriately receive separate recognition. Three major categories of behaviors toward language are discernible within this topical subdivision.

7.3.1   Attitudinal-Affective Behaviors

We know all too little about language-oriented attitudes and emotions (running the gamut from language loyalty—of which language nationalism is only one expression—to language antipathy—of which conscious language abandon-

FIGURE 19. (Population and Housing Census, 1961; Government of Israel, Jerusalem)

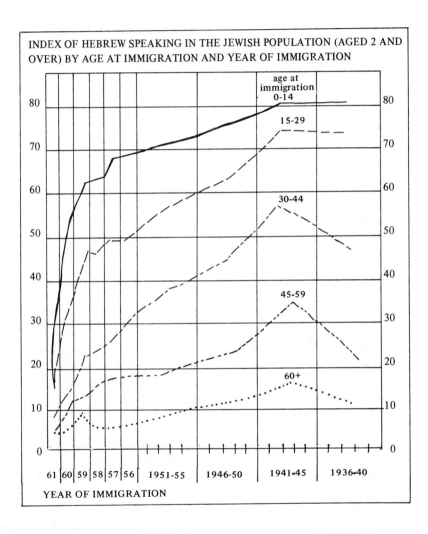

INDEX OF HEBREW SPEAKING IN THE JEWISH POPULATION (AGED 2 AND OVER) BY AGE AT IMMIGRATION AND YEAR OF IMMIGRATION

ment is only one expression) as distinguised from attitudes and emotions toward the "typical" speakers of particular language variants. The features of language that are considered attractive or unattractive, proper or improper, distinctive or commonplace, have largely remained unstudied. However, in multilingual settings, particularly in those in which a variety of "social types" are associated with each language that is in fairly widespread use, languages per se (rather than merely the customs, values, and cultural contributions of their model speakers) are reacted to as "beautiful" or "ugly," "musical" or "harsh," "rich" or "poor," etc. Generally speaking, these are language stereotypes (Fishman 1956). However, the absence or presence of a "kernel of truth" (or of verifiability itself) is entirely unrelated to the mobilizing power of such views.

The manifold possible relationships between language attitudes and language use also remain largely unstudied at the present time. Although Lambert reports a positive relationship between success in school-based second language learning and favorable attitudes toward the second language and its speakers (Lambert et al. 1963), this finding need not be paralleled in all natural multilingual contact settings. Thus, Ruth Johnston reports a very low correlation between subjective and objective (external) assimilation in the language area (1963b). Many older Polish immigrants in Australia identified strongly with English, although they hardly spoke or understood it several years after their resettlement. On the other hand, many young immigrants spoke English faultlessly and yet identified strongly with Polish, although they spoke it very poorly (1963a). Similarly, in summarizing his findings concerning current language maintenance among pre-World War I arrivals in the United States coming from rural Eastern and Southern European backgrounds, Fishman reported a long-term distinction between attitudes and use, namely, an increased esteem for non-English mother tongues concomitant with the increased relegation of these languages to fewer and narrower domains of language use (Fishman 1965f). In the latter case, the particular non-English mother tongues in question were now found to be viewed positively and nostalgically by older first- and second-generation individuals who had formerly character- ized these tongues as ugly, corrupted, and grammarless in pre-World War II days. Younger second- and third-generation individuals were found to view these mother tongues (almost always via translations) with less emotion but with even more positive valence. Instead of a "third generation return" (Hansen 1940) there seemed to be an "attitudinal halo-ization" within large segments of all generations, albeit unaccompanied by increased usage. This development (a negative relationship over time between *use rates* and *attitudinal positiveness*) was not predictable from most earlier studies of language maintenance or language shift in immigrant or nonimmigrant settings. We are far from knowing whether its explanation in American contextual terms (i.e., in terms of the greater acceptability of marginal rather than either primordial or ideologized ethnicity) would also apply to other settings in which similar circumstances might obtain. Recent methodological clarification of the language-attitude area (Fishman and Agheyisi 1970) should now make it possible for workers to move ahead in this area along a broad front of little explored topics and approaches.

7.3.2 Overt Behavioral Implementation of Attitudes, Feelings, and Beliefs
Both language reinforcement ("language movements") and language planning may be subsumed under this heading. Language reinforcement may proceed along voluntary as well as along official routes and encompasses organizational protection, statutory protection, agitation, and creative production. As for language planning, it has not always been recognized that much (if not most) of its activity (codification, regularization, simplification, purification, elaboration, and the implementation and evaluation of all of the foregoing) occurs in the context of language maintenance or language shift (Fishman 1966c, ch. 21).

The possible relationships between language reinforcement (or language planning), on one hand, and the waxing or waning of actual language use (or of other sociocultural processes) on the other are largely unknown at this time. Data from the American immigrant case imply that a number of unexpected relationships may obtain in that novel reinforcements may be introduced as actual language use diminishes. Thus, as even some of the more "exotic" mother tongues (i.e., mother tongues not usually considered to be among the major carriers of European civilization, and therefore hitherto usually associated only with foreign ethnicity in the minds of "average Americans" Hayden 1966) have ceased to be primarily associated with immigrant disadvantages or with full-blown religio-ethnic distinctiveness among their own sometime-and-erstwhile speakers, they have been increasingly introduced as languages of study at the university, college, and public high school levels (Haugen 1953, Kloss 1966b). At the same time, massive displacement seems to have had greater inhibitory impact on language-planning efforts in the American immigrant case than it has had on language-reinforcement efforts. The latter are essentially conservative and seem to require less in the way of highly specialized leadership. The former are frequently innovative and dependent upon expert personnel working in concert with compliance producing or persuasive authority. To what extent this differential impact also holds true in other types of language shift settings is currently unknown but worthy of study.

Advocates of languages that are undergoing displacement are often much more exposed to (and identified with) the values and methods of their linguistic competitors than were their less exposed (and less threatened) predecessors. As a result, they are more likely to adopt organized protective and publicity measures from more "advantaged" coterritorial (other-tongue) models to serve language maintenance purposes (Fishman 1969a). The introduction of a few ethnically infused languages into the curricula of American high schools, colleges, and universities represents just such a recent innovation on behalf of mother-tongue maintenance— and an even more de-ethnicized one (Nahirny and Fishman 1965) one than was the innovative establishment of ethnic group newspapers, schools, cultural organizations, and camps prior to World War I. In contrast, the normal processes of controlled *language change* and the more aroused processes of conscious *language planning* may require more than "last ditch" ingenuity. However, to what extent reinforcement and planning are differently balanced given varying degrees of displacement or augmentation is currently unknown but worthy of study. In addition to its importance in its own right, the over-all study of the relationship between language attitudes and language behaviors (Fishman 1969c) will also gain greatly from attention to topics such as this.

7.3.3 Cognitive Aspects of Language Response

Constantly flitting between the above two categories and overlapping partially with one, with the other, or with both are such matters as: *consciousness* of mother tongue (or "other tongue") as an entity separate from folkways more generally; *knowledge* of synchronic variants, language history, and literature; and *perceptions of language as a component of "groupness."* We have little systematic information concerning the circumstances under which language consciousness, language knowledge, and language-related groupness perceptions do or do not enter into reference group behavior in contact situations. As a result, it is difficult to say at this time whether or when language maintenance and language shift are ideologically mediated as distinguised from their more obvious situational and instrumental determinants discussed thus far. We recognize very gross long-term contrasts in this connection, namely, that there were periods and regions when language "was in no way regarded as a political or cultural factor, still less as an object of political or cultural struggle" (Kohn 1945, p. 6); that there were other periods and regions marked by a sharp increase in such regard, so that language became a principle "in the name of which people . . . [rallied] themselves and their fellow speakers consciously and explicitly to resist changes in either the functions of their languages (as a result of language shift) or in the structure or vocabulary (as a consequence of interference)" (Weinreich 1953a, p. 99), and that there currently seems to be less of this than previously, particularly if we compare African with European nation building. However, gross differentiations such as these are patently insufficient to enable us to clarify the conditions under which language becomes a prominent component in *perceptions* of "own-groupness" and "other-groupness." This topic (language-related groupness perception) is, of course, closely related to one previously mentioned, namely, the role of language in group membership and in group functioning (see subsection 7.2.1.2, above). In the American immigrant case we have seen a growing dissociation between self-perceived ethnic identification and language maintenance. Far from being viewed as necessary components of groupness (whether

TABLE 19a. The Non-English and the Ethnic Group Press, 1910-1960 (Fishman 1966c) Proportions of Types of Publication, 1930 and 1960

Number

Ethnic Groups	1930 Mother Tongue n	%	1930 Mixed n	%	1930 English n	%	1930 Total n	1960 Mother Tongue n	%	1960 Mixed n	%	1960 English n	%	1960 Total n
French	28	80	6	17	1	3	35	13	76	3	18	1	6	17
Spanish	61	81	9	12	5	7	75	31	65	13	27	4	8	48
German	146	59	22	9	78	32	246	41	37	9	8	60	55	110
Jewish	20	21	13	14	62	65	95	15	14	4	4	85	82	104
Hungarian	35	90	4	10	0	0	39	32	94	1	3	1	3	34
Ukranian	6	86	1	14	0	0	7	14	74	3	16	2	10	19
Italian	85	68	38	30	2	2	125	21	16	20	43	5	11	46
Polish	84	95	2	2	2	2	88	37	86	2	5	4	9	43
Greek 15	15	71	4	19	2	10	21	9	47	5	26	5	26	19
Czech	44	98	1	2	0	0	45	19	83	4	17	0	0	23
Other Slavic	53	79	14	21	0	0	67	46	68	19	28	3	4	68
Scandinavian	62	63	17	17	19	19	98	20	43	5	11	21	46	46
Other Germanic	13	56	5	22	5	22	23	1	8	2	15	10	77	13
Other Romance	15	94	1	6	0	0	16	7	88	1	12	0	0	8
Near Eastern	8	89	0	0	1	11	9	10	63	1	6	5	31	16
Far Eastern	18	67	6	22	3	11	27	12	57	8	38	1	5	21
All Others	44	86	6	12	1	2	51	49	78	7	11	7	11	63
Total	737	69	149	14	181	17	1067	377	54	107	15	214	31	698

TABLE 19b. Proportions of Types of Publications, 1930 and 1960

Circulation

Ethnic Groups	1930 Mother Tongue		1930 Mixed		1930 English		1930 Total	1960 Mother Tongue		1960 Mixed		1960 English		1960 Total
	n	%	n	%	n	%	n	n	%	n	%	n	%	n
French	151*	94	10	6	—	—	161	118*	96	5	4	—	—	123
Spanish	298	98	3	1	3	1	304	268	81	54	16	7	2	329
German	1354	67	65	3	598	30	2017	281	10	146	5	2274	84	2701
Jewish	775	72	34	3	264	25	1073	179	9	63	3	1826	88	2068
Hungarian	238	96	9	4	0	0	247	198	95	4	2	6	3	208
Ukranian	51	100	—	—	0	0	51	47	62	27	36	2	2	76
Italian	613	83	114	15	16	2	743	270	56	164	34	47	10	481
Polish	999	96	23	2	15	1	1037	690	96	9	1	18	2	717
Greek	74	77	12	12	10	10	96	65	62	15	14	24	23	104
Czech	513	100	—	—	0	—	513	274	94	17	6	0	0	291
Other Slavic	730	74	167	17	93	9	990	216	45	243	51	17	4	476
Scandinavian	580	85	82	12	21	3	683	120	26	40	9	303	65	463
Other Germanic	22	58	16	42	—	—	38	4	2	15	6	216	92	235
Other Romance	130	100	—	—	0	0	130	25	86	4	4	0	0	29
Near Eastern	38	100	0	0	—	—	38	37	69	6	11	11	20	54
Far Eastern	346	87	52	13	—	—	398	67	57	45	38	6	5	118
All Others	296	98	7	2	—	—	303	253	85	26	9	20	7	299
Total	7216	82	591	7	1023	12	8830	3118	35	889	10	4784	54	8791

* Last three digits have been dropped in all circulation figures.

in the sense of resultants or contributors) non-English mother tongues appear to be viewed increasingly in terms of nonethnic *cultural* and nonethnic *practical* considerations. At the same time, some form of ethnic self-identification is frequently still reported by many of those who no longer claim any facility at ·all in their ethnic mother tongues, implying that in several American immigrant-derived groups some kind of ethnicity usually appears to be a much more stable phenomenon than language maintenance. Indeed, some groups are able to maintain newspapers, schools, and organization long after they have lost their nonethnic mother tongues (Table 19a and Table 19b). Most immigrants became bilingual much before they embarked on de-ethnization or seriously contemplated the possibility of biculturism. However, there were obvisously exceptions to this process, both in the United States and in other contact settings. We certainly

TABLES 20a and 20b. Attitudes and Beliefs with Respect to Spanish among Ordinary Puerto Ricans (OPR) and Intellectuals, Leaders, and Artists (ILA) in the Greater New York Metropolitan Area. (Fishman, 1969e)

TABLE 20a. Is It Necessary To Know Spanish To Be Puerto Rican?

Response	OPR (n= 29)	ILA (n= 20)
No	20 (62%)	2 (10%)
Yes	12 (38%)	18 (90%)

TABLE 20b. Are There Many "Nuyorquinos" Who Do Not Speak Or Understand Spanish?

RESPONSE	OPR (n=29)	ILA (n=20)
Yes (many do not understand)	2 (7%)	1 (5%)
Most understand little and speak poorly	3 (10%)	4 (20%)
Most understand well but speak poorly	3 (10%)	14 (70%)
Most speak and understand without real difficulty	21 (73%)	1 (5%)

do not seem to be in a position to indicate the underlying regularities in this subtle area of inquiry at the present time, except to point out that the segments of the population among which language consciousness, language interest, and language-related groupness perceptions are likely to be in evidence are normally quite small and elitist in nature (Tables 20a and 20b).

We know very little about the interaction *among* the three components of behavior toward language or about the interaction *between* any of these components and the larger psychological, social, and cultural processes discussed earlier. Rather than being a "natural," omnipresent condition, either in monolingual or multilingual settings, heightened and integrated behaviors toward language may be related to somewhat rare and advanced symbolic and ideological extensions of primordial ethnicity. Such extensions may well require a particular level of sociocultural development and a particular group of custodians for their preservation and further elaboration. They almost certainly require a relatively advanced level of elitist concentration on intraelitist concerns, often in advance of elitist concerns for communication within the masses. Nevertheless, none of these desiderata need have invariable consequences for behavior toward language. Even where heightened and integrated behaviors toward language are culturally present, they will not be equally operative in all situations or among all population subgroups. Furthermore, even where they are culturally present they need not be uniformly related to other symbolically elaborated forms of behavior. Thus, this area remains the most unsystematized topical subdivision of the study of language maintenance and language shift. Perhaps it can be clarified in the future as a result of concomitant clarification and constant interrelation in connection with the two other major subdivisions within this field of inquiry.

7.3.4 *Interference and Switching*

Within the topical subdivision of behavior toward language we once again meet the topic of interference and switching, first introduced in subsection 7.1 above. The absence or presence of interference and switching can have cognitive, affective, and overt implementational implications for language maintenance and language shift. Certainly, both interference and switching are related to the domains and variance sources of bilingualism on one hand, and to sociocultural processes and type of interaction on the other hand. Moreover, within this topical subdivision it is appropriate to stress that where attitudes and awareness concerning purism obtain, interference is sometimes viewed as *an imperfection*—not in the speaker or in his productions but *in the language itself.* At the opposite pole, there are multilingual contact situations in which conscious, purposive interference obtains. In these instances speakers attempt to incorporate into their language usage as many elements or features as possible from another language including (in very advanced cases) interference in stress patterns, intonation, and *Denkformen*. In either case (i.e., when interference occurs although it is considered undesirable, or when interference occurs and is considered desirable) interference is not always considered to be all of one piece. Certain occurrences are considered to be more acceptable, excusable, permissible, necessary than others. In either case it can become a factor in hastening language shift, particularly since bilinguals tend to interpret interference in each of the languages known to them quite differently. Finally, at a point when language shift is appreciably advanced, certain sounds and forms of the language undergoing displacement may become so difficult for the average speaker (while errors in connection with them may become so stigmatized among purists) that this in itself may accelerate further shift. All in all, recognition of interference, attitudes toward interference, and the behavioral consequences of interference represent interesting and important topics within the field of language maintenance and language shift.

7.4 A GLANCE BACK AND A GLANCE AHEAD

Various language-maintenance and language-shift phenomena have long been of interest to scholars and to laymen. Several subtopics within this area have undisputed relevance to the daily concerns and joys of millions. Others, of more theoretical interest, are closely related to topics of recognized concern to linguists, anthropologists, sociologists, psychologists, political scientists, educators, etc. Culture contact and language contact will always be with us, and out of these contacts will come modifications in habitual behavior as well as attempts to restrain or channel such modifications. Whether or when language habits change more or less quickly than others, whether or when language loyalties are more or less powerful than others, indeed, whether or when men can live in a supraethnic tomorrow without strong links (linguistic or nonlinguistic) to their ethnic yesterday and today—these are questions to which there are currently no definitive answers. However, interest in sociopsychological aspects of language behavior is currently growing, whether under that name or under the name of sociolinguistics, anthropological linguistics, ethnolinguistics, the ethnography of speaking, the ethnography of communication, the sociology of language, or some other designation. In most instances, there is some recognition of *behavior toward language* as a crucial topic within the field of social behavior through language. This growing interest will undoubtedly contribute answers to many of the currently unanswerable questions within the field of language maintenance and language shift.

Three major subdivisions of the study of language maintenance and language shift have been suggested. The first deals with the precise establishment of habitual language use in a contact situation. This requires instruments just beginning to become available for the measurement of *degree of bilingualism* and of *location of bilingualism* along sociologically relevant dimensions. Degree of bilingualism, hitherto recognizable in terms of automaticity, proficiency, and code intactness at the phonetic, lexical, and grammatical levels, must also be investigated with respect to media variance and overtness variance. *Location of bilingualism* requires investigation with respect to functional diversification in appropriately designated domains of language, each domain being abstracted from patterned role relations, topics, locales, and/or other lower-order phenomena. The complex relationships between the several components of degree of bilingualism and location of bilingualism may be represented by a *dominance configuration*, which, in turn, may or may not be reducible to a single index of direction of bilingualism. The drift of language maintenance or language shift may be established by diachronic measures pertaining to some or all of the above factors.

The second major topical subdivision of the study of language maintenance and language shift deals with psychological, social, and cultural processes that are associated with ascertained changes in habitual language use. No conceptual systematization of these processes is currently available, although several preliminary typologies of "contact situations" exist and require further refinement in cross-cultural perspective.   The greatest encouragement in this topical subdivision comes from the accelerating inter-disciplinary work on sociocultural and politico-operational change (including work on development and modernization). To the extent that the study of language maintenance and language shift will become increasingly linked to ongoing theoretical and empirical refinements in the study of psycho-sociocultural stability and change more generally the more rapidly will mutually rewarding progress occur.

The third (and final) major subdivision of the study of language maintenance and language shift pertains to behavior toward language, including (but not limited to) more focused and conscious behaviors on behalf of maintenance or shift. Three major subtopics within this topic are recognizable: Attitudinal-affective behaviors (loyalty, antipathy, etc.), overt behavioral implementation (control or regulation of habitual language use via reinforcement, planning, prohi-bition, etc.), and (overlapping partially with each of the two foregoing subtopics) cognitive behaviors (language conscious-ness, language knowledge, language-related group percep-tions, etc.).

Two sociolinguistic patterns, that of the urban American immigrant and that of the urban French-Canadian nationalist, have been repeated many times in the past century. The increasing use of Russian alone by Soviet minorities—particularly the smaller ones—whether they be immigrants to large urban centers in other regions or outnumbered by Russians and various other immigrants into their own regions, has followed the same path as the increasing use of English alone by immigrants to the United States, the increasing use of Spanish alone by indigenous Indian populations moving to urban centers throughout Latin America, or the increasing use of Wolof alone by the diverse Senegalese populations that began to move to Dakar more than a generation ago. Similarly, the increasing use of the mother tongue in the domains of education, industry, and government (which had previously "belonged," so to speak, to English), that has increasingly typified French Canada, is not at all unlike the growing displacement of English or another Western language of wider communication in Puerto Rico, Tanzania, Kenya, India, Pakistan, Malaysia, and the Philippines. One group of cases illustrates the general inability of dislocated populations to maintain domain separation, and therefore a sufficiently distinctive functional allocation of codes in their verbal repertoires, so as to render their mother tongues necessary for membership and status even within the home, neighborhood, and other intragroup domains. The other group of cases illustrates the generally far greater ability of sedentary populations to withstand the onslaught of foreign-inspired political, educational, social, and economic domination. If domain separation is maintained, at least between the L domains of home and neighborhood and the H domains of government, education, and religion, a subsequent mobilization of the indigenous population around a new, nationalist protoelite may yet lead to the introduction (or reintroduction) of the vernacular into those domains from which it has been barred or displaced.

In the urban American immigrant case—as in all instances in which severely dislocated populations have been presented with tangible opportunities to share in new role relationships and in vastly improved power and status networks—a new language initially entered the verbal repertoire of the speech community for marginal metaphorical purposes only. Situational *and* metaphorical switching *both* were possible only with respect to several varieties of the ethnic mother tongue or its H + L matrix. However, with the passage of time *intragroup* power, status, and even membership per se, all come to be granted on the basis of mastery of the new language. As a result, the ethnic mother tongue became increasingly relegated to metaphorical purposes (humor, contrast, tenderness), and therefore to oblivion as a third generation arose that had itself directly experienced none of the situations upon which the metaphorical functions of the ethnic mother tongue rested in the usage of "old timers" and the second generation.

In the case of less dislocated populations—where the absence of widespread social mobility or of physical extirpation from established roles and networks helped preserve the distinction between intragroup and extragroup domains—the new language normally gained metaphorical recognition *only* in so far as the majority of intragroup networks and role relations were concerned. As a result, it served primarily as an intergroup H for the few well-placed individuals with intergroup roles. Little wonder then that among the rank and file of such less dislocated populations—including the Alsatians discussed by Tabouret-Keller (1968) and by Verdoodt (1971) and the Swabians discussed by Fishman and Luders (in press)—H varieties do not displace L varieties, and indeed, are themselves easily displaced by yet newer H varieties resulting from the temporary intrusions of new political authorities.

The above sketch is still more suggested than demonstrated. It depends more on theoretical parsimony than on empirical data. The exhaustive study of language maintenance and language shift ultimately requires not merely theory, but also theory tested and revised in the light of hard data. Since the basic instruments and theory required for the establishment of degree and direction of language maintenance or language shift are now beginning to be available (certainly this is true relative to the situation five years ago), it would now seem to be most crucial to devote increasing amounts of theoretical and empirical attention to comparative (cross-network, cross-speech community, cross-policy, and cross-cultural) study of the psychosociocultural antecedents and concomitants of language maintenance and language shift. The next few years will doubtlessly see the greatest progress precisely along these lines, i.e., along lines for which the social anthropologist, social psychologist, and sociologist—rather than the linguist—must take primary responsibility.

SOCIOCULTURAL ORGANIZATION:
LANGUAGE CONSTRAINTS
AND
LANGUAGE REFLECTIONS

One of the major lines of social and behavioral science interest in language during the past century has been that which has claimed that the radically differing structures of the languages of the world constrain the cognitive functioning of their speakers in different ways. It is only in relatively recent years—and partially as a result of the contributions of psycholinguists and sociolinguists—that this view (which we shall refer to as the linguistic-relativity view) has come to be replaced by others: (a) that languages primarily reflect rather than create sociocultural regularities in values and orientations, and (b) that languages throughout the world share a far larger number of structural universals than has heretofore been recognized. While we cannot here examine the work related to language universals (Greenberg 1966; Osgood 1960), since it is both highly technical and hardly socio-linguistic in nature, we *can* pause to consider the linguistic-relativity view itself as well as the linguistic-reflection view which is increasingly coming to replace it in the interests and in the convictions of social scientists. It is quite clear why so much interest has been aroused by the question of language as restraint and language as reflection of sociocultural organizations. Both of these views are undirectional. One posits that language structure and language usage are fundamental and "given" and that all behavior is influenced thereby. The other claims that social organization and behavior are prior and language merely reflects them. A position on one side or another of this argument must be taken by those who are interested in changing or influencing the "real world" of behavior.

8.1 GRAMMATICAL STRUCTURE CONSTRAINS COGNITION

The strongest claim of the adherents of linguistic relativity—whether by Whorf (1940, 1941), Hoijer (1951, 1954), Trager (1959), Kluckhohn (1961), or by others—is that cognitive organization is directly constrained by linguistic structure. Some languages recognize far more tenses than do others. Some languages recognize gender of nouns (and, therefore, also require markers of gender in the verb and adjective systems), whereas others do not. Some languages build into the verb system recognition of certainty or uncertainty of past, present, or future action. Other languages build into the verb system a recognition of the size, shape, and color of nouns referred to. There are languages that signify affirmation and negation by different sets of pronouns, just as there are languages that utilize different sets of pronouns in order to indicate tense and absence or presence of emphasis. Some languages utilize tone and vowel length in their phonological systems, whereas English and most other modern European languages utilize neither. There are languages that utilize only twelve phonemes, while others require more than fifty. A list of such striking structural differences between languages could go on and on—without in any way denying that each language is a perfectly adequate instrument (probably the *most* adequate instrument) for expressing the needs and interests of its speakers. That the societies using these very different languages differ one from the other in many ways is obvious to all. Is it not possible, therefore, that these sociocultural differences—including ways of reasoning, perceiving, learning, distinguishing, remembering, etc.—are directly relatable to the structured differences between the languages themselves? The Whorfian hypothesis claims that this is indeed the case (Fishman 1960).

Intriguing though this claim may be, it is necessary to admit that many years of intensive research have not succeeded in demonstrating it to be tenable. Although many have tried to do so, no one has successfully predicted and demonstrated a cognitive difference between two populations on the basis of the grammatical or other structural differences between their languages alone. Speakers of tone languages and of vowel-length languages and of many-voweled languages do *not* seem to hear better than do speakers of languages that lack all of these features. Speakers of languages that code for color, shape, and size in the very verb form itself do not tend to categorize or classify a random set of items much differently than do speakers of languages whose verbs merely encode tense, person, and number (Carroll and Casagrande 1958). Whorf's claims (namely, that ". . . the background linguistic system [in other words, the grammar] of each language is not merely a reproducing instrument for voicing ideas, but rather is itself the shaper of ideas, the program and guide for the individual's mental activity, for his analysis of impressions, for his synthesis of his mental stock in trade. Formulation of ideas is not an independent process, strictly rational in the old sense, but it is part of a particular grammar and differs, from slightly to greatly, between grammars" 1940) seem to be overstated and no one-to-one correspondence between grammatical structure and either cognitive or sociocultural structure measured independently of language has ever been obtained. Several of the basic principles of sociolinguistic theory may help explain why this is so, although the psychological maxim that most men think about what they are talking about (i.e., that language structure is *always being struggled with via cognitive processes*) should also be kept in mind.

In contrast with the older anthropological-linguistic approach of Whorf, Sapir, Kluckhohn, Korzybski, and others who pursued this problem during the first half of the twentieth century, sociolinguistics is less likely to think of *entire languages or entire societies* as categorizable or typable in an over-all way. The very concepts of linguistic repertoire, role repertoire, repertoire range, and repertoire compartmentalization argue against any such neat classification, once functional realities are brought into consideration. Any reasonably complex speech community contains various speech networks that vary with respect to the nature and ranges of their speech repertoires. Structural features that may be present in the speech of certain interaction networks may be lacking (or marginally represented) in the speech of others. Structural features that may be present in certain varieties within the verbal repertoire of a particular interaction network may be absent (or marginally represented) in other varieties within that very same repertoire. Mother-tongue speakers of language X may be other-tongue speakers of language Y. These two languages may coexist in a stable dislossic pattern throughout the speech community and yet be as structurally different as any two languages chosen at random.

Certainly, all that has been said above about the difficulty in setting up "whole-language" typologies is equally true when we turn to the question of "whole-society" typologies. Role repertoires vary from one interaction network to the next and roles themselves vary from one situation to the next within the same role repertoire. Distinctions that are appropriately made in one setting are inappropriate in another, and behaviors that occur within certain interaction networks do not occur in still others within the same culture. The existence of structured biculturism is as real as the existence of structured bilingualism, and both of these phenomena tend to counteract any neat and simple linguistic relativity of the kind that Whorf had in mind.

Nevertheless, there are at least two large areas in which a limited degree of linguistic relativity *may* be said to obtain: (a) the structuring of verbal interaction, and (b) the structuring of lexical components. The first area of concern points to the fact that the role of language (when to speak, to whom to speak, the importance of speaking per se relative to inactive silence or relative to other appropriate action) varies greatly from society to society (Hymes 1966). However, this type of relativity has nothing to do with the *structure* of language per se in which Whorf was so interested. The second area of concern deals with lexical taxonomies and with their consequences in cognition and behavior. However, these border on being linguistic *reflections* of sociocultural structure rather than being clearly and solely linguistic *constraints* that inevitably and interminably must bring about the particular behaviors to which they are supposedly related. It is to a consideration of these lexical taxonomies that we now turn.

8.2 LEXICAL STRUCTURE CONSTRAINS COGNITION

For many years it was believed that the only tightly structured levels of language were the grammatical (morphological and syntactic) on one hand, and the phonological on the other. These two levels certainly received the brunt of linguistic attention and constituted the levels of analysis of which linguists were most proud in their interactions with other social and behavioral scientists. By contrast, the lexical level was considered to be unstructured and exposed to infinite expansion (as words were added to any language) and infinite interference (as words were borrowed from other languages). A small but hardy group of lexicographers (dictionary makers) and etymologists (students of word origins) continued to be enamored of words per se, but the majority of linguists acted as though the lexicon were the black sheep, rather than a bona fide member in good standing, of the linguistic family. The discovery of structured parsimony in parts of the lexicon has done much to revive linguistic interest in the lexical level of analysis. The discovery as such is one in which psychologists, anthropologists, and sociologists were every bit as active as were linguists themselves, if not more so. This may also explain why the interrelationship between lexical organization *and* behavioral organization has been so prominent in conjunction with the investigation of lexical structure.

The psychological contributions to this area of analysis take us back to one level of the Whorfian hypothesis (see level 2 in Figure 20). Psychologists had long before demonstrated that the availability of verbal labels was an asset in learning, perception, and memory tasks (see e.g., Carmichael et al. 1932; Lehmann 1889; Maier 1930). A new generation of psychologists has recently set out to determine whether this could be demonstrated both interlinguistically (i.e., within a given language) on a structured set of behaviors that corresponded *to a structured portion of lexicon.*

FIGURE 20. Schematic Systematization of the Whorfian Hypothesis (Fishman 1960)

Data of Language Characteristics	Data of (Cognitive) Behavior	
	Language data ("cultural themes")	Nonlinguistic data
Lexical or "semantic" characteristics	Level 1	Level 2
Grammatical characteristics	Level 3	Level 4

Level 1 of the Whorfian ("linguistic relativity") hypothesis predicts that speakers of languages that make certain lexical distinctions are enabled thereby to talk about certain matters (for example, different kinds of snow among speakers of Eskimo and different kinds of horses among speakers of Arabic) that cannot as easily be discussed by speakers of languages that do not make these lexical distinctions. Similarly, Level 3 of the Whorfian hypothesis predicts that speakers of languages that possess particular grammatical features (absence of tense in the verb system, as in Hopi, or whether adjectives normally precede or follow the noun, as in English vs. French) predispose these speakers to certain cultural styles or emphases (timelessness; inductiveness vs. deductiveness). These two levels of the Whorfian hypothesis have often been criticized for their anecdotal nature as well as for their circularity in that they utilized verbal evidence for both their independent (causal) and dependent (consequential) variables. Level 2 of the Whorfian hypothesis predicts that the availability of certain lexical items or distinctions enables the speakers of these languages to remember, perceive, or learn certain nonlinguistic tasks more rapidly or completely than can the speakers of languages that lack these particular lexical items or distinctions. This level of the Whorfian hypothesis has been demonstrated several times—most recently and forcefully in connection with the differing color terminologies of English and Zuni—but it is difficult to argue that the absence of lexical items or distinctions in a particular language is more a *cause* of behavioral differences than a *reflection* of the differing sociocultural concerns or norms of its speakers. As soon as speakers of Zuni become interested in orange (color) they devise a term for it. Language relativity should be more stable and less manipulable than that! Level 4 of the Whorfian hypothesis is the most demanding of all. It predicts that grammatical characteristics of languages facilitate or render more difficult various nonlinguistic behaviors on the part of their speakers. This level has yet to be successfully demonstrated via experimental studies of cognitive behavior.

They chose the color spectrum to work with because it is a real continuum that tends to be environmentally present in all cultures. Nevertheless, the investigators hypothesized that language labels for the color spectrum are culturally idiosyncratic. These labels not only chop up the color continuum into purely conventional segments in every language community, but they probably do so differently in different language communities. By a series of ingenious experiments, Brown and Lenneberg (1954), Lenneberg (1953, 1957), Lantz and Stefflre (1964), and others have demonstrated that this was indeed true. They have demonstrated that those colors for which a language has readily available labels are more unhesitatingly named than are colors for which no such handy labels are available. They have shown that the colors for which a language has readily available labels (i.e., highly codable colors) are more readily recognized or remembered when they must be selected from among many colors after a delay subsequent to their initial presentation. They have demonstrated that somewhat different segments of the color spectrum are highly codable in different language communities. Finally, they have shown that the learning of nonsense-syllable associations for colors is predictably easier for highly codable colors than for less codable colors that require a phrase—often an individually formulated phrase—in order to be named.

All in all, this series of experiments has forcefully shown that the availability of a structured set of terms has both intralinguistic as well as interlinguistic consequences. However, in addition, it has underscored the equally important fact that every speech community has exactly such terms for those phenomena that are of concern to it. Certainly, artists, painters, and fashion buyers have a structured color terminology that goes far beyond that available to ordinary speakers of English. The relative absence or presence of particular color terms in the lexicon of a given speech network is thus not a reflection of the state of that network's *code per se* as much as it is a reflection of the color interests, sensitivities, and conventions of that network at a particular time in its history.

A color terminology is merely one kind of *folk taxonomy* i.e., it is an example of the many *emic* semantic grids that are contained in the lexicons of all speech communities. Other such examples are the kinship terminologies of speech communities, their disease or illness terminologies, their plant terminologies, their terms of address, etc. (Basso 1967; Conklin 1962; Frake 1961, 1962; Pospisil 1965; Friederich 1966; Metzger and Williams 1966; Price 1967; Wittermans 1967; etc.). In each of these instances the particular lexicons involved constitute "un systeme où tout se tient."

Each such system is considered by its users to be both literally exhaustive and objectively correct. Nevertheless, each system is socially particularistic, i.e., for all of its self-evident objectivity ("what other kind of kinship system could there *possibly* be?"—we can imagine the average member of each of the scores of such systems asking himself), it is a reflection of locally accepted conventions rather than a necessary reflection either of nature or of language per se. This last is particularly well demonstrated in the work of Friederich (on Russian kinship terms), Wittermans (on Javanese terms of address), and Basso (on Western Apache anatomical terms and their extension to auto parts; see Figure 21).

The Russian revolution brought with it such fargoing social change that the kinship terms in use in Czarist days had to be changed to some degree. In contrast with the refined stratificational distinctions that existed in Czarist days— distinctions that recognized gradations of power, wealth, and proximity within the universe of kin, not unlike those that were recognized in the larger universe of social and economic

FIGURE 21. Lexical Structure and Social Change*

ndɛ bɩ tsi ("man's body")																	
										ni ("face")		ɛbiyɩ' ("entrails")					
likɔ ("fat")	dɔ ("chin and jaw")	wos ("shoulder")	gən ("hand and arm")	kai ("thigh and buttock")	zɛ' ("mouth")	kɛ' ("foot")	ɣen ("back")	inda ("eye")	čį ("nose")	ta ("forehead")	tsǫs ("vein")	zɩk ("liver")	pɩt ("stomach")	či ("intestine")	jĩ ("heart")	jisolɛ ("lung")

FIGURE A.   Taxonomic Structure of Anatomical Set

Note: Black bars indicate position of additional (unextended) anatomical terms.

Western Apache

nalbil bɩ tsi ("automobile's body")																
									ni*		ɛbiyɩ' ("machinery under hood")					
likɔ ("grease")	dɔ ("front bumper")	wos ("front fender")	gən ("front wheel")	kai ("rear fender")	zɛ' ("gas pipe opening")	kɛ' ("rear wheel")	ɣen ("bed of truck")	inda ("headlight")	čį ("hood")	ta ("front of cab," "top")	tsǫs ("electrical wiring")	zɩk ("battery")	pɩt ("gas tank")	či ("radiator hose")	jĩ ("distributor")	jisolɛ ("radiator")

FIGURE B. Taxonomic Structure of Extended Set

*"Area extending from top of windshield to bumper"

*Keith H. Basso, Semantic Aspects of Linguistic Acculturation, *American Anthropologist*, LXIX (1967), 471-477.

relationships—Soviet society stressed far fewer and broader distinctions. As a result, various kinship terms were abandoned entirely, others were merged, and other were expanded. A very similar development transpired in Javanese with respect to its highly stratified system of terms of address. The impact of postwar independence, industrialization, urbanization, and the resulting modification or abandonment of traditional role relationships led to the discontinuation of certain terms of address and the broadening of others, particularly of those that implied relatively egalitarian status between interlocutors. Howell's review of changes in the pronouns of address in Japan (1967) also makes the same point, as did his earlier study of status markers in Korean (1965). Not only does he indicate how individuals change the pronouns that they use in referring to themselves and to each other, as their attitudes and roles vis-à-vis each other change, but he implies that widespread and cumulative changes of this kind have occurred in Japan since the war, to the end that certain pronouns have been practically replaced by others. Certainly the best known study of this kind is Brown and Gilman's review of widespread Western European social change with respect to the use of informal (T) vs. formal (V) pronouns and verb forms for the third person singular (1960). Feudalism, Renaissance, Reformation, the French Revolution, nineteenth century liberalism, and twentieth century democratization each had recognizable and cumulative impact. As a result, both T and V forms were retained in interclass communication (except in the case of English), but their differential use came to indicate differences primarily in *solidarity* or differences in *solidarity and in power* rather than differences in *power alone* as had been the case in the early Middle Ages (see Figure 22).

Note that the complexities of the prerevolutionary kinship taxonomies in Russia did not keep Russians from thinking about or from engaging in revolution. Note also that the revolution did not entirely scrap the pre-existing kinship taxonomy. Similarly, the Apache anatomical taxonomy did not preclude (but rather assisted) taxonomic organization of automobile parts. Thus, while we are clearly indicating the untenability of any strong linguistic *relativity* position when we show that semantic taxonomies are subject to change,

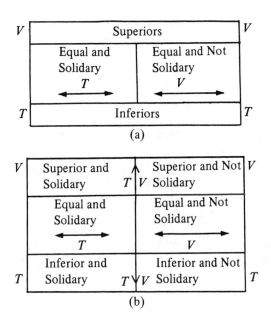

FIGURE 22. The two-dimensional semantic (a) in equilibrium and (b) under tension. (Brown and Gilman, 1960)

Solidarity comes into the European pronouns as a means of differentiating address among power equals. It introduces a second dimension into the semantic system on the level of power equivalents. So long as solidarity was confined to this level, the two-dimensional system was in equilibrium (see Figure 1a), and it seems to have remained here for a considerable time in all our languages. It is from the long reign of the two-dimensional semantic that *T* derives its common definition as the pronoun of either condescension or intimacy and *V* its definition as the pronoun of reverence or formality. These definitions are still current but usage has, in fact, gone somewhat beyond them.

The dimension of solidarity is potentially applicable to all persons addressed. Power superiors may be solidary (parents, elder siblings) or not solidary (officials whom one seldom sees). Power inferiors, similarly, may be as solidary as the old family retainer and as remote as the waiter in a strange restaurant. Extension of the solidarity dimension along the dotted lines of Figure 1b creates six categories of persons defined by their relations to a speaker. Rules of address are in conflict for persons in the upper left and lower right categories. For the upper left, power indicates *V* and solidarity *T*. For the lower right, power indicates *T* and solidarity *V*.

Well into the nineteenth century the power semantic prevailed and waiters, common soldiers, and employees were called *T* while parents, masters, and elder brothers were called *V*. However, all our evidence consistently indicates that in the past century the solidarity semantic has gained supremacy. The abstract result is a simple one-dimensional system with the reciprocal *T* for the solidary and the reciprocal *V* for the nonsolidary.

expansion, and contraction as the sociocultural realities of their users change, we are also demonstrating that their linguistic *reflection* of social reality is also likely to be both slow and partial. Nevertheless, as between the two, the taxonomic *reflection* of sociocultural reality is more likely to have widespread heuristic utility at any given time, however much the existence of such taxonomies is likely to be *constraining* in the momentary cognitive behavior of individual members of sociocultural systems.

The *emic* distinctions which underlie these taxonomies are differentially constraining for various interaction networks within any speech community. Some networks (e.g., the networks of quantitative scientists) can repeatedly rise above the cognitive constraints of the taxonomies current in their speech communities. These networks are likely to be the ones that are most actively engaged in social change and in taxonomic change as well. Other networks are unable to break out of the sociocultural taxonomies that surround them. In such cases, as, e.g., in connection with Kantrowitz' race relations taxonomy among white and Negro prison inmates (1967; see Figure 23), or Price's botanical taxonomies among the Huichols (1967), these taxonomies may be taken not only as useful *reflections* of the cognitive world of the speech community from which they are derived, but also as forceful *constraints* on the cognitive behavior of most, if not all, of the individual members of these networks.

8.3 LEXICAL STRUCTURE REFLECTS SOCIAL ORGANIZATION

There are, however, more pervasive (and, therefore, seemingly less systematic) ways in which lexicons in particular and languages as a whole are reflective of the speech communities that employ them. In a very real sense a language variety is an inventory of the concerns and interests of those who employ it at any given time. If any portion of this inventory reveals features not present in other portions this may be indicative of particular stresses or influences in certain interaction networks within the speech community as a whole or in certain role relationships within the community's total role repertoire. Thus, Epstein's study of

FIGURE 23. Selected Examples of Vocabulary Used by White and Negro Prison Inmates (N. Kantrowitz, American Dialect Society, Chicago, 1967).

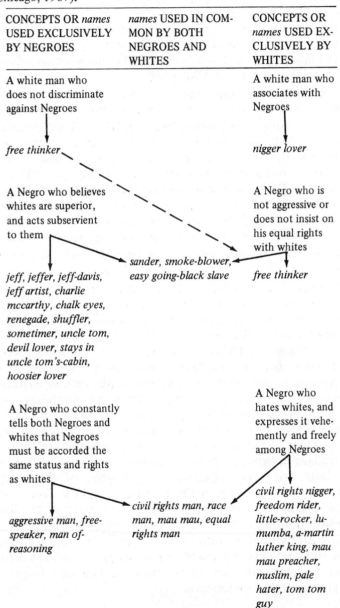

CONCEPTS OR *names* USED EXCLUSIVELY BY NEGROES	*names* USED IN COMMON BY BOTH NEGROES AND WHITES	CONCEPTS OR *names* USED EXCLUSIVELY BY WHITES
A white man who does not discriminate against Negroes		A white man who associates with Negroes
free thinker		*nigger lover*
A Negro who believes whites are superior, and acts subservient to them		A Negro who is not aggressive or does not insist on his equal rights with whites
jeff, jeffer, jeff-davis, jeff artist, charlie mccarthy, chalk eyes, renegade, shuffler, sometimer, uncle tom, devil lover, stays in uncle tom's-cabin, hoosier lover	*sander, smoke-blower, easy going-black slave*	*free thinker*
A Negro who constantly tells both Negroes and whites that Negroes must be accorded the same status and rights as whites		A Negro who hates whites, and expresses it vehemently and freely among Negroes
aggressive man, free-speaker, man of-reasoning	*civil rights man, race man, mau mau, equal rights man*	*civil rights nigger, freedom rider, little-rocker, lumumba, a-martin luther king, mau mau preacher, muslim, pale hater, tom tom guy*

linguistic innovation on the Copperbelt of Northern Rhodesia (1959) revealed that the English and other Western influences on the local languages were largely limited to matters dealing with urban, industrial, and generally nontraditional pursuits and relationships. Similarly, M. Weinreich's meticulous inquiry into the non-Germanic elements in Yiddish (1953) sheds much light on the dynamics of German-Jewish relations in the eleventh century Rhineland.

Like all other immigrants to differently speaking milieus, Jews, learning a variety of medieval German in the eleventh century, brought to this language learning task sociolinguistic norms which incorporated their prior verbal repertoire. In this case the repertoire consisted of a vernacular (Loez, a variety of Romance) and a set of sacred languages (Hebrew-Aramaic). However, the pre-existing sociolinguistic norms did not impinge upon the newly acquired Germanic code in either a random fashion or on an equal-sampling basis. Quite the contrary. Both the Romance and the Hebraic-Armanic elements in Yiddish were overwhelmingly retained to deal with a specific domain: traditional religious pursuits and concerns. The Christological overtones of many common German words, for example, *lesen* (to read) and *segnen* (to bless), were strong enough to lead to the retention of more neutral words of Romance origin (*levenen and bentshn*) in their stead. Similarly, Hebrew and Aramaic terms were retained not only for all traditional and sanctified objects and ceremonies, but also in doublets with certain Germanic elements in order to provide contrastive emphases: *bukh* (book) vs. *seyfer* (religious book, scholarly book); *lerer* (teacher) vs. *melamed* or *rebi* (teacher of religious subjects) etc. Thus, Yiddish is a wonderful example of how *all* languages in contact borrow from each other selectively and of how this very selectivity is indicative of the primary interests and emphases of the borrowers and the donors alike (for examples pertaining to early Christianity see Knott 1956, Mohrman 1947, 1957). Indeed, M. Weinreich has conclusively demonstrated (1953, 1967, etc.) that a language not only reflects the society of its speakers, but conversely, that societal data per se is crucial if language usage and change are to be understood.

Findling's work too (1969) is interpretable in this fashion, demonstrating as it does that Spanish and English among Puerto Rican youngsters and adults in the Greater New York Metropolitan area reflect different psychosocial needs and conflicts. In word-association tasks Findling found his subjects mentioning human beings more frequently in English than in Spanish and more frequently in the work and education domains than in the home and neighborhood domains (Table 21a and 21b). According to various previous

TABLE 21a. Analysis of Variance of Human Ratio (Need Affiliation) Scores (Findling 1969)

Source of Variance	Sum of Squares	df	Mean Square	F	F_{95}	F_{99}
Between subjects	19,573.09	31				
Occupation (C)	110.73	1	110.73	.17	4.17	7.56
Error (b)	19,463.08	30	648.77			
Within subjects	65,904.10	288				
Language (A)	701.69	1	701.69	3.78*	4.17	7.56
Domain (B) (B)	12,043.27	4	3,010.82	12.10**	2.44	3.47
AB	239.49	4	59.87	.48	2.44	3.47
AC	181.84	1	181.84	.98	4.17	7.56
BC	1,855.50	4	463.87	1.86	2.44	3.47
ABC	446.16	4	111.54	.89	2.44	3.47
Error (w)	50,436.15	270				
$Error_1$ (w)	5,571.17	30				
$Error_2$ (w)	29,851.83	120	248.77			
$Error_3$ (w)	15,013.15	120	125.11			
Total	85,477.19	319				

8p

*

$*p > .07$
$**p > .01$

TABLE 21b. Mean Need Affiliation Ratio Scores by Language and Domain

Language		DOMAIN				
	Work	Education	Religion	Neighborhood	Home	Total
English	33	24	20	17	14	22
Spanish	28	23	17	13	14	19
Total	30	23	18	15	14	20

studies in the area of personality theory, the prevalence of human terms in such unstructured tasks is indicative of "need affiliation," that is, the need to be accepted into positive relationships with others. Findling therefore maintains that the language of Puerto Ricans in New York reveals this need to be stronger (because less gratified) in English interactions and in Anglo-controlled domains than in Spanish interactions and Puerto Rican controlled domains. Knowing, or suspecting, as we do from other sources, that Puerto Ricans in New York are struggling for acceptance in an Anglo-dominated world, Findling's interpretations seem reasonable and intriguing indeed.

8.4 LANGUAGE BEHAVIOR AND SOCIETAL BEHAVIOR: A CIRCULAR PROCESS OF MUTUAL CREATIONS

The difference between the language-constraint view and the language-reflection view is related to the difference between being interested in language as langue and language as parole. It is also related to the difference between being interested in intercultural variation and being interested in intrasocietal variation. Obviously, the sociology of language is more fully at home with the latter level of analysis, in both cases, than with the former. However, the latter level too can be overstated, particularly if it is claimed that not only is language behavior a *complete* index to social behavior, but also that it is nothing more than an index of such behavior. While indices are merely passive, language behavior is an active force as well as a reflective one. Language behavior feeds back upon the social reality that it reflects and helps to reinforce it (or to change it) in accord with the values and goals of particular interlocutors.

When Weinreich relates that Yiddish (then Judeo-German) came to be the vernacular of Rhineland Jewry because Jews and non-Jews on the eastern shore of the Rhine shared open networks and because higher status in these Jewish-Gentile networks also came to provide Jews with higher status in their own closed networks, he is saying much more than that language usage reflects social interaction. Of course, Judeo-German was a reflection of the fact that Jews and Gentiles participated in common open networks. However,

Judeo-German also helped implement and reinforce these networks, and thus became a coparticipant in creating or preserving the social reality that it reflected. Similarly, when Weinreich tells us that Judeo-German became increasingly more indigenously normed (and therefore increasingly more Yiddish and less Judeo-German), he is referring to much more than a linguistic reflection of the primacy of its closed networks for this Jewish community. He is also telling us that the uniquely Jewish aspects of Yiddish (in phonology, lexicon, and grammar) also helped foster the primacy of Jewish closed networks for its speakers. As a result, Yiddish not only reflected (as it does today) the cohesiveness and separateness of its speakers, but it helped to preserve and to augment these characteristics as well.

Thus, both unidirectional views are outgrowths of an artificial search for independent variables and original causes. The original cause of any societal behavior may well be of some interest, but it is a historical interest rather than a dynamic one with respect to life as it continues round about us. If we can put aside the issue of "what first caused what," we are left with the fascinating process of ongoing and intertwined conversation and interaction. In these processes language and societal behavior are equal partners rather than one or the other of them being "boss" and "giving orders" to the other.

APPLIED SOCIOLOGY
OF LANGUAGE

One of the wisest maxims that Kurt Lewin bequeathed to social psychology is that which claims that "nothing is as practical as a good theory." In addition, social science theory is undoubtedly enriched by attempting to cope with the real problems of the workaday world. Thus, if social science theory is *really* any good (really powerful, really correct), it should have relevance for practitioners whose work brings them into contact with larger or smaller groups of human beings. Applied sociology of language attempts both to enrich the sociology of language and to assist in the solution of societal language problems. The applied sociology of language is of particular interest whenever: (a) language varieties must be "developed" in order to function in the vastly new settings, role relationships, or purposes in which certain important networks of their speakers come to be involved, or (b) whenever important networks of a speech community must be taught varieties (or varieties in particular media or uses) that they do not know well (or at all), so that these networks may function in the vastly new settings, role relationships, or purposes that might then become open (or more open) to them. In many instances (a) and (b) co-occur, that is, language varieties must be both developed and taught in order that important networks within a speech community may be fruitfully involved in the new settings, role relationships, and purposes that have become available to them. This is but another way of saying that planned language change and planned social change are highly interrelated activities, and that the sociology of language is pertinent to their interaction.

Comments on the uses of sociology of language must keep in mind four separate categories of actual and potential users, namely, linguists and sociologists on one hand, and the users of linguistics as well as the users of sociology on the other hand. The sociology of language as a hybrid or bridge-building specialization is useful not *only* as it pertains to the front line of contact between science and society, but *also* as it enables those in theoretical heartlands to understand their basic fields afresh and in refreshing ways. Application and applicability are themselves an endless array of concentric circles that surround all immediate problems in an ever-widening and interlocking flow. It is never wise to rigidly declare some knowledge "useful" and other "useless," for neither knowledge nor usefulness (nor even the very problems to which both are referred) hold still long enough for such judgments to be more than myopic indicators of how near or far we stand with respect to a particular and often fleeting goal. All knowledge is useful, and if at any point in time we nevertheless grope toward a consideration of the "uses of X," it is merely because for some particular purposes at some particular time some knowledge may seem *more useful* than other.

This Section proceeds by reviewing a few recognized topics within applied linguistics in order to illustrate and document a point of view with respect to the usefulness of the sociology of language. Its point of departure is Charles A. Ferguson's well-known attempt to divide applied linguistics into its six most common American branches: the creation and revision of writing systems, literacy efforts, translation work, language teaching efforts, and language policy efforts (Ferguson 1959a; for a German and a Soviet view see Kandler 1955 and Andreev and Zinder 1959). Although it will be impossible to give equally detailed attention to all six of these branches of applied linguistics here, it would seem that essentially similar questions must be addressed to each of them, namely, what has been accomplished *without* formal sociolinguistic awareness and sophistication?; what has the sociology of language *contributed* to more recent applied linguistic efforts in these topical areas?; finally, what more *could* the sociology of language contribute to these (and even to other) applied linguistic concerns if its practitioners were to really take *both* parts of this hybrid field with *equal seriousness* and with the deep technical and theoretical proficiency that they *both* require?

9.1 THE CREATION OF WRITING SYSTEMS

The sophistication of phonological theory, both that of the early part of this century as well as that of very recent years, and the recent linguistic interest in theories of writing systems and in the relations between such systems and spoken language are, and have long been, powerful linguistic contributions to the world-wide efforts to create writing systems for preliterate peoples. However, the very sophistication of the linguist's professional skills in code description and code creation merely intensified the separation trauma when it became obvious that it was necessary to go outside the code and to confront the real world if writing systems were not only to be devised (this being the only apparent concern of Pike 1947 and Ray 1963) but also *employed*. The first steps in this direction were moderate indeed. These consisted of Vachek's (1945/49 and 1948) and Bolinger's (1946) protests (among others) that the writing system must be viewed separately from the spoken code, i.e., that it could not properly be viewed as merely the phonetic transcription of the spoken code, and that it was basically a "visual system" (being not unlike the language interaction of the deaf in this respect) with regularities all its own.

The reverberations of these early protests are still with us. As Berry has pointed out (1958), new alphabets have clearly become less purely phonemic and more inclined to the "use of reason and expedience" (rather than to rely on phonemicization alone) in their pursuit of acceptance. Indeed, the latter concern, that of acceptance, has tended to replace the former, that of "reduction to writing," and as a result, arguments pertaining to intra-(written) code phenomena have tended to recede evermore into the background. While "phonetic ambiguity" is still considered a "bad" thing, and while it is generally agreed that "words pronounced differently should be kept graphically apart" (Bradley 1913/14), it is considered to be an even "worse thing" if alphabets of exquisite perfection remain unused or unaccepted. More and more work on the creation of writing systems has shown awareness of the fact that such non-acceptance is only to a relatively minor degree governed by intracode ambiguities, inconsistencies, or irrelevancies (all of these being rampant characteristics of the most widely used writing systems today and throughout history). Time and again in recent years the greater importance of extracode phenomena has been hinted at (Gelb 1952, Bowers 1968), pointed to (Sjoberg 1964, 1966, Walker 1969), and finally, even listed and catalogued (Nida 1954, Smalley 1964).

9.2 DESIRED SIMILARITY AND DISSIMILARITY

Perhaps because their attention is basically directed toward intracode factors, linguists and applied linguists were quickest to notice those extracode factors in the adoption or rejection of writing systems which indicated societal preferences or antipathies for writing conventions associated with some other language or languages. Thus, among the "practical limitations to a phonemic orthography" Nida (1954) discussed the fact that both the Otomi and the Quechua "suffer from cultural insecurity" and want their writing systems not only to "look like Spanish," but to operate with the same graphemic alternances as does Spanish, *whether these are needed or not* in terms of their own phonemic system. In a related but crucially different vein Hans Wolff recommended (1954) that Nigerian orthographies be created not only in terms of tried and true technically linguistic criteria (such as "accuracy, economy, and consistency"), but that "similarity to the orthographies of related languages" also be used as a guide. Of course, Wolff was merely following in the footsteps of the Westermann Script of the late 1920's, which in its fuller, more generally applicable form became the All-Africa Script of the International African Institute (Anon. 1930).

However, he was also following in the tradition that placed the linguist or other outside expert in the position of judging not only *which languages* were sufficiently related in order to deserve a common writing system, but that placed him in the position of deciding whether such similarity in writing systems was or was not a "good thing" and whether it was or was not desired by the speech communities involved.

However, once having stepped outside of the charmingly closed circle of intracode considerations, Pandora's box had been opened never again to be shut. In very recent days, to mention only such examples, Serdyuchenko has assured us that the Cyrillic alphabet is used as the model in "the creation of new written languages in the USSR" only because of the widespread and still growing interest in subsequently more easily learning Russian, just as Sjoberg (1966) mentions Tlingit insistence that their orthography "follow the rather chaotic orthographic patterns of English wherever possible in order to conform to the demands of the broader society" (p.217), and the Institut Français d'Afrique Noire concludes that speakers of African vernaculars in Francophone countries want their orthographies to look as French as possible (Smalley 1964). Walker (1969), like Serdyuchenko before him (1962), is quite willing to champion such modeling at the explicit expense of maximal phonemic efficiency. Recently the Bamako Meeting on the Use of the Mother Tongue for Literacy (February 28 - March 5, 1966, UNESCO sponsored) went a step further. It not only recommended that new writing systems be similar to those of *unrelated but important languages for the learners* (Bowers 1968), but it also warned of "possible repercussions of a technical and economic nature" following upon the adoption of non-European diacritics and special letters in the standard transcriptions of West African languages (Ferru 1966). Such letters and diacritics, it is pointed out, increase the cost of printing and typing, as well as the cost of manufacturing printing and typing equipment, and do so at the time when the per capita cost of printed or typed material is already likely to be troublesomely high in view of the limited number of consumers available for them in newly literate societies. On these same grounds the Institut d'Afrique Noire insisted as far back as 1959 that "when symbols have to be made up

they should be typable on a standard French typewriter"
(Smalley 1959).

The obverse case has been less fully documented, namely,
that in which newly literate communities have desired a more
distinctive writing system, one that they could call *their own*
or one that would more effectively differentiate their
language from others with respect to which they sought not
similarity but rather *dissimilarity.* Dickens's (1953) discussion of the Ashante rejection of the Akuapem-based
writing system for standard Twi (in the late 1930's and early
1940's) is one such case. Another is Ferguson's brief
reference to the fact that St. Stefan of Perm (fourteenth
century) purposely created a separate alphabet for the Komi
giving "some of the letters an appearance suggestive of the
Tamga signs in use among the Komi as property markers and
decorations" (1967, p. 259) "so that the Komi could regard
the writing system as distinctively theirs and not an alphabet
used for another language." There must be many examples of
this kind, e.g., St. Mesrop's creation of the Armenian
alphabet in the fifth century, utilizing in part characters like
those of far-distant brother-Menophysite Christians in
Ethiopia with whom contact had probably been made
(according to Olderogge) as a result of the presence of both
Armenian and Ethiopian churches in Jerusalem. Another
such example is Sequoyah's syllabary, which was "not
associated with aliens but developed within the Cherokee
language community itself" (Walker 1969, p. 149; also see
White 1962). Finally, to the above cases there must be added
the few preliminary studies of indigenous African and Asian
scripts of relatively small communities that weathered
competitive pressures precisely because of their real or
assumed local origins (e.g., Dalby 1967, 1968, Hair 1963,
Stern 1968, Stewart 1967). Perhaps the relative reluctance to
document such cases is not unrelated to the more general
reluctance of those who practice applied linguistics upon
others to recognize the frequent desires of nonliterate
peoples to be themselves (albeit "in a modern way"), rather
than merely to be imitative copies of *ourselves* (whether we
be Chinese, Russian, Arab, French, British, American,
Spanish, or Portuguese).

9.3 "A LITTLE MORE COMPLICATED THAN THAT"

If economics answers all questions with "supply and demand," psychology with "stimulus and response," and education with "it all depends," then the first contribution of the sociology of language to applied linguistics is doubtlessly to stress the fact that the relations and interpenetrations between language and society are "a little more complicated than that," whatever *that* may be. Indeed, although it is nearly half a century since Radin first implied that the adoption (actually, the borrowing) of an alphabet by an aboriginal people was a fascinatingly complex and internally differentiated chain of social processes, we have not to this very day seriously followed up this seeming complexity, let alone tried to reduce it to some underlying set of basic dimensions. Our technical expertise and theoretical sophistication lead us more readily to agree with Burns's (1953) early conclusion, based on sad experience with the failure of "linguistics without sociology" in Haiti, that the choice of an orthography has widespread social and political implications. They also lead us to continually admire Garvin's accounts (1954, also see 1959) of his attempts to achieve consumer consensus and participation in the creation of a standard orthography for Ponape, and to share his disappointment that even this was not enough to assure the use of that orthography. Beyond such agreement and admiration, however, we can only suggest that the process of gaining acceptance for technically sound writing systems is even "a little more complicated than that." In spelling out this complexity applied sociology of language uniquely stresses that it is cruical to systematically look *outside* of the linguistic system itself if one is to locate the reasons for the differential acceptance or rejection of programs of linguistic change. Modern sociology of language can contribute most by linking this particular topic of applied linguistics with the body of theory and practice that has grown up in connection with the acceptance of other systematic innovations, the planning of social change more generally, and the amelioration of the inevitable dislocations that follow upon the introduction of innumerable innovations and changes of which new writing systems are merely symptomatic.

The creation of writing systems is itself necessarily an outgrowth of culture contact, if not of political and economic domination from outside. Thus, the creation of a writing system is singularly unlikely to be viewed dispassionately, and its propagation and acceptance by indigenous networks are necessarily viewed as having implications for group loyalty and group identity. Latinization, Arabization, Cyrillization, or Sinoization are not merely fargoing indications of desired (and frequently of subsidized or directed) social change and cognitive-emotional reorganization, but they have immediate consequences for the relevance of traditional elitist skills and implications for the distribution of new skills and statuses related to literacy and to the philosophy or ideology which is the carrier of literacy.

The creation of writing systems is significant only in so far as it leads to the acceptance and implementation of writing systems. The latter are broadly revolutionary rather than narrowly technical acts. They succeed or fail far less on the basis of the adequacy of their intracode phonological systems or on the basis of their fidelity to model systems, than on the basis of the success of the larger revolutions with which they are associated; revolutions in the production and consumption of economic goods (leading to new rural-urban population distributions, new jobs, new training programs, new avocations, new pastimes, and new purposive social groups) are revolutions in the distributions of power and influence. All of these both lead to and depend upon an increasing number of new texts and new written records. Thus, when sociolinguistic attention is finally directed to the creation of writing systems, it will be focused upon the organization, functioning, and disorganization of an increasingly literate society. This is potentially a very useful addition to the linguist's disciplinary focus, because even more than writing changes speech (via "spelling pronunciations"), literacy changes speakers and societies. It is this perspective on the creation of writing systems — as always, a perspective which is outside of the linguistic system alone — that is part of the programmatic promise of the sociology of writing systems.

How will such attention improve or alter the creation of writing systems? Precisely by relating the problem of creation to the problem of acceptance, of impact, of possible dislocation, of possible manipulation, of possible exploitation, of possible redistribution of power, and in general, of the dependency of the very best writing system on revolutionary processes at their most pragmatic as well as at their most symbolic.

9.4 ORTHOGRAPHIC REFORM

To some extent such liberation and immersion are more advanced with respect to the study and planning of orthographic *reforms*, perhaps because the truly vast amount of technical linguistic effort invested in these reforms has yielded such meager results. Even though orthographic reform may be so sweeping as to involve the complete replacement of one writing system by another (and in that sense, it may be viewed as a subcategory of the topic just reviewed), it deals with already literate networks, and as a result, more clearly reveals the societal ramifications and reverberations of seemingly technical linguistic adjustments.

If the introduction of a newly created writing system easily threatens to change established lines of relative advantage and disadvantage, practical and symbolic, the revision of traditional orthographies most often obviously *attempts* to do so. Orthographic change represents departure from an established written tradition, and as such, it *must* cope with the gatekeepers of that written tradition, the poets, priests, principals, and professors, and the institutions and symbols that they create and serve, or be destined to oblivion. Indeed, the greater and grander the tradition of literacy, literature, and liturgy in an orthographic community, the less likely that even minor systematic orthographic change will be freely accepted and the less likely that any orthographic change will be considered minor.

In this connection we have a larger number of rather detailed, and to some extent, *sociolinguistically oriented* descriptions, than is the case for the creation of writing systems, but as yet we have no sociological analyses or hypotheses per se. The socioculturally contextualized descriptions of orthographic reforms in the USSR (Kolarz 1967, Orenstein 1959, Quelquejay and Bennigsen 1961,

Serdyuchenko 1965, Weinreich 1953b, Winner 1952), Turkey (Rossi 1927, 1929, 1935, 1942, 1953, Heyd 1954, Ozmen 1967, Gallagher 1967 and 1969), Norway (Haugen 1966a, which contains an exhaustive bibliography of other studies), and Vietnam (Haudricourt 1943, Nguyen dinh Hoa 1960, Thompson 1965) again point to the literally revolutionary nature of the societal processes that have often accompanied system-wide orthographic change. On the other hand, the available descriptions of far less successful attempts to bring about orthographic change under less dramatic circumstances, e.g., in Japan (DeFrancis 1947, Holton 1947, Meyenburg 1934, Scharshmidt 1924, Toshio 1967), Haiti (Valdman 1968, Burns 1953) and Israel (Rabin 1969), or to bring about the orthographic unification of closely related languages in the absence of accompanying societal unification, e.g., in India (Anon. 1963, Jones 1942, Ray 1963), Africa (Dickens 1953, Ward 1945), and Indonesia-Malaysia (Alisjahbana 1969 and in press), all indicate the difficulties encountered and the failures experienced thus far.

However, there is no justification for interpreting the above cited investigations as implying "revolutionary success and nonrevolutionary failure" as the proper summation of experience with orthographic reform. In earlier centuries a great deal of orthographic reform seems to have been accomplished both quietly and successfully without the involvement of mobilized populations or, indeed, of any other population segments than "the authorities" whose business it was to make wise decisions for the community. The initial orthographic distinctions between Serbian and Croatian, or between Ruthenian (Ukrainian) and Polish, were decided upon by representatives of God and/or Caesar who sought to cultivate differences between speech communities that were otherwise "in danger" of religious, political, and linguistic unification. Indeed, the Ausbau languages (in Kloss's sense, 1952) are all instances of the success of applied linguistics and should be carefully studied as such. The restoration of written Czech (and Slovak) in Latin script was engineered by Count Sedlnitzsky, the administrative director of the Austro-Hungarian police and one of the most influential officials under the Emperor Francis (early nineteenth century), by subsidizing the publication of the

Orthodox prayer book in Latin letters as "an important
device to fight the political danger of the pro-Russian
Pan-Slav movement" (Fischel 1919, p. 57). The Roumanian
shift from Cyrillic to Latin script in 1863 was accomplished
by a painless edict which sought to further that nation's
self-defined Latinizing and Christianizing role in the heathen
"Slavo-Moslem" Balkans (Kolarz 1946). In more recent days
Irish orthography has been changed without arousing unusual
interest or opposition (Macnamara 1969), as was the type
font (from an "Irish looking" font to an ordinary Roman
font). Indeed, the relative ease with which these changes were
made may be a reflection of the lack of widespread Irish
interest or concern for the language revival.

Not only *has* there been much successful orthographic
reform without revolutionary change (particularly where
mass mobilization along language-related lines was absent for
one reason or another), but there has also been a good bit of
unsuccessful orthographic reform even when these have been
accompanied by revolutionary social changes. Thus, the
Soviet "rationalization" of Yiddish orthography (Szajkowski
1966) initially aimed at both the *phonetization* of words of
Hebrew-Aramaic origin, as well as at the *discontinuation* of
the social final letters of the traditional Hebrew alphabet.
However, twenty-five years after the October Revolution, the
names of the grandfathers of modern Yiddish literature were
neither spelled

שאָלעמ אַלייכעמ, ייצכאַק לייבוש פּערעצ און מענדעלע מויכער ספּאָרימ

(as they *had* been throughout the 1920's and 1930's), nor
were they spelled

שלום עליכם, יצחק לייבוש פּרץ און מענדעלע מוכר־ספרים

(as they *had* been before the Revolution and continued to be
everywhere outside of the Soviet Union), but rather, in an
attempt to reach a compromise that would maximize the
propaganda value of the few permitted Yiddish publications
primarily distributed to and published for readers outside of
the USSR:

שאָלעם אַלייכעם, ייצכאָק לייבוש פּערעץ און מענדעלע מויכער ספּאָרים

However, even in its heyday the Soviet revolution in Yiddish orthography could not overcome the visual traditions of the orthographic community. The initial silent aleph at the beginning of words that would otherwise begin with the vowels ˈ and ˌ was *never* dropped, regardless of its phonemic uselessness, perhaps because the initial silent aleph in such cases was considered to be too strong a visual convention to be tampered with (Hebrew writing itself − i.e., the visual precursor to written Yiddish − never beginning words with vocalic ˈ or ˌ).

A far more widely renowned revolutionary attempt at orthographic reform which has failed (certainly thus far) is the once promised phonetization of (Northern Mandarin) Chinese. While the basic sources available to us in English (DeFrancis 1950 and 1968, Mills 1956, and Hsia 1956) all agree that the Latinized new writing was abandoned some-time late in the fifties, the reason for this abandonment can still only be surmised.

By 1956 it had become necessary to defend the "Han (Chinese) language phonetization draft plan" as being concerned with an alphabet (Latin) which was truly progressive and international rather than necessarily related to any antiproletarian class (Chinese Writers Language Reform Committee 1956, Wu Yu-chang 1956). By 1959 Chou En-lai had officially demoted phonetization from its original goal of immediate "liberations and development of the whole Chinese language from the shackles of the monosyllabic Chinese characters" (Ni Hai-shu 1949, cited by DeFrancis 1968) to third place and the indefinite future, after both simplification of the traditional characters and adoption of a spoken standard for "Common Speech" had been attained (Chou En-lai 1965). While work on the first two tasks is constantly going on in a very direct fashion (see, e.g., Wu Yu-chang 1965), work on the latter is primarily nominal (that is, phonetization is kept alive as a distant goal but is not substantively advanced) and indirect (i.e., phonetization is utilized for subsidiary purposes, such as annotating novel or complex Chinese characters in technical texts, furthering instruction in the Common Speech among speakers of other regional languages, or creating "initial alphabetic scripts" for illiterate non-Chinese-speaking minorities). Indeed, while phonetization has recently been reported to be superior for such special purposes as telegraphic communication (Wu Yu-chang 1964) and minority group initial literacy (Li Hui 1960), the traditional characters have again been proclaimed as superior in connection with general education for the bulk of the population, among whom these characters are viewed as symbolic of education and the standard pronunciation (Serruys 1962)! The goal of phonetization is seemingly still a long way off and may or may not be reached any more rapidly than the withering away of the state (see several references to this effect in Kwan-wai Chiu 1970).

From the foregoing examples it is clear that if we but dichotomize both "success" (acceptance) and "revolutionary social change" we have examples of all four possible types of co-occurrences: successful orthographic revision with and without revolutionary social change and revolutionary social change with and without successful follow-through of planned orthographic revision. The discussions of revolutionary social change thus far encountered in studies of either the creation of writing systems or the revision of orthographies is still far too crude to be considered as more than rough labeling. As sociolinguistic description it is regrettably out of touch with the sizable modernization literature in economics, political science, sociology, and anthropology. It lacks both the concepts and the technical data collection methods and data analysis skills needed to inquire into the intensity, extensity, or continuity of the change forces and processes or the counterchange forces and processes that underly the gross labels so frequently encountered.

It is also unfortunate that there are *so few* localized case studies of *variation in subgroup reactions* to new writing systems or to revised orthographies, and conversely, proportionally *so many* commentaries, studies, evaluations, and recommendations that deal with entire countries, continents, and even the world at large. The result is an imbalance with respect to the usual mutual stimulation between microanalysis and its emphases on process and function concerns on one hand, and macroanalysis and its emphases on structure, quantification, compositing, and weighing of parameters on the other hand. Either type of study, when pursued too long without correction from the other, becomes myopic, and therefore dangerous for theory as well as (or even more so) for application. However, whereas both macro and micro studies are equally necessary for the growth of general sociolinguistic theory, the future of *applied* sociology of language is particularly tied to *within-context* studies (within nation X, within region Y, within district Z), and therefore to ever more detailed studies of differential acceptance processes, rather than to studies of large-scale between-context variation (the latter not having as immediate applied significance for any particular within-context problem).

9.5 LANGUAGE PLANNING

Perhaps the area of applied linguistics which most clearly illustrates the full complexity of societal phenomena which the sociology of language may someday enable us to understand is that which is concerned with language planning. Just as sociolinguistic inquiry into the creation of writing systems and into the revision of orthographies permits us to first recognize and to then refine our appreciation of the magnitudes of social change and social planning (if not social dislocation) with which such activities are commonly associated, so the systematic sociolinguistic study of language *planning* as a whole (incorporating the creation of writing systems and the revision of orthographies, but going beyond them to conscious governmental efforts to manipulate both the structure and the functional allocation of codes within a polity) enables us to appreciate the societal complexity impinging on the determination, implementation, and evaluation of language *policy* as a whole. The study of language planning is the study of organized efforts to find solutions to societal language problems (Jernudd and Das Gupta 1971). As such, it is necessarily most dependent—of all the fields of applied language concerns—on the sociology of language and on the social sciences as a whole in order to move from theory to informed practice (Figure 24).

Of the language planning studies recently completed or currently under way a few have dealt with the cost-benefit analysis of alternative or hypothetically alternative decisions between which governmental or other bodies must choose

FIGURE 24. Article from *Le Travailleur* June 7, 1969   *187*

Les grandes enquêtes de l'Office du Vocabulaire français de Paris

Depuis quelques années, l'opinion publique est alertée sur les dangers que court la langue française, et divers organismes, tant officiels que privés, ont été créés pour assurer la défense d'un idiome parlé par la communauté sans cesse grandissante des francophones: 90 millions aujourd'hui, ils seront 200 millions avant l'an 2000. Mais comment obtenir que la langue français, ciment de cette francophonie dont on parle tant, ne s'altère pas, ne dégénère pas, ne devienne pas un jargon à la syntaxe désordonnée et au vocabulaire truffé de néologismes mal assimilés?

Les règles du bon langage, on peut les connaître. Les atteintes au bon langage, tout le monde les connaît également, ou peut les connaître à la lecture de maints ouvrages ou articles de presse. Ce que l'on connaît mal, c'est le moyen d'obtenir que les règles soient mieux respectées et l'invasion des néologismes contenue. L'opinion sait que l'usage est à corriger selon les principes d'une norme raisonnable. Mais elle ignore comment la norme, une fois établie, peut descendre jusqu'à l'usage, c'est-à-dire comment l'usage peut être orienté, sinon dirigé par la norme de manière efficace.

Précisément, la troisième Biennale de la langue français a inscrit á l'ordre du jour de ses prochains travaux une formule significative d'enquête: De la norme à l'usage.

L'Office du Vocabulaire français, qui, on le sait, est à l'origine des Biennales, entend participer à cette recherche et fournir aux orateurs de la Biennale qui désireront s'informer sur l'opinion du grand public éclairé une riche documentation. Celle-ci sera puisée à la meilleure source qui soit: le groupe que constituent les membres consultants de l'Office du Vocabulaire français.

C'est pourquoi nous vous demandons de bien vouloir répondre au questionnaire que voici:

1. Pensez-vous, d'une manière très générale, qu'il soit possible d'agir sur les habitudes de langage d'une grande communauté humaine ?

N. B.—A cette première question, les membres de l'Office du Vocabulaire français répondront, de toute évidence, par un «oui». Mais toute personne qui répondra «non» devra développer ses raisons, qui pourront être constructives.

2. Pensez-vous que l'Enseignement soit le seul dispensateur de la norme et que nulle action sur l'usage ne soit concevable hors de l'école?

3. Croyez-vous que les adultes puissent recevoir un enseignement prolongé de la langue française, de la même manière qu'ils reçoivent, par les publications spécialisées, par les revues de vulgarisation scientifique ou technique, un enseignement prolongé en histoire, en physique, en histoire naturelle, en géographie . . . et même en astronautique?

Nous vous serions reconnaissants de bien vouloir répondre à cès questions, en portant en tête de votre lettre vos nom et prénom, profession, adresse.

Vous voudrez bien ajouter, également en tête de votre réponse, selon votre choix:

J'accepte que mon nom figure dans un compte rendu de synthèse (signature);

Je désire garder l'anonymat (id.).

Les réponses devront être adressées au secrétariat de

l'Office du Vocabulaire français, 17, rue du Montparnasse, Paris-Vle, France

(Jernudd 1970, Thurburn 1970). Others have discussed the pressure functions focused upon decision-making/decision-implementing bodies in the language field (whether the latter be legislative-executive within government or political-religious-literary-academic outside of government) from a variety of special interest groups running the gamut from professional associations of educators to manfuacturers of typewriters and publishers of textbooks, and to spokesmen for literary, journalistic, and ideological groupings, etc. (Das Gupta 1971). There are now several theoretical models (happily commensurable) of the interaction of sentimental and instrumental integrative and disintegrative forces in the language planning process (Kelman 1971, Fishman 1971). There are recent critiques and integrations of the literature on the evaluation of planned change in education, industry, agriculture, and other areas of conscious societal planning, in an effort to suggest evaluative methods that might be most fruitfully adopted for the evaluation of success or failure in language planning (Macnamara 1971, Rubin 1971). A four-country study has recently got under way (involving linguists, anthropologists, political scientists, sociologists, psychologists, and educationists) in order to obtain roughly comparable data concerning the processes of language plan-ning per se in each of the above contexts (decision making, pressure functions, national integration, implementation, and evaluation). Obviously, the study of language planning is rapidly moving away from intracode efficiency considera-tions alone (the latter being the primary emphasis of Tauli 1968) and moving steadily into ever-richer contextual concerns. Hopefully, as language planning and social planning agencies become more aware of the possible contributions of applied sociology of language they may become more inclined to involve sociolinguists and other language specialists in *guiding* the decision-making *process* itself rather than merely in *implementing* decisions *already reached.* Several signs already point in this direction. Thus, the several nations of East Africa are interested in the current "Survey of Language Use and Language Teaching" (Prator 1967) in order to adopt (or revise) language operations in schools, mass media, public services, etc., on the basis of more precise information as to the age, number, location, and interactions of the speakers of various local languages. Similarly, the Philippine government has long followed a policy of evaluating language policy in the area of education via research projects dealing with such matters as the advisability of initiating education in the local mother tongues and introducing the national language (Filipino) only in some optimal subsequent year (Ramos et al. 1967). The Irish government has sponsored "motivation research" and opinion polls in order to determine how its citizens view the Irish language and how they react to the government's efforts to "restore" it to wider functions (Anon. 1968). One of the most widely cited guides to governmental language policies and their educational implications is an applied sociolinguistic report issued by UNESCO and dealing with "The Use of the Vernacular in Education" (Anon. 1953). Once a policy is adopted it is then necessary to implement it. Such implementation not only takes the obvious route of requiring and/or encouraging the functional reallocation of varieties, but also their phonological, lexical, and grammatical realization along prescribed lines. Language agencies, institutes, academies, or boards are commonly authorized to develop or plan the variety selected by policy makers. Such agencies are increasingly likely to seek feedback concerning the effectiveness or the acceptability of the "products" (orthographies, dictionaries, grammars, spellers, textbooks, translation series, subsidized literary works, etc.) that they have produced. Sociologists of language have already produced many studies which language agencies are likely to find extremely useful in terms of their implications for the work that such agencies conduct.

The difficulties encountered and the lessons learned in planned lexical expansion to cope with the terminology of modern technology education, government, and daily life are recounted by Alisjahbana (1962, 1965, 1971), Bacon (1966), Morag (1959), Passin (1963), and Tietze (1962) in their accounts of language planning in Indonesia, Central Asia, Japan, Israel, and Turkey, respectively. The problems of planned language standardization have been illuminated by Ferguson (1968), Garvin (1959), Guxman (1960), Ray (1963), U. Weinreich (1953b), Havranek (1964), Valdman (1968), and Twaddell (1959) in sufficiently general terms to be of interest in any speech community where this process needs to be set in motion.

Even the very process of government involvement in language issues has begun to be documented. In this connection one must mention the reports of the Irish government on its efforts to restore the Irish language (Anon. 1965); Goodman's review of Soviet efforts to provide—as well as deny—indigenous *standard* languages to the peoples under their control (Goodman 1960); Haugen's many insightful reports of the Norwegian government's attempts to cope with language conflict by both protecting and limiting the linguistic divergence of its citizenry (Haugen 1961, 1966a, 1966b); Heyd's account of language reform in modern Turkey (Heyd 1954); Lunt's account of the studied efforts in Titoist Yugoslavia to separate Macedonian from Serbian and from Bulgarian (Lunt 1959) and Mayner's comments on the attempts to fuse Serbian and Croatian in that country (Mayner 1967); the contrasts between different parts of Africa noted by Mazrui (1967), Armstrong (1968), Polome (1968), and Whiteley (1968); Mills's report of how Communist China advanced and retreated in connection with the writing reform it so desperately needs (Mills 1956); Wurm's descriptions of the very beginnings of language policy in reference to Pidgin English ("Neo-Melanesian" in New Guinea (Wurm and Laycock 1961/62), and several others (e.g., Brosnahan 1963b, LePage 1964, Fishman 1968c) of more general or conceptual relevance.

One of the most necessary areas of applied sociology of language is that which deals with educational problems related to language policy formulation or evaluation. In this connection there have been studies of the organization and operation of bilingual schools (Gaarder 1967); of the academic consequences of compulsory education via the weaker language for most learners (Macnamara 1966, 1967; of different approaches to teaching hitherto untaught mother tongues (Davis 1967); of varying South American and West Indian approaches of teaching both local and "wider" languages (Burns 1968, LePage 1968, Rubin 1968); of difficulties in teaching English (as the compulsory school language for non-English speakers) encountered by teachers who are themselves nonnative speakers of English (Lanham

1965); and more specifically, of the problem of teaching standard English to speakers of very discrepant, nonstandard varieties of that language (Stewart 1964, 1965). A more generalized interest in applied sociology of language is that shown by the recent Canadian Royal Commission on Bilingualism and Biculturism (Royal Commission 1965, 1967, 1968). It authorized studies not only on bilingual schooling but also on bilingualism in broadcasting, in industrial operations, in military operations, and in the operation of various other societal enterprises.

Notwithstanding the obvious recent strengthening of applied sociology of language, several nations throughout the world are currently engaged in language planning without anything like the information available to them in other areas of planning. Sociolinguistic research on language planning must aim, first, to locate then to apportion the variation in behavior-toward-language which is to be observed in language planning contexts. It must seek detailed knowledge of how orthographic decisions (or script decisions, or national language decisions, or nomenclature decisions, etc.) are arrived at, how they are differentially reacted to or followed up by agencies inside and outside government, how they are differentially accepted or resisted by various population segments, how they are differentially evaluated, and how subsequent policies and plans are differentially modified as a result of feedback from prior policy and planning. The sociology of language is just now beginning to describe the variation that constantly obtains in all of these connections. After this has been done sufficiently well and in sufficiently many contexts, it should begin to successfully account for this variation, and at that point, be able to offer suggestions that are useful from the point of view of those seeking to influence, implement, or evaluate language planning in the future.

9.6 SOME STRAWS IN THE WIND

However, even in the absence of the amount of detail and sophistication that is needed before practical information becomes available, "sociolinguistically motivated" changes in applied linguistics are clearly on the increase. Not only are such topics as the creation of writing systems, the reform of orthographies, and language planning more generally marked (as we have seen) by a constantly increasing awareness of societal interpenetration and of the need for truly professional competence (which is more than simply being either critical or admiring) if one is to understand, let alone influence, the societal forces at work, but such awareness is growing in most other fields of applied linguistics as well.

The planning, implementation, and evaluation of literacy campaigns increasingly ceased being merely applied linguistics plus education (pedagogy) plus ethnography as the period of immediate post World War II exuberance was left behind (Smith 1956). What is currently being developed in this field goes beyond advice on how to establish proper local contacts and obtain official cooperation (Young 1944, Russell 1948), important though such advice undoubtedly is. It goes beyond care to adopt programs to local needs (Jeffries 1958), to utilize a variety of methods on a variety of fronts (Ivanova and Voskresensky 1959), or to evaluate outcomes broadly enough to include health, economic, and other pertinent indices (UNESCO 1951). Current efforts to advance literacy are increasingly based upon efforts to more fully understand the meaning and impact of literacy via small pilot studies which seek to recognize and weigh alternatives (Correa and Tinbergen 1962, Lewis 1961, McClusker 1963) and clarify the societal dimensions of literacy enterprises in different contexts (Goody 1963, Hayes 1965, Nida 1967, Schofield 1968, Wurm1966).

A similar systematic intrusion of societal considerations has become noticeable in the field of *translation*. It is here, in particular, that sociolinguistic differentiation of language into varieties and of speech communities into situations is beginning to be felt, perhaps more so than in any other field of applied linguistics. One cannot read Catford's *Linguistic Theory of Translation* (1965) without being delighted by the fact that it is far broader than "immaculate linguistics" alone, and one cannot read Wonderly's *Bible Translations for Popular Use* (1968) without wishing that its sensitivity to social varieties and social occasions were part of the professional orientation of translation for far more worldly purposes as well. Certainly the deep concern with recognizing the significance of functional variation in language variety use, the sensitivity shown with respect to the *situational analysis* of repertoires of social and linguistic behavior— viewing Bible reading and listening as kinds of situations that may require particular kinds of language—and the repeated attention given to the contextual-functional differences between written and spoken language (and the multiple varieties of each) must sooner or later feed back into religious work on the creation of writing systems and on literacy more generally. This is, indeed, the beginning of technical socio- linguistic utility for an applied field. Having once embarked along the path or recognizing that all of the factors influencing communicative appropriateness in a particular speech community also influence the acceptability and the impact of translations in that community, the probability of mutual enrichment between application and theory for both fields of endeavor (translation and sociology of language) is indeed very great.

The same may yet be the case for the huge field of language teaching, where the contacts with the sociology of language are still far more tenous, if only because the contacts between an elephant and a sparrow must always be rather incomplete. Nevertheless, although the problems and prospects of language teaching could easily swallow up or trample underfoot not only all of the sociology of language, but also all of sociology, psychology, and linguistics per se, first linguistics, and more recently, the sociology of language *have* had some impact on the beast. A valuable introduction to sociology of language has been presented to language teachers generally by Halliday, McIntosh, and Strevens (1964). In this introduction teachers are urged to recognize the different uses (and therefore the different varieties) of language that coexist within speech communities rather than, as has usually been the case thus far, to persist in the erroneous and deadening fiction that there is always *only one* (and always the *same* one) correct variety.

More recently we have witnessed a deluge of "socio- linguistically oriented" interest in the language of disadvan- taged speakers of non-standard English with Bernstein's work (e.g., 1964) being best known in England and Labov's (1965) or McDavid's (1958) in the United States. Most of the products of this interest seek to contrastively highlight the basic structure of the speech of such communities so that teachers may be able to more successfully recognize and overcome the difficulties that learners will encounter when confronted with the phonological and grammatical structures of standard (school) English (e.g., Labov 1966d, 1968b, Wulfram 1969, Baratz and Shuy 1969). Nevertheless much (if not all) of what is currently offered to teachers in this connection is merely "sociolinguistically oriented" (in that it recognizes that minority group members often utilize varieties of English unfamiliar to others) rather than sociology of language proper (Fishman 1969b, Fishman and Lueders, in press). "Sociolinguistically oriented" advice is now also being directed toward teachers of bilinguals (Anderson 1969, Boyd 1968, Gaarder 1965). Such teachers are admonished that learners should be encouraged to maintain or acquire repertoires (incorporating several varieties) in each of their languages, rather than to displace all nonstandard varieties in favor of one artificial standard version of each. Teachers of bilinguals are being urged to enable their students to select from each repertoire in accord with the norms for communicative appropirateness of the particular networks with which they (the pupils) seek mutually accepting interaction (Fishman and Lovas 1970, Mackey 1970). Nevertheless, the teachers of bilinguals (particularly in countries of mass immigration) have just begun to be shown how to influence the bilingual settings in which they and their students live and in which one or another of their languages may be roundly ignored, if not attacked, as soon as school is over (Andersson and Boyer 1970, John and Horner 1971).

Of course, the distance is still considerable between "sociolinguistically oriented" advice or sensitivity training for teachers and any more complete interrelationship between teaching methodology and sociology of language. Thus the education of bilinguals is still viewed primarily within the context of disadvantaged and dislocated minorities (whose lot in life will be far easier if only they learn English, French, Russian, etc.) rather than within the broader context of world-wide experience with bilingual education—whether in conjunction with elitist bilingualism, traditional bilingualism, or more generally, widespread and stable (i.e., nondislocated) bilingualism. As a result, the education of speakers of nonstandard English is being pondered without awareness, for example, of the fact that most students entering German, French, Italian, and other schools during the past century have also been speakers of nonstandard varieties of their respective languages. A true meeting of education and the sociology of language will enable *both* to discover why proportionally so many dialect speakers *do* and *did* seem to become readers and speakers of the standard language (and even of classical languages) in other parts of the world whereas so few seem to accomplish this in the United States today (Fishman and Lueders, in press). As with many other social science fields, a severe test of the power of the sociology of language will be its ability to be useful in the world of affairs. The education of nonliterates, of bilinguals, and of nonstandard speakers are all fields about which the sociology of language must have more to say if it is really a discipline worth listening to at all.

SECTION X

LINGUISTICS:
THE SCIENCE OF CODE DESCRIPTION...
AND MORE

(Addendum for Non-linguists)

If one part of sociolinguistics comprises the "study of the characteristics of language varieties" then we must turn to that science that has specialized in the systematic description of language: linguistics. To attempt to describe and analyze language data, in this day and age, without a knowledge of linguistic concepts and methods is to be as primitive as to try to describe and analyze human behavior more generally (or the functions of language varieties and the characteristics of their speakers) without knowledge of psychological and sociological concepts and methods.

It is no more possible to provide an adequate introduction to linguistics "in one easy lesson" than to provide one for sociology or psychology. Nevertheless, it may be possible to briefly sketch some of the major concerns and methods of linguistics that bear upon sociolinguistics. The purpose of the next few pages, therefore, is to bring about "linguistics appreciation," and of a very selective sort at that, rather than to present a full-fledged introduction to a very technical and complicated science which intersects the humanities, the social sciences, and the natural sciences in its various subdivisions. The specialist knows full well that "music appreciation" is not the same as music mastery. Similarly, "linguistics appreciation" is not the same as linguistics mastery. Nevertheless, it is a beginning.

As a formal discipline, particularly in so far as the American academic scene is concerned, linguistics is a very recent field of specialization. The Linguistic Society of America was founded only in 1924. (The oldest linguistic society in the world, that of Paris, was founded in 1864.) Even today, when the number of linguists and linguistics programs in American universities is greater than ever before, there are only some two score graduate linguistics departments in the United States. Nevertheless, this discipline has not only come to be of prime interest to a growing band of dedicated scholars and practitioners within linguistics per se, but it has also in very recent years forcefully come to the attention of all other disciplines that recognize the centrality of verbal interaction in human affairs. Interdisciplinary contacts between linguistics and anthropology have been well established since the very appearance of linguistics in American universities. The anthropological linguist is a well recognized and highly regarded specialist among linguists and anthropologists alike. Indeed, linguistics is recognized as a "branch" of anthropology in many textbooks and training programs. Of more recent vintage is psycholinguistics. Most recent of all is sociolinguistics, an interdisciplinary field which is just now beginning to train specialists that can bridge linguistics and sociology-social psychology in such a manner as to expand the horizons of both.

10.1 DESCRIPTIVE LINGUISTICS

The basic field in which most (if not all) linguists have been trained is that which is known as descriptive or synchronic linguistics. As its names imply, this field focuses upon the systematic description of a given language in a given time and place. It is not historical; it is not comparative; it is not prescriptive. Its emphasis is definitely on *spoken language,* the assumption being that written language is both derivative and different from natural language or speech.

It is common for the uninitiated to think of a language as being well represented by an unabridged dictionary. This view implies that the way to describe a language is to consider its components to be words. Any careful or consistent and exhaustive presentation and definition of the words of a language (which may be exactly what dictionaries attempt to do) would, therefore, from this point of view, be considered a description of that language. For most linguists, however, there are two other kinds of systematic presentations which are considered even more basic to their goal of describing language: the sound system of a language and the grammatical system of that language.

The branch of linguistics that is concerned with the systematic description of the sounds (phones) of a language is *phonology*. Some of the more general subspecialties within phonology are articulatory phonetics (how tongue, lips, teeth, vocal chords, velum, nasal passage, and other speech organs produce the sounds of language) and acoustic phonetics (the physical properties of the sound waves or signals emitted by the speaker). Linguists have devised for purposes of phonetic notation the International Phonetic Alphabet, which is roughly adequate for the transcription of speech in all languages, although minor adjustments or additions to it are required in most individual cases.

On the foundation of these more general branches of phonology linguistics has been able to establish the study of *phonemics*, i.e., the study of those sounds that enter into meaningful contrasts or combinations in a given language, as compared to all of the physically differentiable sounds of a language (which are of interest in *phonetics*). A skilled phonetician differentiates far more fine shades of language sounds than do the native speakers of any particular language. Phonetic analysis is now sufficiently refined to demonstrate that no two speakers of a given language pronounce their words in exactly the same way. Indeed, the degree of refinement available to phonetic analysis has gone so far that it is possible to show that even an idiolect (the way of speaking that characterizes an individual) is not entirely consistent. The same individual does not pronounce the same word in the same way on all occasions of the same type. Into this endless series of successively refined analysis of language sound differences *phonemics* seeks to introduce the parsimony that derives from a knowledge of those sound differences that are meaningfully distinctive (i.e., that serve to distinguish between linguistic signs and their meanings) for the native speakers of a particular language. The following brief example may illustrate the phonemic approach to demonstrable phonetic differences.

Let us consider the "b" sound in English, Arabic, and Bengali. That each of these languages has some sound that the American man in the street would unhesitatingly represent by the letter *b* is, for linguistics, a nonstructural comment, and therefore one of no particular interest. It *is* of interest, however, to point out that in English *aba* and *apa* are differentiated, the voiced bilabial stop ("b") in the first being considered clearly different from the unvoiced bilabial stop ("p") in the second because the difference between *b* and *p* is crucial to recognizing the difference in meaning between "bit" and "pit," "bet" and "pet," and hundreds of other meaningful contrasts. In Arabic, on the other hand, no such meaningful substitutions of *b* and *p* are made. The native speaker of Arabic says only *aba* and uses a *p* sound only under special conditions, such as before *s* or *t*. More generally put, whatever sound differences exist in the *p-b* range in Arabic are not distinctive, i.e., they do not regularly signal meaning differences.

Thus, it is not enough to say that both English and Arabic have a *b* sound, for the sound functions far differently in the two languages. In English *b* and *p* function as phonemically different sounds (and, therefore, are notated /p/ and /b/); in Arabic they do not.

The absence or presence of a meaningful contrast between *b* and *p* takes on even greater linguistic significance if Bengali is examined. Not only are /b/ and /p/ differentiated by the ordinary native speaker of Bengali, but in addition, an *unaspirated p* (as in the English *spin*) is differentiated from an *aspirated p* (as in the English *pin*). Similarly, an *unaspirated b* is regularly differentiated from an *aspirated b*.

Note, that while English recognizes a phonemic (meaning-related) difference between two sounds (one voiced and one unvoiced) that represent only a meaningless difference in Arabic, Bengali recognizes a further phonemic difference between two pairs of sounds (each with an aspirated and an unaspirated component) that represent only meaningless phonetic differences in English. Furthermore, as the English and Bengali languages change over time, changes in their "b" sounds will presumably be correlated with changes in their "p" sounds, precisely because these sounds are systematically related to each other.

It is in this last respect—i.e., in terms of systematic inter-relationships—that descriptive linguistics is interested in the sounds of a language. This is also why descriptive linguistics is sometimes referred to as structural linguistics. It is not merely the sounds of a language that are of interest to linguistics, nor even the meaningfully different sounds, but above all, the systematic links that exist between the meaningfully different sounds of a language. The phonemes of a language, like all other features of a language at a given point in time, are part of a system (a "structure") that operates as a whole. Changes in one part of the structure affect the other parts; indeed, in true Gestalt fashion, any phonemic part can be truly appreciated only in terms of the phonological whole. A famous linguist of the first part of this century was the first to emphasize that language is a system in which every part has its (interlinked) place ("un systeme ou tout se tient"; de Saussure 1916) and this structural dictum has since then come to characterize not only descriptive linguistics but other branches of linguistics as well.

So basic is descriptive linguistics to linguistic science as a whole that another example of its concerns, this time at the level of grammatical analysis, is in order. Such an example is particularly desirable because the grammatical structure of language is completely interwoven with its sound structure, so much so that some linguists claim that phonological analysis depends on and must be part of an exhaustive grammatical analysis (although most linguists consider phonology, grammar, lexicon, and semantics as quite separate *levels* of analysis).

Just as there is a minimal unit of meaningful sound (actually, of substitutionally meaningful sound, since the sounds in question are not meaningful per se), the phoneme, so is there a minimal unit of meaningful grammatical (i.e., of ordered or environmental) form, the *morpheme*. As a result, one branch of grammatical study is known as *morphology*. It studies the ordered relationships between small meaningful segments such as occur within words. (Syntax, on the other hand, studies the ordered relationships between units such as words in a phrase or utterance.) Thus, many English verbs form the past tense by adding a morpheme, which may be represented as {d}, to the present tense of the verb: I open—I opened. {d} means past tense in English. Similarly, many English nouns form their plural by adding a morpheme, which may be represented as {z}, to their singular: car—cars. In both of these instances, however, the morphemes in question occur in several different forms that also differ somewhat as to their sound. Functionally equivalent alternatives of the same morpheme are referred to as *allomorphs*, precisely because there is no functional difference between them, however much they may differ in sound, just as sounds that revealed no functional difference were referred to earlier as *allophones*. The allomorphs of {d} for the common, productive English verbs may sound like a *d* (as in opened), like a *t* (as in laughed), or like *ed* (as in mended). However, these allomorphs are not used at random. How would linguistics provide a rule to indicate when the native speaker of English employs which? What would such a rule be like?

To begin with, linguists would list as many verbs as possible that utilize each variant of the {d} morpheme. Such a list might initially look like that shown in Table 1. After inspecting the array of final sounds in each of the columns of that table a linguist is able to do that which no ordinary native speaker of English can do: formulate a very few rules which summarize the systematic variation in the three allomorphs of {d}. Such rules might proceed as follows:

TABLE 22. Allomorphs of {d} in the past tense of some common, productive English verbs

ed	t	d
mend	bank	open
lift	cook	use
boot	drop	save
raid	help	bomb
kid	walk	mail
tend	laugh	try
sift	shop	play
hoot	stamp	radio
shade	rank	hinge
hand	staff	rig

1. If the verb stem ends in /t/ or /d/ the past tense ends in *ed*, (with the exception of a small number of verbs that retain the same form in past and present: cut, hit, put),

2. If the verb stem ends in a voiceless stop (other than /t/) or in a voiceless spirant, the past tense ends in *t*,

3. Otherwise, the past tense ends in *d*.

The above three brief rules pertain to the phonological conditioning of allomorphs. The allomorphs of [d] are realized according to their phonological environment. Thus, variations in grammatical form and variations in phonological form may and frequently do coincide. In general, linguistics has traditionally pursued two kinds of structured variation: variation relatable to change in meaning (such as the substitutional meaning that underlies phonemic analysis) and variation relatable to change in environment (such as the positional meaning that underlies morphemic analysis). Further synchronic variation in language, i.e., variation that cannot be identified either with change in meaning (i.e., change in referent) or with change in linguistic environment, when geographic area is held constant, has traditionally been thought of as "free variation," i.e., as variation (not to say "irregularity") due to factors outside of *langue* (the latent structure underlying speech) and therefore outside of the descriptive rules pertaining to *langue*. It is in some of the kinds of free variation—in variations which may co-occur with differences in a speaker's alertness or emotional state, with differences in topic, role relationship, communicational setting, or interpersonal purpose—that sociolinguistics (and other interdisciplinary studies of language usage) attempts to discover additional regularity.

Linguistics has long been aware that "free variation" might have a structure of its own. However, *that* structure (when and if it obtains) has usually been considered as being part of the structure of the speech event rather than part of the structure of the speech code per se. Although descriptive linguistics has emphasized the spoken language, the *speech act* itself was long considered to be outside of the domain of linguistics, for the speech act, just like the message content of speech, was considered to be part of "communication" (long considered by linguists to be an outer or surface phenomenon) rather than part and parcel of *langue* per se (the heart of the matter). Many famous linguists have warned against confusing the two.

Thus, if it appeared that certain phonemic, morphological, syntactic, or lexical regularities were not *always* as regular as one would hope (time and place remaining constant) this was attributed to the irregularity of *parole* (speaking, behavioral realization) as distinct from the systematic and abstract purity of *langue* (language, underlying structure) with which linguists should really be concerned. *Parole* is subject to many factors that produce variation (among those not previously mentioned: fatigue, anger, limitation in memory span, interruptions, etc.). These are all factors of "degree," of "more or less," of "sometimes." It was thought that the goal of linguistics was to cut through these psychological and sociological sources of "static" and to concern itself with matters that were clear-cut enough to be viewed as all or none phenomena: the basic code which, at any given time and place, might be considered to be one and the same for all who employed it. Thus, not only were linguists warned to distinguish sharply between *parole* and *langue* (de Saussure 1916), but they were also admonished to keep their distance from psychological or sociological data and theories which were viewed as inherently more concerned with the highly variable and seemingly irregular processes of verbal interaction and communication (and therefore with the messy data of *parole*) than with the pure code underlying these processes (Bloomfield 1933). It is only in more recent days, when the traditionally rigid distinction between *langue* and *parole* has come to be re-examined and when the varying interaction between them has come to be pursued that larger groups of linguists and of social scientists have found things to say to each other.

10.2 OTHER BRANCHES OF LINGUISTICS

Other branches of linguistics—some of them older than descriptive linguistics (even though the latter has come to be so central to all linguistic pursuits)—have long been on friendlier terms with the social sciences. *Historical* (diachronic) *linguistics,* for example, in studying the changes that occur in a given code over time (sound changes, grammatical changes, and word changes) has of necessity been interested in human migrations, intergroup contacts (conquest, trade), and any other diversification within a speech community that leads some of its members to interact with each other differentially (rather than equally or randomly), or that leads some of its members to interact with outsiders much more than do the rest. Historical linguistics (also known as *comparative linguistics*) focuses on tracing how one, earlier, parent ("proto") code subsequently divided into several related but separate ("sister" or "daughter") codes, or alternatively, how several codes were derived from one pre-existing code. Although time is the crucial dimension in the development of *families of languages* between which *genetic relationships* can be shown to exist, as it is in the reconstruction of all common ancestries, nevertheless historical linguists realize full well that the language changes that occurred were due to differential interaction and contact processes that occurred as time passed, rather than to the mere passing of time per se. As a result, historical linguistics has interacted fruitfully with history, archeology, and anthropology, and with other disciplines that can provide information concerning coterritorial influences between populations. In recent years, the fluctuating interaction between *langue* and *parole* (e.g., how one of the alternative systems of speaking available to a speech community spreads through the entire speech community, and increasingly displacing other alternatives, becomes an unvarying part of its basic code) has been studied by linguists working with social science concepts and methods of data collection and data analysis on what would once have been considered a "purely" comparative problem (Labov 1963; Haugen 1961). The ties between comparative linguistics and the social sciences become stronger as the *dynamics* of language change come under increasing linguistic scrutiny, as distinct from the static, step-wise contrasts between the written records of one century and those of another that formerly dominated this field of study.

Another branch of linguistics that has frequently maintained close ties to the social sciences is *dialectology* (also known as *linguistic* or *dialect geography*). In comparison to historical linguistics this branch is concerned with variation in language on some dimension *other than time*. The achronic dimension with which dialectologists have most commonly been concerned has been geographic space or distance. Languages that are employed over considerable expanses are often spoken somewhat differently (or even quite differently) in different parts of their speech areas. These differences may be phonological, such as President Kennedy's "Cuber" (for Cuba) and "vigah" (for vigor), where a Philadelphian would have said "Cubah" and "vigor" while many a Southerner would have said "Cubah" and "vigah." Dialect differences may also apply to the lexicon (milk shake vs. frappe; soda vs. pop) and even to parts of the grammatical system. Dialectologists have traditionally prepared *linguistic atlases* to show the geographic distribution of the linguistic features that have been of interest to them. Such atlases consist of maps on which are indicated the geographical limits within which certain usages are current. These limits are known as isoglosses (Weinreich, U. 1962; Herzog 1965).

However, dialectologists are well aware that the variations that are of interest to them are not due to geographical distance per se, but rather to the interactional consequences of geographic and other kinds of "distance." Phonological, lexical, and grammatical uniformity may obtain over large geographic expanses when settlement is simultaneous and when verbal interaction as well as common identification are frequent. On the other hand, major language differences (sometimes referred to as "social dialects" or "sociolects") may arise and be maintained within relatively tiny geographic areas (e.g., in many cities) where the above conditions do not obtain. Considerations such as these have led many dialectologists, particularly those who have been interested in urban language situations, to be concerned with educational, occupational, religious, ethnic, and other social groups and societal processes (although all or most of these groups may, in part, be traceable to originally diverse geographic origins) rather than with geographic distance per se. As a result, the ties between dialectologists and social scientists (not to mention sociolinguists) have been many and strong, particularly in recent years (Blanc 1964; Ferguson and Gumperz 1960), when the entire speech act—rather than merely the code rules abstracted from the speech act—has come to be of interest to an increasing number of dialectologists (Hymes 1962).

Of late, many linguists have taken to examining the structure of language—rather than the structure of particular languages—and to doing so in order to discover the nature of those fundamental human capacities which make for the competence of native speakers. Native speakers possess a rare gift which they themselves usually overlook: the ability to generate sentences that are recognized as structurally acceptable in their speech communities, and what is more, to generate only such sentences. Many linguists now believe that a linguistic theory that can specify an adequate grammar (i.e., the rules that native speakers implicitly grasp and that constitute their native speaker competence) will also specify the language acquiring and language using nature of man. These linguists say that only an adequate theory of human capacity to acquire and use language will yield an adequate theory of what language itself is (Chomsky 1957, 1965).

Sociolinguistics may ultimately serve similarly basic purposes in the on-going quest of the social sciences to understand communicative competence as a fundamental aspect of the social nature of man. The sociolinguistic theory that can specify adequate communicative competence (i.e., the rules that native members of speech communities implicitly grasp and that constitute their native member sociolinguistic behavior) will also specify the nature of social man as an acquirer and utilizer of a repertoire of verbal and behavioral skills. Man does not acquire or use his communicative competence in a single-code or single-norm community. Indeed, pervasively homogeneous communities with respect to communicative and other social behaviors do not exist except in the simplified worlds of some theorists and experimenters. Ultimately, sociolinguistics hopes to go beyond comfortably simple theory concerning the nature of communicative competence in the conviction that only an adequate theory of human capacity to acquire and to use a repertoire of interlocking language varieties and their related behaviors will yield an adequate theory of what communicative competence in social man really is.

Just as there are branches of linguistics that seek to study *langue* and *langue* alone (indeed, to study language at its "deepest," most abstract, and, therefore, at its socially most uninvolved), so are there branches of linguistics that have departed from a strict separation between *langue* and *parole* (since *parole* too has its very definite structure, since *parole* constantly influences *langue,* and since the individual's meaningful differentiation must be referred to, even though these are outside of *langue* per se, in order to establish a description of phonemic and other distinctions). Similarly, some branches of social psychology (and other social sciences as well) have moved closer to linguistics. Many sociologists and social psychologists now realize (whereas few did so a decade ago) that the norms that apply to and that may be thought of as generating human verbal interaction pertain not only to the communicative *content* and *context* of that interaction, but to its linguistic *form* as well. As linguistics is developing outward—in the hopes of some: to become an all-encompassing science of language behavior—sociology and social psychology are developing toward increasing technical competence in connection with language description and analysis. The sociology of language is one of the by-products of these two complementary developments and, as such, it must refer not only to the work of linguists, but must attend as well to those topics that are essentially sociological and social psychological and to which few linguists have, as yet, paid much attention.

ADDENDUM FOR LINGUISTS

Sociolinguistic Reflections on Chomskian Linguistics

It is a curious fact that the past decade has marked both the major impact of Chomsky and the more minor impact of sociology of languages (SOL) on the language sciences without these two very different forces or directions having been brought into overt confrontation with each other. It would be even more curious if the latter and quieter force were ultimately to turn out to be the more continuing.

Differences in focus

The two schools of thought have focused on different problems, and, as a result, have differed methodologically and philosophically. Whereas generative-transformational linguistics (GTL) has focused upon the similarities between the deep structure characteristics of all human language and upon the underlying linguistic competence of all human speakers, SOL has focused upon the differences between surface characteristics of particular varieties in the repertoires of particular speech networks or speech communities. Whereas GTL has focused upon syntactic structure devoid of communicational intent, SOL has focused upon communicative appropriativeness relative to deversified social functions. GTL has stressed innate communalities, SOL has stressed socialized differences. Both, of course, have sought *laws* or *regularities*, but they have been attracted to far different aspects of language. If GTL had deigned to look at SOL during the past decade (or decade and a half since the appearance of *Syntactic Structures* in 1957) it would have subjected it to many of the same criticisms heaped upon structural linguistics (classificatory, performance oriented, surface oriented, discovery oriented, etc.). However, there are a number of similarities between the two that should also be pointed out.

Everyday language—everyday life

Chomsky and Chomkyites have repeatedly pointed to the ambiguities which are so characteristic of real language and to the fact that these have largely been overlooked by structural linguistics. The anomalies that others have ignored or even ruled out of court as being of no consequence have become in their hands the crucial building blocks of basic theoretical advances and orientational redirections. GT linguists constantly provide examples and arguments that cannot derive from working with an informant and that must derive from a sensitivity to the ways people naturally talk, to the seeming irregularity of much talk, to the constant innovativeness of live-talk. While GTL does not collect ethnographic or interview data on how people talk, it does show an intuitive grasp for the complexity of such talk as well as for the listener's versatility in handling that complexity. SOL too, particularly in the work of its more ethnomethodological and microsociolinguistic devotees, has been oriented toward real talk and to its seemingly endless variability. Obviously the two schools have had quite different reactions to what they have noticed. The one has sought to go below or beyond real talk to the regularities in language structure and in human cognitive structure that must underlie all the observed irregularity of everyday talk. The other has focused on and systematically gathered the data of real talk itself and has demonstrated that its supposed "free variation" is highly patterned, both internally (in terms of linguistic co-occurrences that made up varieties) and externally (in terms of situational/functional and linguistic co-occurrences).

Chomsky has often been compared to Freud in the sense of revolutionary impact and redirection of attention. There is indeed a similarity, even in connection with attention to little noticed "everyday" data. However, Freud's *Psychopathology of Everyday Life* was not merely syntactic (that is, relational and derivational with respect to structures) but it was also dynamic (that is, purposive, motivational, intentional, interactional, or, ultimately, functional). In this sense SOL has been much more Freudian than Chomskian in its handling of everyday data.

Whorfianism

Both GTL and SOL have been profoundly non-Whorfian (or even anti-Whorfian), explicitly or by implication. Chomsky's stress that syntax is devoid of communicational purpose or consequence and that communicational purpose is independent of syntactic consequences is certainly as far away from Whorf's relativistic linguistic determinism re cognitive processes as one can get. Whorf was looking for intercultural differences in cognitive views, styles or processes. Chomsky's entire quest is for the fundamental, universal or cross-cultural similarities in *faculté de langage*. Obviously their views on the impact of syntax on cognition or on the relevance of the one for understanding the other must differ.

SOL, too, is non-Whorfian, at least to the extent that Whorf operated in terms of one speaker = one language = one cognitive pattern. Given its stress on language repertoires and on role repertoires, SOL is particularly sensitive to the fact that members of speech communities or networks may well utilize structurally quite different varieties for quite different cognitive (and non-cognitive) purposes. In some situations these varieties may be kept quite distinct (compartmentalized) from each other and in others they may be quite interactive with each other. Fundamentally, therefore, the notion of language in society must posit the ongoingness of bi-directional influences, of language characteristics influencing behavioral process and of behavioral processes influencing language characteristics. Thus, if SOL does not directly contradict Whorf, it does considerably expand and loosen up the directionality hypothesis with which Whorf is most generally associated.

Generative semantics and SOL

The coming of generative semantics (GS) and speech act theory augurs for a brand of GT linguistics in the future that will, of necessity, be more attentive to SOL. Their interests in the interaction between form and function, in structure and use, in the competence to perform, in the intention to communicate, all are quite clearly in harmony with (and indeed, part and parcel of) basic sociolinguistic principles.

Thus, if there will remain a set of fundamental differences between GS and SOL these will probably depend largely on the extent to which the former stresses *innateness* and the latter *socialization* with respect to the acquisition of situational functionalism or intentiveness. To the extent that GS must always be somewhat closer to psychology it must always give proportionately greater attention to the pan-human and unvarying characteristics of language use. SOL will probably always be more oriented toward socialization processes and societal differences. It is, of course, necessary to appreciate and to master both areas of concern. I personally doubt that one is more correct than the other or that, without specifying the exact problem to be answered, that one is basically more useful than the other. As long as both are *data* oriented, the proof of the pudding will be in the eating.

Innateness and heritability

It is striking to note the GT penchant for innateness as an explanatory vehicle or goal at a time when the other social sciences are moving away from it even as a useful hypothetical construct, let alone as a useful explanatory principle. The nature-nurture, heredity-environment, genotype-phynotype discussions of the 30's have been revived as a result of Jensen's and Shockley's interpretations. Given reanalyses and reinterpretations, the distinctions between the polar extremes have generally lessened. Heritability is no longer viewed as only that component in behavior which is entirely independent of treatment; rather, it is viewed as also applying to behavior which is a consequence of reactions to inherited characteristics. The black child's responses to his teacher's reactions-to-his-blackness are viewed as heritable behavior. Thus, there is no hereditary behavior devoid of social environment and no social environment that does not impinge upon (limit, channel) innate mechanisms. To stress innateness per se or alone as an explanatory principle is to make the explanation of human social behavior (and, therefore, of communicative behavior) impossible. Perhaps GS will be able to see this more clearly than did GTL.

The power of weakness

Very much like most intellectual revolutions GTL did not so much succeed in solving all problems related to its discipline as in directing mass attention away from some problems and toward others. SOL as a much quieter, less powerful and less iconoclastic "new departure" has probably been less dislocative with respect to either of its parental disciplines. In a sense, it has served to supplement other interests and approaches rather than to displace them. If, now, GS and SOL too can supplement each other it may be that the broader behavioral perspective and larger scale of analysis that some practitioners of the latter have to offer will receive a bit more attention. I cannot believe that the study of language in society will remain content with explicating conversations, let alone sentences. I cannot believe that it will long continue to view larger scale language behaviors as "merely community problems" that are of no theoretical importance to the language sciences regardless of what their pragmatic centrality may be. Having spent so many years really listening to how people talk and, now beginning more and more to listen to what people talk about and noting why, it cannot be too long before most students of SOL realize that there are more to languages than sentences and that not only sentences have intensions but societies do as well. The recognition of a more inclusive SOL is coming and when it arrives the language sciences will move on to an awareness of language in society as it really is, i.e. on beyond the sentence. Perhaps this will happen so naturally and effortlessly that no revolution and no hero will be associated with it, for there is no holding back an idea when its time has come. Perhaps that is what Chomsky means by innateness.

The Sociolinguistic Revolution

If GTL has forever changed our view of language-in-general or language-at-its-most-fundamental, in the direction of focusing upon the *underlying cognitive structures* that generate any and all languages, then SOL has added an equally basic dimension to our understanding of language and language behavior, namely *societal function*. These two, cognitive structure and societal function, are complementary rather than contradictory, in that they both point to factors outside of the code per se which tend to mold it in particular ways.

The dimension of societal function ultimately leads students of language and language behavior to abandon two simplistic concepts: that of *"The X language"* (in favor of the construct *"repertoire of societally allocated varieties of X"*) and that of man as merely *"implementer of language as it is"* (in favor of "societal networks that can be every bit as consciously at work on changing their language varieties and their societal allocations as any other aspect of their social environment"). It is difficult for me to believe that two such fundamental insights cannot help linguistics better understand language structure and language change.

While the deep-structure of language-in-general may well depend on pan-human cognitive structures about which social man can do very little, the societal functions and markers of language varieties depend on the active (indeed, on the oft times contentious) processes of norm definition and redefinition about which modern societies can do and are doing much more than was heretofore dreamt to be possible. Thus, SOL helps us understand man and society as active and purpose entities, not only vis-à-vis the functions of language varieties but also vis-à-vis their structured characteristics. This may well be a more basic contribution of SOL than its broadening impact on linguistics per se.

REFERENCES

Alisjahbana, S. Takdir. "The Modernization of the Indonesian Language in Practice," in his *Indonesian Language and Literature: Two Essays:* Yale University, Southeast Asia Studies, 1962, New Haven, Conn., 1-22.

———. "New National Languages: A Problem Modern Linguistics Has Failed to Solve," *Lingua,* XV (1965), 515-530.

———. "Some Planning Processes in the Development of the Indonesian/Malay Language," *Consultative Meeting on Language Planning Processes.* Honolulu, IAP, 1969; subsequently in Joan Rubin and Bjorn Jernudd (eds.), *Can Language be Planned?* East-West Center Press, Honolulu, 1971.

——— (ed.), *The Modernization of the Languages of Asia,* University of Malaysia Press, Kuala Lumpur, 1971.

Andersson, Theodore. "Bilingual Schooling: Oasis or Mirage?" *Hispania,* LII (1969) 69-74

———, and Mildred Boyer (eds.), *Bilingual Schooling in the United States.* 2 vols., USGPO, Washington, D.C., 1970.

Andreev, N. D., and L. R. Zinder. "Osnovnye problemy prikladnoj lingvistiki," *Voprosy Jazykoznaiya,* IV (1959), 1-9.

Anon. *Practical Orthography of African Languages.* International Institute of African Languages and Cultures, Memorandum 1. Oxford University Press, London, 1930, revised edition.

———. *The Use of Vernacular Languages in Education.* UNESCO, Paris 1953.

———. *A Common Script for Indian Languages.* Ministry of Scientific Research and Cultural Affairs, Delhi, 1963.

———. *The Restoration of the Irish Language.* The Stationery Office, Dublin, 1965. Also note *Progress Report for the Period Ended 31 March, 1966* and *Progress Report for the Period Ended 31 March, 1968.* The Stationery Office, Dublin, 1966 and 1968.

———. *A Motivational Research Study for the Greater Use of the Irish Language,* 2 vols., Ernest Dichter International Institute for Motivational Research. Croton-on-Hudson (N.Y.), 1968.

Armstrong, Robert. "Language Policies and Language Practices in West Africa," in J. A. Fishman, C. A. Ferguson, and J. Das Gupta (eds.), *Language Problems of Developing Nations.* Wiley, New York, 1968, 227-236.

Bacon, Elizabeth E. "Russian Influence on Central Asian Languages," in her *Central Asians under Russians Rule.* Cornell University Press, Ithica, N.Y., 1966.

Baratz, Joan, and Roger W. Shuy. *Teaching Black Children to Read.* Center for Applied Linguistics, Washington, D.C., 1969.

Barker, George C., "Social Functions of Language in a Mexican-American Community," *Acta Americana*, V (1947), 185-202.

Basso, Keith H. Semantic Aspects of Linguistic Acculturation. *American Anthropologist,* LXIX (1967), 471-477.

Bell, Daniel. *The End of Ideology.* New York, Collier, 1961.

Bernstein, Basil. Elaborated and Restricted Codes: Their Social Origins and Some Consequences. *American Anthropologist*, LXIV, vi, 2 (1964), 55-69.

———. "Elaborated and Restricted Codes: An Outline," *Sociological Inquiry*, XXXVI (1966), 254-261.

Berry, Jack. "The Making of Alphabets," *Proceedings of the International Congress of Linguistics.* Oslo University Press, Oslo, 1958, 752-764; also reprinted in J. A.

Fishman (ed.), *Readings in the Sociology of Language.* Mouton, The Hague, 1968, pp. 737-753.

Blanc, Chaim. *Communal Dialects in Baghdad.* Harvard, Cambridge, Mass., 1964.

Blom, Jan Peter, and John J. Gumperz. "Some Social Determinants of Verbal Behavior," in John J. Gumperz and Dell Hymes (eds.), *The Ethnography of Communication: Directions in Sociolinguistics.* Holt, New York, in press.

Bloomfield, Leonard. *Language.* Holt, New York, 1933.

Bock, Philip K. "Social Structure and Language Structure," *Southwestern Journal of Anthropology,* XX (1964), 393-403; also in J. A. Fishman (ed.), *Readings in the Sociology of Language.* Mouton, The Hague, 1968, 212-222.

Bolinger, D. L. "Visual Morphemes," *Language,* XX (1946), 333-340.

Bonjean, Charles M. "Mass, Class and the Industrial Community: A Comparative Analysis of Managers, Businessmen and Workers," *American Journal of Sociology,* LXXII (1966), 149-162.

Bottenberg, R. A., and K. H. Ward, Jr. *Applied Multiple Linear Regression.* Lackland AF Base PRL-TDR-63-6, Lackland, Texas, 1963.

Boulding, Kenneth. "The Death of the City: A Frightened Look at Post-Civilization," in Oscar Handlin and John Burchard (eds.), *The Historian and the City.* M.I.T. and Harvard, Cambridge, Mass., 1963, p.145.

Bowers, John. "Language Problems and Literacy," in J. A. Fishman, C. A. Ferguson, and J. Das Gupta (eds.), *Language Problems of Developing Nations,* Wiley, New York, 1968, pp. 381-401.

Boyd, Dorothy L. "Bilingualism as an Educational Objective," *The Educational Forum,* XXXII (1968), 309-313.

Bradley, Henry. "On the Relation between Spoken and Written Language," *Proceedings of the British Academy,* VI (1913/14), 212-232.

Bright, William. "Animals of Acculturation in the California Indian Languages," *University of California Publications in Linguistics,* IV, iv (1960), 215-246.

Broom, Leonard, and Norval D. Glenn. "Negro-White Differences in Reported Attitudes and Behavior," *Sociology and Social Research*, L (1966), 187-200.

Brosnahan, L. F. "Some Historical Cases of Language Imposition," in Robert Spencer (ed.), *Language in Africa*. Cambridge, London, 1963a, 7-24.

–––. "Some Aspects of the Linguistic Situation in Tropical Africa," *Lingua*, XII (1963b), 54-65.

Brown, Roger W., and Albert Gilman. "The Pronouns of Power and Solidarity," in Thomas A. Sebeok (ed.), *Style in Language*. M.I.T., Cambridge, Mass., and Wiley, New York, 1960, pp. 253-276; also in J. A. Fishman (ed.), *Readings in the Sociology of Language*. Mouton, The Hague, 1968, pp. 252-275.

–––, and Eric H. Lenneberg. "A Study in Language and Cognition," *Journal of Abnormal and Social Psychology*, XLIX (1954), 454-462.

Burns, Donald. "Social and Political Implications in the Choice of an Orthography," *Fundamental and Adult Education*, V,ii (1953), 80-85.

–––. "Bilingual Education in the Andes of Peru," in J. A. Fishman, C. A. Ferguson, and J. Das Gupta (eds.), *Language Problems of the Developing Nations*. Wiley, New York, 1968, pp. 403-414.

Carmichael, L., H. P. Hogan, and A. A. Walter. "An Experimental Study of the Effect of Language on the Perception of Visually Perceived Form," *Journal of Experimental Psychology*, XV (1932), 73-86.

Carroll, John B., and J.B. Casagrande. "The Function of Language Classifications in Behavior," in E. Maccoby, T. Newcomb and E. Hartley. (eds.), *Readings in Social Psychology,* Holt, New York; 1958, pp. 18-31.

Catford, J. C. *A Linguistic Theory of Translation*. Oxford University Press, London, 1965.

Chinese Written Language Reform Committee. "Several Points concerning the Han Language Phoneticization Plan (Draft) Explained," *Current Background*, no. 380 (March 15, 1956), 4-13.

Chomsky, Noam. *Syntactic Structures*. Mouton, The Hague, 1957.

Chou En-lai. "Current Tasks of Reforming the Written Language," in *Reform of the Chinese Written Language*. Foreign Language Press, Peking, 1965, 7-29.

Cohen, Jack. "Some Statistical Issues in Psychological Research," in B. B. Wolmand (ed.), *Handbook of Clinical Psychology*. McGraw-Hill, New York, 1965, pp. 95-121.

———. "Prognostic Factors in Functional Psychosis: A Study in Multivariate Methodology." Invited address at the New York Academy of Sciences, March 18, 1968a, mimeographed.

———. "Multiple Regression as a General Data-Analytic System," *Psychological Bulletin*,LXX (1968b), 426-443.

Conklin, Harold C. "Lexicographic Treatment of Folk Taxonomies," in Fred W. Householder and Sol Saporta (eds.), *Problems in Lexicography*, Indiana University Research Center in Anthropology, Folklore and Linguistics, Publication 21, Bloomington, 1962, 119-141.

Cook, S.F. "The conflict between the California Indian and White Civilization," *Ibero-Americana*, XXI (1943), 1-194; XXII (1943), 1-55;XXIII (1943), 1-115; XXIIV (1943), 1-29.

Corpas, Jorge Pineros. "Inconvenientes de la enseñanza bilingüe a la luz de la fisiología cerebral," *Noticias Culturales*, no. 99, Bogotá, 1969, 1-4.

Correa, Hector, and Jan Tinbergen. "Quantitative Adaptation of Education to Accelerated Growth," *Kyklos*, XIV (1962), 776-785.

Dalby, David. "A Survey of the Indigenous Scripts of Liberia and Sierre Leone: Vai, Mende, Loma, Kpelle and Bassa," *African Languages Studies*, VIII (1967), 1-51.

———. "The Indigenous Scripts of West Africa and Surinam: Their Inspiration and Design," *African Languages Studies*, IX (1968), 156-197.

Das Gupta, Jyotirindra. "Religious Loyalty, Language Conflict and Political Mobilization," *Consultative Meeting on Language Planning Processes*. EWC-IAC, Honolulu, 1969; subsequently in Joan Rubin and Bjorn Jernudd (eds.), *Can Language be Planned?* East-West Center Press, Honolulu, 1971.

———. and Joshua A. Fishman. "Interstate Migration and Subsidiary Language-Claiming: An Analysis of Selected

Indian Census Data," *International Migration Review,* 1971.

Davis, Frederick B. *Philippine Language-Teaching Experiments.* (Philippine Center for Language Study, no. 5), Alemar-Phoenix, Quezon City, 1967.

DeFrancis, John. "Japanese Language Reform: Politics and Phonetics," *Far Eastern Survey,* XVI, xix (1947), 217-220.

―――. *Nationalism and Language Reform in China,* Princeton University Press, Princeton, N.J., 1950.

―――. "Language and Script Reform (in China)," *Current Trends in Linguistics.* Mouton, The Hague, 1968, 130-150; also in J. A. Fishman (ed.), *Advances in the Sociology of Language II,* Mouton, The Hague, 1972.

de Saussure, Ferdinand. *Course in General Linguistics* (translated by Wade Baskin). Philosophical Library, 1959. New York, original (French) publication: 1916.

Deutsch, Karl W. "The Trend of European Nationalism―the Language Aspect," *American Political Science Review,* XXXVI (1942), 533-541.

―――. *Nationalism and Social Communication.* M.I.T., Cambridge, Mass., 1966, (2nd edition).

Dickens, K. J. "Unification: The Akan Dialects of the Gold Coast," in *The Use of Vernacular Languages in Education.* UNESCO, Paris, 1953, pp. 115-123.

Dohrenwend, Bruce P., and Robert J. Smith., "Toward a Theory of Acculturation," *Southwest Journal of Anthropology*, XVIII (1962), 30-39.

Dozier, Edward P. "Resistance to Acculturation and Assimilation in an Indian Pueblo," *American Anthropologist*, LIII (1951), 56-66.

Edelman, Martin, Robert L. Cooper, and Joshua A. Fishman. "The Contextualization of School Children's Bilingualism," *Irish Journal of Education*, II (1968), 106-111.

Ellis, Dean S. "Speech and Social Status in America."*Social Forces*, XLV (1967), 431-437.

Epstein, A. L. "Linguistic Innovation and Culture on the Copperbelt, Northern Rhodesia," *Southwestern Journal of Anthropology*, XV (1959), 235-253; also in J. A. Fishman (ed.), *Readings in the Sociology of Language.* Mouton, The Hague, 1968, pp. 320-339.

Ervin, Susan M., and Charles E. Osgood. "Second Language Learning and Bilingualism," *Journal of Abnormal and Social Psychology,* XLIX (1954), Supplement, 139-146.

Ervin-Tripp, Susan. "An Analysis of the Interaction of Language, Topic and Listener," *American Anthropologist,* LXVI, ii, (1964), 86-102; also in J. A. Fishman (ed.), *Readings in the Sociology of Language,* Mouton, The Hague, 1968, pp. 192-211.

―――. "Sociolinguistics," in L. Berkowitz (ed.), *Advances in Experimental Social Psychology,* vol. 4, Academic Press, New York, 1969, pp. 91-165; also in J. A. Fishman (ed.), *Advances in the Sociology of Language I,* Mouton, The Hague, 1971.

Ferguson, Charles A. "Diglossia," *Word,* XV (1959a), 325-340.

―――. "Myths about Arabic," *Monograph Series on Languages and Linguistics (Georgetown University),* XII (1959b), 75-82; also in J. A. Fishman (ed.) *Readings in the Sociology of Language.* Mouton, The Hague, 1968, pp. 375-381.

―――, and Raleigh Morgan, Jr. "Selected Readings in Applied Linguistics," *Linguistic Reporter,* 1959c, Supplement 2, 4pp.

―――. "Directions in Sociolinguistics: Report on an Interdisciplinary Seminar," *SSRC Items,* XIX, i (1965), 1-4.

―――. "St. Stefen of Perm and Applied Linguistics," in *To Honor Roman Jacobson.* Mouton, The Hague, 1967; also in J. A. Fishman, C. A. Ferguson, and J. Das Gupta (eds.), *Language Problems of Developing Nations.* Wiley, New York, 1968, pp. 253-266.

―――. "Language Development," in J. A. Fishman, C. A. Ferguson, and J. Das Gupta (eds.), *Language Problems of Developing Nations.* Wiley, New York, 1968.

―――, and John J. Gumperz (eds.), "Linguistic Diversity in South Asia: Studies in Regional, Social and Functional Variation," *International Journal of American Linguistics,* IV, i (1960) (entire issue).

Ferru, Jean Louis. "Possible Repercussions of a Technical and Economic Nature of the Adoption of Particular Letters for the Standard Transcription of West African Languages," *Bamako/Mali/Meeting on the Standard-*

ization of African Alphabets, February 28-March 5, 1966. UNESCO/CLT Baling.

Findling, Joav. "Bilingual Need Affiliation and Future Orientation in Extragroup and Intragroup Domains," *Modern Language Journal,* LIII (1969), 227-231; also in J. A. Fishman, *Advances in the Sociology of Language II,* Mouton, The Hague, 1972.

Fischel, A. *Der Panslawismus bis zum Weltkrieg.* Cotta, Stuttgart/Berlin, 1919.

Fischer, John L. "Social Influences in the Choice of a Linguistic Variant," *Word,* XIV (1958), 47-56.

Fishman, Joshua A. "The Process and Function of Social Stereotyping," *Journal of Social Psychology,* XLIII (1956), 27-66.

–––. "A Systematization of the Whorfian Hypothesis," *Behavioral Science,* VIII (1960), 323-339.

–––. "Language Maintenance and Language Shift as a Field of Inquiry," *Linguistics,* IX (1964), 32-70.

–––. *Yiddish in America.* Indiana University Research Center in Anthropology, Folklore and Linguistics, Publication 36, Bloomington, 1965a.

–––. "Bilingualism, Intelligence and Language Learning," *Modern Language Journal,* XLIX (1965b), 227-237.

–––. "Varieties of Ethnicity and Language Consciousness," *Georgetown University Monograph Series on Languages and Linguistics,* XVIII (1965c), 69-79.

–––. "Who Speaks What Language to Whom and When?" *Linguistique,* II (1965d), 67-88.

–––. "Language Maintenance and Language Shift: The American Immigrant Case Within a General Theoretical Perspective," *Sociologus,* XVI (1965e), 19-38.

–––. Language Maintenance and Language Shift in Certain Urban Immigrant Environments: The Case of Yiddish in the United States. *Europe Ethnica,* XXII (1965f), 146-158.

–––. "Bilingual Sequences at the Societal Level," *On Teaching English to Speakers of Other Languages,* II (1966a), 139-144.

–––. "Some Contrasts between Linguistically Homogeneous and Linguistically Heterogeneous Polities," *Sociological Inquiry,* XXXVI (1966b), 146-158. Revised and expanded in J. A. Fishman, C. A. Ferguson and J. Das Gupta (eds.), *Language Problems of Developing Nations.* Wiley, New York, 1968, 53-68.

―――. *Language Loyalty in the United States.* Mouton, The Hague, 1966c.

―――, "Planned Reinforcement of Language Maintenance in the United States: Suggestions for the Conservation of a Neglected National Resource," in J. A. Fishman, *Language Loyalty in the United States.* Mouton, The Hauge, 1966d, Chap. 21.

―――. "The Breadth and Depth of English in the United States," *University Quarterly*, March, 1967a, 133-140.

―――. "A Sociology of Language (Review)," *Language*, XLIII (1967b), 586-604.

―――. *Readings in the Sociology of Language.* Mouton, The Hague, 1968a.

―――. "Sociolinguistic Perspective on the Study of Bilingualism," *Linguistics*, XXXIX (1968b), 21-50.

―――. "Sociolinguistics and the Language Problems of Developing Nations," *International Social Science Journal*, XX (1968c), 211-225.

―――. "National Language and Languages of Wider Communication in the Developing Nations," *Anthropological Linguistics*, XI (1969a), 111-135.

―――. "Literacy and the Language Barrier," *Science*, CLXV (1969b), 1108-1109.

―――. "Bilingual Attitudes and Behaviors," *Language Sciences*, no. 5, 1966c, 5-11; also in J. A. Fishman, R. L. Cooper, Roxana Ma, et al., *Bilingualism in the Barrio*, Yeshiva University, New York, 1968, Final Report to DHEW under contract no. OEC-1-7-062817-0297, and Bloomington (Ind.), Language Sciences Series, 1971.

―――. "A Sociolinguistic Census of a Bilingual Neighborhood," in J. A. Fishman, R. L. Cooper, Roxana Ma, et al., *Bilingualism in the Barrio*, Yeshiva University, New York, 1968, Final Report to Department of Health, Education, and Welfare under contract no. OEC-1-7-062817-0297; also *American Journal of Sociology* LXXV (1969d), 323-339.

―――. "The Links between Micro- and Macro-sociolinguistics in the Study of Who Speaks What Language to Whom and

When," in Dell Hymes and John J. Gumperz (eds.), *The Ethnography of Communication: Directions in Sociolinguistics.* Holt, New York, in press, also in J. A. Fishman, R. L. Cooper, and Roxana Ma, et al. *Bilingualism in the Barrio.* Bloomington (Ind.) Language Sciences Series, 1971.

——. "The Impact of Nationalism on Language Planning: Some Comparisons between Early 20th Century Europe and Subsequent Developments in South and South-East Asia," *Consultative Meeting on Language Planning Processes.* Honolulu, East-West Center, Institute of Advanced Projects, 1969; also in Joan Rubin and Bjorn Jernudd (eds.) *Can Language be Planned?* East-West Center Press, Honolulu, 1971.

——. "Puerto Rican Intellectuals in New York: Some Intragroup and Intergroup Contrasts," *Canadian Journal of Behavioral Sciences,* I (1969e), 215-226.

——, and Rebecca Agheyisi, "Language Attitude Studies," *Anthropological Linguistics,* XII (1970), 215-226.

——, Robert C. Cooper, Roxana Ma, et al. *Bilingualism in the Barrio.* Final Report on contract OEC-1-7-062817-0297 to DHEW. New York, Yeshiva University, 1968; also Bloomington (Ind.), Language Sciences Series, 1971.

——, and Lawrence Greenfield., "Situational Measures of Normative Language Views in Relation to Person, Place and Topic among Puerto Rican Bilinguals," *Anthropos,* 1970; also in J. A. Fishman (ed.), *Advances in the Sociology of Language II,* Mouton, The Hague, 1972.

——, and Eleanor Herasimchuk. "The Multiple Prediction of Phonological Variables in a Bilingual Speech Community," *American Anthropologist,* LXXI (1969), 648-657.

——, and John C. Lovas. "Bilingual Education in Sociolinguistic Perspective," *TESOL Quarterly* (1970), 215-222.

——, and Erika Lueders. "What Has the Sociology of Language to Say to the Teacher? (On Teaching the Standard Variety to Speakers of Dialectal or Sociolectal Varieties)," in C. Cazden, V. John, and D. Hymes (eds.), *The Functions of Language.* Teachers College Press, New York, 1972.

———, and Vladimir C. Nahirny. "The Ethnic Group School in the United States," in J. A. Fishman et al. *Language Loyalty in the United States*, Mouton, The Hague, 1966, chap. 6; also *Sociology of Education*, XXXVII (1964), 306-317.

———, and Charles Terry. "The Validity of Census Data on Bilingualism in a Puerto Rican Neighborhood," *American Sociological Review*, XXXIV (1969), 636-650.

Frake, Charles O. "The Diagnosis of Disease among the Subanun of Mindanao," *American Anthropologist*, LXIII (1961), 113-132.

———. "The Ethnographic Study of Cognitive Systems," in T. Gladwin and William C. Sturtevant (eds.), *Anthropology and Behavior*, Anthropological Society of Washington, Washington, D.C., 1962, pp. 77-85; also in J. A. Fishman (ed.), *Readings in the Sociology of Language*. Mouton, The Hague, 1968, pp. 434-446.

Friederich, Paul. "The Linguistic Reflex of Social Change: From Tsarist to Soviet Russian Kinship," *Sociological Inquiry*, 1966, 36, XXXVI (1966), 159-185.

———. "Language and Politics in India," Daedalus, Summer, 1962, 543-559.

Gaarder, A. Bruce. "Teaching the Bilingual Child: Research, Development and Policy," *The Modern Language Journal*, XLIX (1965), 165-175.

———. "Organization of the Bilingual School," *Journal of Social Issues*, XXIII (1967), 110-120.

Gallagher, Charles F. "Language Rationalization and Scientific Progress." Paper prepared for Conference on Science and Social Change, California Institute of Technology, October 18-20, 1967.

———. "Language Reform and Social Modernization in Turkey," *Consultative Meeting on Language Planning Processes*, Honolulu, EWC-IAP, 1969; subsequently in Joan Rubin and Bjorn Jernudd (eds.), *Can Language be Planned?*, East-West Center Press, Honolulu, 1971.

Garfinkel, Harold. *Studies in Ethnomethodology*. Prentice-Hall, Englewood Cliffs, N.J., 1967.

———, and H. Sachs (eds.). *Contributions in Ethnomethodology*. Indiana University Press, Bloomington, in press.

Garvin, Paul L. "Literacy as Problem in Language and Culture," *Georgetown University Monograph Series on Languages and Linguistics*, 7, 1954, 117-129.

―――. "The Standard Language Problem: Concepts and Methods," *Anthropological Linguistics*, I, ii (1959), 28-31.

Geertz, Clifford. "Linguistic Etiquette," in his *Religion of Java*. Glencoe Press, New York, 1960; also in J. A. Fishman (ed.), *Readings in the Sociology of Language*, Mouton, The Hague, 1968, 282-295.

Gelb, I. J. *A Study of Writing*. The University of Chicago Press, Chicago, 1952.

Gerullis, Georg. "Muttersprache und Zweisprachigkeit in einem preussischlitauischen Dorf," *Studi Baltici*, II (1932), 59-67.

Glenn, Norval D. "The Trend in Differences in Attitudes and Behavior by Educational Level," *Sociology of Education*, XXXIX (1966), 255-275.

―――, and J. L. Simmons. "Are Regional Cultural Differences Diminishing?" *Public Opinion Quarterly*, XXXI (1967a), 176-193.

―――. "Differentiation and Massification: Some Trend Data from National Surveys," *Social Forces*, XLVI (1967b), 172-179.

Goodenough, Ward H. "Rethinking Status and Role: Toward a General Model of the Cultural Organization of Social Relationships," in M. Banton (ed.), *The Relevance of Models for Social Anthropology*. Praeger, New York, 1965, pp. 1-24.

Goodman, Elliot R. "World State and World Language," in his *The Soviet Design for a World State*. Columbia University Press, New York, 1960, pp. 264-284; also in J. A. Fishman (ed.), *Readings in the Sociology of Language*. Mouton, The Hague, 1968, pp. 717-736.

Goody, Jack. *Literacy in Traditional Societies*. Cambridge, London, 1963.

Greenberg, Joseph R. *Universals of Language*, 2nd edition. M.I.T., Cambridge, Mass., 1966.

―――. Urbanism, Migration and Language, in Hilda Kuper, (ed.), *Urbanization and Migration in West Africa*. University of California Press, Berkeley, 1965, pp. 50-59.

Greenfield, Lawrence. "Situational Measures of Language Use in Relation to Person, Place and Topic among Puerto Rican Bilinguals," *Bilingualism in the Barrio*. Final Report to DHEW re Contract No. DEC-1-7-062817-0297. Yeshiva University, New York, 1968.

Grimshaw, Allen D. "Sociolinguistics and the Sociologist," *The American Sociologist*, IV (1969), 312-321.

———. "Some Social Sources and Some Social Functions of Pidgin and Creole Languages," in D. Hymes (ed.), *Proceedings of the Social Science Research Council Conference on Creolization and Pidginization*. Cambridge, London, 1971.

Gulick, John. "Language and Passive Resistance among the Eastern Cherokees," *Ethnohistory*, V (1958), 60-81.

Gumperz, John J. "Dialect Differences and Social Stratification in a North Indian Village," *American Anthropologist*, LX (1958), 668-682.

———. "Speech Variation and the Study of Indian Civilization," *American Anthropologist*, LXIII (1961), 976-988.

———."Types of Linguistic Communities," *Anthropological Linguistics*, IV, i (1962), also in J. A. Fishman (ed.), *Readings in the Sociology of Language*. Mouton, The Hague, 1968, pp. 460-476.

———. "Linguistic and Social Interaction in Two Communities," *American Anthropologist*, LXVI, ii (1964a), 37-53.

———. "Hindi-Punjabi Code Switching in Delhi," in Morris Halle (ed.), *Proceedings of the International Congress of Linguistics*. Mouton, The Hague, 1964b.

———. "On the Ethnology of Linguistic Change," in William Bright (ed.), *Sociolinguistics*. Mouton, The Hague, 1966, pp. 27-38.

———. "The Linguistic Markers of Bilingualism." *Journal of Social Issues*, XXIII, ii (1967), 48-57.

Guxman, M. M. "Some General Regularities in the Formation and Development of National Languages," in M. M. Guxman (ed.), *Vaprosy Formirovanija Nacional'nyx Jazykov*. Moscow, 1960, pp. 295-307; also in J. A. Fishman (ed.), *Readings in the Sociology of Language*. Mouton, The Hague, 1968, pp. 766-779.

Hair, P. E. H. "Notes on the Discovery of the Vai Script, with a Bibliography," *Sierra Leone Language Review,* II (1963), 36-49.

Hall, Robert A., Jr. "Bilingualism and Applied Linguistics," *Zeitschrift für Phonetik und allgemeine Sprachwissenschaft,* VI (1952), 13-30.

Halliday, M. A. K., Angus MacIntosh, and Peter Strevens. *The Linguistic Sciences and Language Teaching.* Longmans, London, 1964.

———, ———, and ———. "The Users and Uses of Language," in M. A. K. Halliday, A. McIntosh, and P. Strevens (eds.), *The Linguistic Sciences and Language Teaching.* Longmans, London, 1964; also in J. A. Fishman (ed.), *Readings in the Sociology of Language.* Mouton, The Hague, 1968, pp. 139-169.

Hamilton, Richard F. "Affluence and the Worker: The West German Case," *American Journal of Sociology,* LXXI (1965), 144-152.

Hansen, Marcus L. *The Immigrant in American History* (Arthur M. Schlesinger, ed.) Harvard, Cambridge, 'Mass., 1940.

Haudricourt, A. G. De L'origine des particularites de l'alpha-bet Vietnamien. *Dan Vietnam,* No. 3, 1943, 61-68.

Haugen, Einar. *The Norwegian Language in America; A Study in Bilingual Behavior.* University of Pennsylvania Press, Philadelphia, 1953, 2 vols.; 2nd ed., Indiana University Press, Bloomington, 1969.

———. "Language Planning in Modern Norway," *Scandinavian Studies,* XXXIII (1961), 68-81; also in J. A. Fishman (ed.), *Readings in the Sociology of Language.* Mouton, The Hague, 1968, 673-687.

———. *Language Planning and Language Conflict; the Case of Modern Norwegian.* Harvard, Cambridge, Mass., 1966a.

———. "Linguistics and Language Planning," in Wm. Bright (ed.), *Sociolinguistics.* Mouton, The Hague, 1966b, pp. 50-66.

———. "Dialect, Language, Nation," *American Anthropologist,* LXVIII (1966c), 922-935.

Havranek, Bohuslav. "The Functional Differentiation of the Standard Language," in Paul L. Garvin (ed.), *A Prague School Reader on Esthetics, Literary Structure and Style.* Georgetown University Press, Washington, D.C., 1964, pp. 1-18.

Hayden, Robert G., and Joshua A. Fishman. "The Impact of Exposure to Ethnic Mother Tongues on Foreign Language Teachers in American High Schools and Colleges," in J. A. Fishman et al., *Language Loyalty in the United States.* Mouton, The Hague, 1966, Chap. 13; also, *Modern Language Journal,* XLVIII (1964), 262-274.

Hayes, Alfred S. *Recommendations of the Work Conference on Literacy,* Center for Applied Linguistics, Washington, D. C., 1965.

Herman, Simon N. "Explorations in the Social Psychology of Language Choice," *Human Relations,* XIV (1961), 149-164; also in J. A. Fishman (ed.), *Readings in the Sociology of Language.* Mouton, The Hague, 1968, pp. 492-511.

Hertzler, Joyce O. *The Sociology of Language.* Random House, New York, 1965.

Herzog, Marvin I. *The Yiddish Language in Northern Poland: Its Geography and History.* Indiana University Research Center in Anthropology, Folklore and Linguistics, Publication 37, Bloomington, 1965.

Heyd, Uriel. *Language Reform in Modern Turkey.* Israel Oriental Society, Jerusalem, 1954.

Hodges, Harold M. *Social Stratification: Class in America.* Schenkman, Cambridge, Mass., 1964.

Hofman, John E. "Mother Tongue Retentiveness in Ethnic Parishes," in Joshua A. Fishman et al. *Language Loyalty in the United States.* Mouton, The Hague, 1966a, chap. 9.

———. "The Language Transition in some Lutheran Denominations," in J. A. Fishman et al. *Language Loyalty in the United States.* Mouton, The Hague, 1966b, chap. 10; also in J. A. Fishman (ed.), *Readings in the Sociology of Language.* Mouton, The Hague, 1966, pp. 620-638.

———, and Haya Fisherman. "Language Shift and Maintenance in Israel," *International Migration Review,* 1971.

Hohenthal, W. D., and T. McCorkle, "The Problem of Aboriginal Persistence," *Southwestern Journal of Anthropology,* XII (1955), 288-300.

Hoijer, H. "Cultural Implications of the Navaho Linguistic Categories," *Language,* XXVII (1951), 111-120.

———. "The Sapir-Whorf Hypothesis," in H. Hoijer (ed.), *Language in Culture.* American Anthropological Association, Memoir No. 79, The University of Chicago Press, Chicago, 1954, pp. 92-104.

Holton, Daniel C. "Ideographs and Ideas," *Far Eastern Survey,* XVI, xix (1947), 220-223.

Howell, Richard W. "Linguistic Status Markers in Korean," *Kroeber Anthropological Society Papers,* LIV (1965), 91-97.

———. "Terms of Address as Indices of Social Change." Paper presented at American Sociological Association Meeting, San Francisco, Sept. 1967.

Hsia, Tao-tai. *China's Language Reforms.* Yale, New Haven, Conn., 1956.

Huffine, Carol L. "Inter-Socio-Economic Clan Language Differences: A Research Report," *Sociology and Social Research,* L, iii (1966), 351-355.

Hughes, Everett C. "The Linguistic Division of Labor in Industrial and Urban Societies." *Georgetown University Monograph Series on Languages and Linguistics,* 1970 in press; also in J. A. Fishman (ed.), *Advances in the Sociology of Language II,* Mouton, The Hague, 1972.

Hymes, Dell H. "The Ethnography of Speaking," in T. Gladwin and W. C. Sturtevant (ed.), *Anthropology and Human Behavior.* Anthropology Society of Washington, Washington, D. C., 1962, pp. 13-53; also in J. A. Fishman (ed.), *Readings in the Sociology of Language.* Mouton, The Hague, 1968, pp. 99-138.

———. "Two Types of Linguistic Relativity," in Wm. Bright (ed.), *Sociolinguistics.* Mouton, The Hague, 1966, pp. 114-157.

———. "Why Linguistics Needs the Sociologist," *Social Research,* XXXIV, vii (1967a), 632-647.

———. "Models of Interaction of Language and Social Setting," *Journal of Social Issues,* XXXIII, ii (1967b), 8-28.

Ivanova, A. M. and V. D. Voskresensky. "Abolition of Adult Illiteracy in USSR, 1917-1940," *Fundamental and Adult Education,* XI,iii (1959), 131-186.

Jeffries, W. F. "The Literacy Campaign in Northern Nigeria," *Funding and Adult Education,* X, i (1958), 2-6.

Jernudd, Bjorn H., and Tommy Willingsson. "A Sociolectal Study of the Stockholm Region," *Svenska Landsmal och Svenskt Folkliv,* CCLXXXIX (1968), 140-147.

———. "Notes on Economic Analysis and Language Planning," *Consultative Meeting on Language Planning Processes.* EWC-IAP, Honolulu, 1969; subsequently, in Joan Rubin and Bjorn Jernudd (eds.), *Can Language be Planned?* East-West Center Press, Honolulu, 1971.

———, and J. Das Gupta, "Towards a Theory of Language Planning," *Consultative Meeting on Language Planning Processes.* EWC-IAP, Honolulu, 1969; subsequently, in Joan Rubin and Bjorn Jernudd (eds.), *Can Language be Planned?* East-West Center Press, Honolulu, 1971.

John, Vera, and Vivian Horner. *Early Childhood Bilingual Education.* Modern Language Association, New York, 1971.

Johnston, Ruth. *Factors in the Assimilation of Selected Groups of Polish Post-War Immigrants in Western Australia.* Unpublished Ph. D. dissertation, University of Western Australia (Perth), 1963a; subsequently: *Immigrant Assimilation; A Study of Polish People in Western Australia.* Paterson Brokensha, Perth, 1965.

———. "A New Approach to the Meaning of Assimilation," *Human Relations,* XIV (1963b), 295-298.

Jones, D. *Problems of a National Script for India.* Hartford Seminary Foundation, Hartford, Conn., 1942.

Jones, Frank E. and Wallace E. Lambert, "Attitudes toward Immigrants in a Canadian Community," *Public Opinion Quarterly,* XXIII (1959), 538-546.

Joos, Martin. "Description of Language Design," *Journal of the Acoustical Society of America,* XXII (1950), 701-708.

Reprinted in his *Readings in Linguistics,* American Council of Learned Societies, Washington, D. C., 1958, pp. 349-356.

———. "The Isolation of Styles." *Georgetown University Monograph Series on Languages and Linguistics,* XII (1959), 107-113; also in J. A. Fishman (ed.), *Readings in the Sociology of Language,* Mouton, The Hague, 1968, pp. 185-191.

Kandler, C. Zum Aufbau der angewandten Sprachwissenschaft. *Sprachforum,* I (1955), 3-9.

Kandori, Takehiko. Study of dialects in Japan. *Orbis,* XVII (1968), 47-56.

Kantrowitz, Nathan. "The Vocabulary of Race Relations in a Prison." Paper presented at American Dialect Society Meeting, Chicago, December, 1967.

Kaye, Alan S. "Modern Standard Arabic and the Colloquials," *Lingua,* XXIV (1970), 374-391.

Kelman, Herbert C. "Language as Aid and Barrier to Involvement in the National System." Consultative Meeting *on Language Planning Processes,* EWC-IAP, Honolulu, 1969; subsequently, in Joan Rubin and Bjorn Jernudd (eds.), *Can Language be Planned?* East-West Center Press, Honolulu, 1971; also in J. A. Fishman (ed.), *Advances in the Sociology of Language.* Mouton, The Hague. 1972.

Kimple, James, Jr., Robert L. Cooper, and Joshua A. Fishman. "Language Switching in the Interpretation of Conversations," *Lingua,* XXIII (1969), 127-134.

Kloss, Heinz. "Sprachtabellen als Grundlage für Sprachstatistik, Sprachenkarten und für eine allgemaine Soziologie der Sprachgemeinschaften," *Vierteljahrsschrift für Politik und Geschichte,* 1 (7), 1929, 103-117.

———. *Die Entwicklung Neuer Germanischer Kultursprachen.* Pohl, Munich, 1952.

———. "Types of Multilingual Communities: A Discussion of Ten Variables," *Sociological Inquiry,* XXXV (1966a), 135-145.

———. "German-American Language Maintenance Efforts," in

J. A. Fishman et al. *Language Loyalty in the United States.* Mouton, The Hague, 1966b, chap. 15.

———. "'Abstand' languages and 'Ausbau' languages," *Anthropological Linguistics,* IX, vii (1967), 29-41.

Kluckhohn, Clyde. "Notes on Some Anthropological Aspects of Communication," *American Anthropologist,* LXIII (1961), 895-910.

Knott, Betty I. "The Christian 'Special Language' in the Inscriptions," *Vigiliae Christianae,* X (1956), 65-79.

Kohn, Hans. *The Idea of Nationalism: A Study of Its Origin and Background.* Macmillan, New York, 1945.

Kolarz, Walter. *Myths and Realities in Eastern Europe.* Lindsay Drummond, London, 1946.

———. *Russia and Her Colonies.* Archon/Shoe String, Hamden, Conn., 1967 (originally published in 1952).

———. *The Peoples of the Soviet Far East.* Archon/Shoe String, Hamden, Conn., 1969 (originally published in 1954).

Kuhn, Walter. *Die jungen deutschen Sprachinselm in Galizien: ein Beitrag zur Methode der Sprachinselforschung.* Aschendorffsche Verlagsbuchhandlung, Munster, 1930.

———. *Deutsche Sprachinselforschung.* Gunther Wolff, Plauen, 1934.

Kwan-wai Chiu, Rosaline. *Language Contact and Language Planning in China (1900-1967); A Selected Bibliography.* Les Presses de l'Universite Laval, Quebec, 1970.

Labov, William. "The Social Motivation of a Sound Change," *Word,* XIX (1963), 273-309.

———. "Phonological Correlates of Social Stratification," *American Anthropologist,* LXVI, ii (1964), 164-176.

———. "On the Mechanism of Linguistic Change," *Georgetown University Monograph Series in Language and Linguistics,* XVIII (1965), 91-114.

———. "The Effect of Social Mobility on Linguistic Behavior," *Sociological Inquiry,* XXXVI (1966a), 186-203.

———. "Hypercorrection by the Lower Middle Class as a Factor in Linguistic Change," in Wm. Bright (ed.), *Sociolinguistics.* Mouton, The Hague, 1966b, pp. 84-101. 84-101.

———. *The Social Stratification of English in New York City.* Center for Applied Linguistics, Washington, D.C., 1966c.

———. "Stages in the Acquisition of Standard English," in Roger W. Shuy (ed.), *Social Dialects and Language Learning.* NCTE, Champaign, 1966d.

———. "The Reflection of Social Processes in Linguistic Structures," in J. A. Fishman (ed.), *Readings in the Sociology of Language.* Mouton, The Hague, 1968a, pp. 240-251.

———. Paul Cohen, Clarence Robins, and John Lewis. *A Study of the Non-Standard English of Negro and Puerto Rican Speakers in New York City.* Final Report, Cooperative Research Project No. 3288, Columbia University, New York, 1968b, 2 vols.

Lambert, Wallace E., R. C. Gardner, H. C. Barick, and K. Tunstall. "Attitudinal and Cognitive Aspects of Intense Study of a Second Language," *Journal of Abnormal and Social Psychology*, LXVI (1963), 358-368.

Lanham, L. W. "Teaching English to Africans: A Crisis in Education," *Optima*, XV (Dec. 1965), 197-204.

Lantz, De lee, and Volney Stefflre. "Language and Cognition Revisited," *Journal of Abnormal and Social Psychology*, XLIX (1964), 454-462.

Lehmann, A. "Über Wiedererkennen," *Philos. Stud.,* V (1889), 96-156.

Lenneberg, Eric H. "Cognition in Ethnolinguistics," *Language,* XXIX (1953), 463-471.

———. "A Probabilistic Approach to Language Learning," *Behavioral Science*, II (1957), 1-12.

LePage, Robert. *The National Language Question.* Oxford, London, 1964.

———. "Problems to Be Faced in the Use of English as the Medium of Education in Four West Indian Territories," in J. A. Fishman, C. A. Ferguson, and J. Das Gupta (eds.), *Language Problems of Developing Nations.* Wiley, New York, 1968, pp. 431-441.

Levine, William L., and H. J. Crockett. "Speech Variation in a Piedmont Community: Postvocalic r." *Sociological Inquiry*, XXXVI (1966), 204-226.

Lewis, E. Glynn. "Migration and Language in the USSR," *International Migration Review,* 1971; also in J. A. Fishman (ed.), *Advances in the Sociology of Language II,* Mouton, The Hague, 1972.

Lewis, W. Arthur. "Education and Economic Development," *Social and Economic Studies* X, ii (1961), 113-127.

Li Hui. "The Phonetic Alphabet–Short Cut to Literacy," *Peking Review*, XIII, xxviii (July 12, 1960).

Liebêrson, Stanley. "Bilingualism in Montreal: A Demographic Analysis," *American Journal of Sociology*, LXXI (1965), 10-25; also in J. A. Fishman (ed.), *Advances in the Sociology of Language.* Mouton, The Hague, 1971.

–––, and T. J. Curry, "Language Shift in the United States: Some Demographic Clues," *The International Migration Review,* 1971.

Lind, Andrew W. "Race Relations in New Guinea," *Current Affairs Bulletin* (Sydney, Australia), XLIV, iii (1969), 34-48.

Lindenfeld, Jacqueline. "The Social Conditioning of Syntactic Variation in French," *American Anthropologist*, LXXI (1969), 890-898; also in J. A. Fishman (ed.), *Advances in the Sociology of Language II,* Mouton, The Hague, 1972.

Lunt, Horace G. "The Creation of Standard Macedonian: Some Facts and Attitudes," *Anthropological Linguistics*, I, v (1959), 19-26.

Ma, Roxana, and Eleanor Herasimchuk. "The Linguistic Dimensions of a Bilingual Neighborhood." In J. A. Fishman R. L. Cooper, Roxana Ma, et al. *Bilingualism in the Barrio*, Yeshiva University, New York 1968, Final Report to Department of Health, Education and Welfare under Contract No. OEC-1-7-062817-0297; also Bloomington (Ind.) Language Sciences, 1971; also in J. A. Fishman (ed.), *Advances in the Sociology of Languages II,* Mouton, The Hague, 1972.

Mackey, William F. "The Description of Bilingualism," *Canadian Journal of Linguistics*, VII (1962), 51-85.

–––. "A Typology of Bilingual Education," *The Foreign Language Annals,* III (1970), 596-608; also in J. A. Fishman (ed.), *Advances in the Sociology of Language II,* Mouton, The Hague, 1972.

Macnamara, John. *Bilingualism in Primary Education.* Edinburgh University Press, Edinburgh, 1966.

———. "The Effects of Instruction in a Weaker Language," *Journal of Social Issues,* XXIII (1967), 121-135.

———. "Successes and Failures in the Movement for the Restoration of Irish," *Consultative Meeting on Language Planning Processes.* EWC-IAP, Honolulu, 1969; subsequently in Joan Rubin and Bjorn Jernudd (eds.), *Can Language be Planned?* East-West Center Press, Honolulu, 1971.

Maier, Norman R. F. "Reasoning in humans. I. On direction," *Journal of Comparative Psychology,* X (1930), 115-143.

Manuel, Herschel T. *The Preparation and Evaluation of Interlanguage Testing Materials,* University of Texas Press, Austin, 1963. Mimeographed report, Cooperative Research Project Number 681.

Mayner, Thomas F. "Language and Nationalism in Yugoslavia," *Canadian Slavic Studies.* I (1967), 333-347.

Mazrui, Ali A. "The National Language Question in East Africa," *East Africa Journal,* III (1967), 12-19.

McClusker, Henry F., Jr. *An Approach for Educational Planning in the Developing Countries.* Stanford Research Institute, Menlo Park, Calif., 1963.

McCormack, William. "Social Dialects in Dharwar Kannada," in C. A. Ferguson and J. J. Gumperz (eds.), "Linguistic Diversity in South Asia," IV, i (1960), *IJAL,* 79-91.

———. "Occupation and Residence in Relation to Dharwar Dialects," in M. Singer and B. S. Cohn (eds.), *Social Structure and Social Change in India.* Viking Fund, New York, 1968, pp. 475-486.

McDavid, Raven I. "The Dialects of American English," in W. N. Francis (ed.), *The Structure of American English.* Ronald, New York, 1958.

Metraux, Ruth W. "A Study of Bilingualism among Children of U.S.-French Parents," *French Review,* XXXVIII (1965), 650-655.

Metzger, Duane, and Gerald E. Williams. "Some Procedures and Results in the Study of Native Categories: Tzeltal 'firewood'," *American Anthropologist,* LXVIII (1966), 389-407.

Meyenburg, Erwin. "Der heutige Stand der Romazi-Bewegung in Japan," *Forschungen und Fortschritte,* X, nos. 23-24 (1934).

Mills, H. C. "Language Reform in China," *Far Eastern Quarterly*, XV (1956), 517-540.

Mohrmann, Christine. "Le latin commun et le latin des Chretiens," *Vigiliae Christiannae*, I (1947), 1-12.

———. "Linguistic Problems in the Early Christian Church," *Vigiliae Christiannae*, XI (1957), 11-36.

Morag, Shelomo. "Planned and Unplanned Development in Modern Hebrew," *Lingua*, LXXXVIII (1959), 247-263.

Nader, Laura. "A Note on Attitudes and the Use of Language," *Anthropological Linguistics*, IV, vi (1962), 24-29; also in J. A. Fishman (ed.). *Readings in the Sociology of Language*. Mouton, The Hague, 1968, pp. 276-281.

Nahirny, Vladimir C., and Joshua A. Fishman. "American Immigrant Groups: Ethnic Identification and the Problem of Generations," *Sociological Review*, XIII (1965), 311-326.

Nelson, Lowry. "Speaking of tongues," *American Journal of Sociology*, LIV (1947), 202-210.

Nguyen dinh Hoa. *The Vietnamese Language*. Department of National Education, Vietnam Culture Series, no. 2, Saigon, 1960.

Nida, Eugene A. "Practical Limitations to a Phonemic Orthography," *Bible Translator*, V (1954), 35-39 and 58-62.

———. "Sociological Dimensions of Literacy and Literature," in Floyd Shacklock et al. (eds.), *World Literacy Manual*. New York, Committee on Literacy and Christian Literature, 1967, chap. 11.

Orenstein, Jacob. "Soviet Language Policy: Theory and Practice," *Slavic and East European Journal*, XVII (1959), 1-24.

Osgood, Charles E. "The Cross-Cultural Generality of Visual-Verbal-Synestetic Tendencies," *Behavioral Science*, V (1960), 146-149.

Owens, Roger C. "The Patrilocal Band: A Linguistically and Culturally Hybrid Social Unit," *American Anthropologist*, LXVII (1965), 675-690.

Özmen, Yücel. "A Sociolinguistic Analysis of Language Reform in Turkey 1932-1967, with Special Reference to the Activities of the Turk Dil Kurumu." MS Thesis, Georgetown University, 1967 (unpublished).

Passin, Herbert. "Writer and Journalist in the Transitional Society," in Lucian W. Pye (ed.), *Communication and Political Development.* Princeton University Press, Princeton, N.J. 1963, pp. 82-123; also in J. A. Fishman, C. A. Ferguson, and J. Das Gupta (eds.), *Language Problems of Developing Nations.* Wiley, New York, 1968, pp. 442-458.

Pike, Kenneth L. *Phonemics: A Technique for Reducing Languages to Writing.* The University of Michigan Press, Ann Arbor, 1947.

Polome, Edgar. "The Choice of Official Languages in the Democratic Republic of the Congo," in J. A. Fishman, C. A. Ferguson, and J. Das Gupta (eds.) *Language Problems of Developing Countries.* Wiley, New York, 1968, pp. 295-312.

Pool, Jonathan. "National Development and Language Diversity," *La Monda Lingvo- Problemo,* I (1969), 129-192; also in J. A. Fishman (ed.), *Advances in the Sociology of Language II,* Mouton, The Hague, 1972.

Pospisil, Leopold. "A Formal Semantic Analysis of Substantive Law: Kapauka Papuan Laws of Land Tenure," *American Anthropologist,* LXVII, pt. 2 (1965), 186-214.

Prator, Clifford H. "The Survey of Language Use and Language Teaching in Eastern Africa," *Linguistic Reporter,* IX, viii (1967).

Price, P. David. "Two Types of Taxonomy: A Huichol Ethnobotanical Example." *Anthropological Linguistics,* IX, vii (1967), 1-28.

Quelquejay, C., and A. Bennigsen. *The Evolution of the Muslim Nationalities of the USSR and Their Linguistic Problems.* Central Asian Research Center, London, 1961.

Rabin, Chaim. "Spelling Reform: Israel, 1968," *Consultative Meeting on Language Planning Processes.* EWC-IAP, Honolulu, 1969; subsequently in Joan Rubin and Bjorn Jernudd (eds.), *Can Language be Planned?* East-West Center Press, Honolulu, 1971.

Radin, Paul. "The Adoption of an Alphabet by an Aboriginal People," *Cambridge University Reporter* (Proceedings of the Cambridge Philological Society), Nov. 25, 1924, 27-34.

Ramos, Maximi, Jose V. Aguilar, and Bonifacio P. Sibayan. *The Determination and Implementation of Language Policy* (=Philippine Center for Language Study, Monograph 2). Alemar-Phoenix, Quezon City, 1967.

Ray, Punya Sloka. *Language Standardization.* (Chap. 9: Comparative Description and Evaluation of Writing Systems, pp. 106-120), Mouton, The Hague, 1963.

Read, Allen Walker. "The Splitting and Coalescing of Widespread Languages," *Proceedings of the Ninth International Congress of Linguistics,* 1967, 1129-1134.

Reissman, Leonard. *The Urban Process: Cities in Industrial Societies.* Free Press, New York, 1964.

Ross, Allan S. C. "U and Non-U: An Essay in Sociological Linguistics," in N. Mitford (ed.), *Noblesse Oblige.* Hamish Hamilton, London, 1956, 11-38.

Rossi, Ettore. "La questione dell' alfabeto per le lingue turche," *Oriente Moderno,* VII (1927), 295-310.

———. "Il nuovo alfabeto latino introdotto in Turchia," *Oriente Moderno,* XI (1929), 32-48.

———. "La riforma linguistica in Turchia," *Oriente Moderno,* XV (1935), 45-57.

———. "Un decennio di riforma linguistica in Turchia," *Oriente Moderno,* XXII (1942), 466-477.

———. "Venticinque anni di rivoluzione dell'alfabeto e venti di riforma linguistica in Turchia," *Oriente Moderno,* XXXIII (1953), 378-384.

Royal Commission on Bilingualism and Biculturism. *A Preliminary Report.* Queen's Printer, Ottawa, 1965.

———. *Book I: General Introduction, The Official Languages.* Queen's Printer, Ottawa, 1967.

———. *Book II: Education.* Queen's Printer, Ottawa, 1968.

Rubin, Joan. "Bilingualism in Paraguay," *Anthropological Linguistics.* IV, i (1962), 52-58.

———. "Language and Education in Paraguay," in J. A. Fishman, C. A. Ferguson, and J. Das Gupta (eds.), *Language Problems in Developing Nations.* Wiley, New York, 1968, pp. 477-488.

———. "Education and Language Planning," *Consultative Meeting on Language Planning Processses.,* EWC-IAP,

Honolulu, 1969; subsequently in Joan Rubin and Bjorn Jernudd (eds.), *Can Language be Planned?* East-West Center Press, Honolulu, 1971; also in J. A. Fishman (ed.), *Advances in the Sociology of Language II,* Mouton, The Hague, 1972.

Russell, J. K. "Starting a Literacy Campaign," *Books for Africa.* XVIII, ii (1948), 17-20.

Rustow, Dankwart A. *A World of Nations: Problems of Political Modernization.* Brookings Institution, Washington, 1967; also, adapted as "Language, Modernization and Nationhood —an Attempt at Typology," in J. A. Fishman, C. A. Ferguson, and J. Das Gupta (eds.), *Language Problems of Developing Nations,* Wiley, New York, 1968, pp. 87-106.

Samora, Julian, and Wm. N. Deane. "Language Usage as a Possible Index of Acculturation." *Sociology and Social Research,* XL (1956), 307-311.

Scharshmidt, Clemens. "Schriftreform in Japan: Ein Kulturproblem," *Mitteilungen des Seminars für Orientalische Sprachen,* XXVI/XXVII, i (1924), 183-186.

Schegloff, Emanuel A. Sequencing in Conversational Openings, *American Anthropologist,* LXX (1968), 1075-1095; also in J. A. Fishman (ed.), *Advances in the Sociology of Language.* Mouton, The Hague, 1971.

Schermerhorn, Richard A. "Toward a General Theory of Minority Groups," *Phylon,* XXV (1964), 238-246.

Schofield, R. S. "The Measurement of Literacy in Pre-Industrial England," in Jack Goody (ed.), *Literacy in Traditional Societies,* Cambridge, London, 1968.

Selk, Paul. *Die sprachlichen Verhaltnisse in deutsch-danischen Sprachgebiet sudlich der Grenze.* Verlag Heimat und Erbe, Flensburg, 1937 (Erganzungsband, 1940).

Serdyuchenko, G. P. "The Eradication of Illiteracy and the Creation of New Written Languages in the U.S.S.R.," *International Journal of Adult and Youth Education,* XIV, (1962), 23-29.

———. *Elimination of Illiteracy among the People Who Had no Alphabets.* Commission for UNESCO, Ministry of Education, RSFSR, Moscow, 1965, 16p.

Serruys, Paul L. M. *Survey of the Chinese Language Reform and the Anti-Illiteracy Movement in Communist China (Studies in Communist Chinese Terminology,* No. 8), Center for Chinese Studies, Berkeley, Calif., 1962.

Shnore, Leo. "The Rural-Urban Variable: An Urbanite's Perspective," *Rural Sociology,* XXI (1966), 137.

Shuy, Roger W. (ed.), *Social Dialects and Language Learning.* NCTE, Champaign, 1966.

Sjoberg, Andree F. "Writing, Speech and Society: Some Changing Interrelationships," in *Proceedings of the Ninth International Congress of Linguists.* Mouton, The Hague, 1964, pp. 892-897.

–––. "Socio-Cultural and Linguistic Factors in the Development of Writing Systems for Preliterate Peoples," in Wm. Bright (ed.), *Sociolinguistics.* Mouton, The Hague, .1966, pp. 260-276.

Smalley, William A. *Orthography Studies: Articles on New Writing Systems.* United Bible Societies, London, 1964 (Help for Translators, vol. 6).

Smith, Alfred G. "Literacy Promotion in an Underdeveloped Area," University of Wisconsin, Madison. Unpublished Ph.D. thesis, 1956.

Sorensen, Arthur P., Jr. "Multilingualism in the Northwest Amazon," *American Anthropologist,* LXIX (1967), 670-684.

Spencer, John (ed.), *Language in Africa.* Cambridge, London, 1963.

Stern, Theodore. "Three Pwo Karen Scripts: A Study of Alphabet Formation," *Anthropological Linguistics,* X, i (1968), 1-39.

Stewart, Gail. "Present-day Usage of the Vai Script in Liberia," *African Language Review,* VII (1967), 71-74.

Stewart, Wm. A. *Non-Standard Speech and The Teaching of English.* Center for Applied Linguistics, Washington, D.C., 1964.

–––. "Sociolinguistic Factors Affecting English Teaching," in Roger W. Shuy (ed.), *Social Dialects and Language Learning.* NCTE, Champaign, 1965, pp. 10-18.

–––. "A Sociolinguistics Typology for Describing National Multilingualism," in J. A. Fishman (ed.), *Readings in the*

Sociology of Language. Mouton, The Hague, 1968, pp. 531-545.

Szajkowski, Zosa. *Catalogue of the Exhibition on the History of Yiddish Orthography from the Spelling Rules of the Early Sixteenth Century to the Standardized Orthography of 1936.* Yivo Institute for Jewish Research, New York, 1966.

Tabouret-Keller, Andree. "Sociological Factors of Language Maintenance and Language Shift: A Methodological Approach Based on European and African Examples," in J. A. Fishman, C. A. Ferguson, and J. Das Gupta (eds.), *Language Problems of Developing Nations,* Wiley, New York, 1968, pp. 107-118.

Tanner, Nancy. "Speech and Society among the Indonesian Elite: A Case Study of a Multilingual Community," *Anthropological Linguistics*, IX, iii (1967), 15-40.

Tauli, Valter. *Introduction to a Theory of Language Planning.* Acta Universitatis Upsaliensis, Studia Philologiae Scandinavicae Upsaliensia, Uppsala, 1968.

Thompson, Laurence C. *A Vietnamese Grammar.* University of Washington Press, Seattle, 1965.

Thorburn, Thomas. "Cost-benefit Analysis in Language Planning," *Consultative Meeting on Language Planning Processes.* EWC-IAP, Honolulu, 1969; subsequently, in Joan Rubin and Bjorn Jernudd (eds.), *Can Language be Planned?* East-West Center Press, Honolulu, 1971; also in J. A. Fishman (ed.), *Advances in the Sociology of Language II,* Mouton, The Hague, 1972.

Tietze, Andreas. "Problems of Turkish Lexicography," *IJAL,* XXVIII (1962), 263-272.

Toshio, Yamada. "The Writing System: Historical Research and Modern Development," *Current Trends in Linguistics,* II (1967), 693-731.

Trager, George L. "The Systematization of the Whorf Hypothesis." *Anthropological Linguistics,* I, i (1959), 25-31.

Twadell, W. I. "Standard German," *Anthropological Linguistics,* I, iii (1959), 1-7.

UNESCO. *The Haiti Pilot Project.* UNESCO, Paris, 1951.

Vachek, Joseph. "Some Remarks on Writing and Phonetic Transcription," *Acta Linguistica* (Copenhagen), V (1945-1949), pp. 86-93.

———. "Written Language and Printed Language," *Recueil Linguistique de Bratislava,* I (1948), pp. 67-75. Reprinted in J. Vachek (ed.), *A Prague School Reader in Linguistics.* Indiana University Press, Bloomington, 1964, pp. 453-560.

Valdman, Albert. "Language Standardization in a Diglossia Situation: Haiti," in J. A. Fishman, C. A. Ferguson, and J. Das Gupta (eds.), *Language Problems of Developing Nations.* Wiley, New York, 1968, pp. 313-326.

Verdoodt, Albert. "The Differential Impact of Immigrant French Speakers on Indigenous German Speakers: A Case Study in the Light of Two Theories," *International Migration Review,* 1971, also in J. A. Fishman (ed.), *Advances in the Sociology of Language II,* Mouton, The Hague, 1972.

Walker, Willard. "Notes on Native Writing Systems and the Design of Native Literacy Programs," *Anthropological Linguistics,* XI, v (1969), 148-166.

Ward, Ida C. *Report of an Investigation of Some Gold Coast Language Problems.* Crown Agents for the Colonies, London, 1945.

Weinreich, Max. "Yidishkayt and Yiddish: On the Impact of Religion on Language in Ashkenazic Jewry," in *Mordecai M. Kaplan Jubilee Volume.* Jewish Theological Seminary of America, New York, 1953; also in J. A. Fishman (ed.), *Readings in the Sociology of Language.* Mouton, The Hague, 1968, pp. 382-413.

———. "The Reality of Jewishness versus the Ghetto Myth: The Sociolinguistic Roots of Yiddish," in *To Honor Roman Jacobson.* Mouton, The Hague, 1967, pp. 2199-2211.

Weinreich, Uriel. "Research Problems in Bilingualism, with Special Reference to Switzerland," unpublished Ph.D. Dissertation. Columbia University, New York, 1951.

———. *Languages in Contact.* Linguistic Circle of New York, New York, 1953a.

———. "The Russification of Soviet Minority Languages," *Problems of Communism,* II, vi (1953b), 46-57.

———. "Multilingual Dialectology and the New Yiddish Atlas," *Anthropological Linguistics.* IV, i (1962), 6-22.

White, John K. "On the Revival of Printing in the Cherokee Language," *Current Anthropology,* III (1962), 511-514.

Whiteley, W. H. "Ideal and Reality in National Language Policy: A Case Study from Tanzania," in J. A. Fishman, C. A. Ferguson, and J. Das Gupta (eds.), *Language Problems of Developing Nations,* Wiley, New York, 1968, pp. 327-344.

Whorf, Benjamin L. "Science and Linguistics," *Technology Review,* XLIX (1940), 229-231, 247-248.

———. "The Relation of Habitual Thought to Behavior and to Language," in L. Speier, (ed.), *Language Culture and Personality.* Sapir Memorial Publication Fund, Menasha, Wisc., 1941, pp. 75-93.

Willems, Emilio. "Linguistic Changes in German-Brazilian Communities," *Acta Americana,* I (1943), 448-463.

Winner, T. G. "Problems of Alphabetic Reform among the Turkic Peoples of Soviet Central Asia," *Slavonic and East European Review,* 1952, 132-147.

Wittermans, Elizabeth P. "Indonesian Terms of Address in a Situation of Rapid Social Change. *Social Forces,* XLVI (1967), 48-52.

Wolff, Hans. *Nigerian Orthography.* Gaskiya Corp., Zaria, 1954.

Wolfram, Walter A. *A Sociolinguistic Description of Detroit Negro Speech.* Washington, D.C., Center for Applied Linguistics, 1969.

Wonderly, William L. *Bible Translation for Popular Use.* United Bible Societies, London, 1968.

Wu Yu-chang. "Concerning the Draft Han Language Phonetization Plan," *Current Background,* no. 380, Mar. 15, 1956, 4-20.

———. "Widening the Use of the Phonetic Script," *China Reconstructs,* XIII, vi (1964), 29-31.

———. "Report of the Current Tasks of Reforming the Written Language and the Draft Scheme for a Chinese Phonetic Alphabet," in *Reform of the Chinese Written Language.* Foreign Language Press, Peking, 1965.

Wurm, S. A. "Language and Literacy," in E. D. Fisk (ed.), *New Guinea on the Threshold.* Australian National University, Canberra, 1966, 135-148.

———. and D. C. Laycock. "The Question of Language and Dialect in New Guinea," *Oceania,* XXXII (1961/62), 128-143.

Young, R. R. "An Adult Literacy Campaign in Sierra Leone," *Oversea Education,* XIV, iii (1944), 97-100.

READING LIST: INTRODUCTION TO LINGUISTICS

I. *A Few Popular Introductions and Overviews*
  1. Hall, Robert A., Jr. *Linguistics and Your Language.* Doubleday, New York, 1960.
  2. Orenstein, Jacob, and Wm. W. Gage. *The ABC's of Language and Linguistics.* Chilton, Philadelphia, 1964.
  3. Bolinger, Dwight. *Aspects of Language.* Harcourt, Brace & World, New York, 1967.

II. *Some Traditional American Texts*
  1. Bloomfield, Leonard. *Language.* Holt, New York, 1933.
  2. Gleason, H. A., Jr. *An Introduction to Descriptive Linguistics* (rev.). Holt, New York, 1961.
  3. Hockett, Charles F. *A Course in Modern Linguistics* (rev.). Macmillan, New York, 1963.
  4. Sapir, Edward. *Language.* Harcourt, Brace, New York, 1921. (Paperback: Harvest Books, New York, 1955).

III. *One Classic and Three Recent Texts by European Authors*
  1. de Saussure, Ferdinand. *Course in General Linguistics* (translation of 1916 French original by Wade Baskin). Philosophical Library, New York, 1959.
  2. Martinet, André. *Elements of General Linguistics* (translation of 1960 French original by Elisabeth Palmer). University of Chicago Press, Chicago, 1964.
  3. Halliday, M. A. K., Angus McIntosh, and Peter Strevens. *The Linguistics Sciences and Language Teaching.* Longmans, Green, London, 1964.
  4. Robins, Robert H. *General Linguistics: An Introductory Survey.* Indiana University Press, Bloomington, 1966.

IV. *Examples of the Newer "Transformationalist" Approach*

1. Bach, Emmon W. *An Introduction to Transformational Grammars.* Holt, New York, 1964.
2. Chomsky, Noam. *Aspects of the Theory of Syntax.* M.I.T. Press, Cambridge, Mass., 1965.
3. Langacker, Ronald W. *Language And its Structure.* Harcourt, Brace & World, New York, 1968.

V. *Journals to Glance at*

1. *Language*
2. *Lingua*
3. *Linguistics*
4. *Linguistic Reporter*
5. *International Journal of American Linguistics*

VI. *References*

1. Rutherford, Phillip R. *A Bibliography of American Doctoral Dissertations in Linguistics,* 1900-1964. Center for Applied Linguistics, Washington, D.C., 1968.
2. *Linguistic Information.* Center for Applied Linguistics, Washington, D.C., 1965.
3. Cartter, Allan M. "Doctoral Programs in Linguistics," in his *An Assessment of Quality in Graduate Education.* American Council on Education, Washington, D.C., 1966.
4. Various articles on linguistic topics in the new *International Encyclopedia of the Social Sciences.* Macmillan, New York, 1968. (See the review of these topics in *Language,* XLV (1969), 458-463.)